Life in the Spin Cycle

by
Rolf Gunnar Hauge

"The point of the journey is not to arrive." (Neil Peart)

It was quite a moment in my life when I was detained in a holding room at the airport in Oslo, Norway; to then be asked to squat naked over a mirror on the floor with three security guard's eyes upon me...

INTRO

Welcome to *Life in the Spin Cycle.* This book is a raw, unedited, truthful account of many experiences, adventures, and setbacks I've endured throughout my life thus far. The *Spin Cycle* represents various aspects of my life that are molded into one noteworthy concoction of interesting material to read. The first segment of chapters focus on my upbringing and experiences from adolescence into young adulthood. The next set of chapters contain many examples and stories of amazing adventures and tormenting circumstances I've lived through. And the final chapters make up a collective array of thought-provoking ideas, analogies, and various constituents that represent how my brain perceives things in general; which are all a representation of my warm heart, creative mind, reputable attitude, and interminable persistence. Let's just say my journey so far has been very interesting and quite barmy.

If I had to dedicate this book to anyone it would be to those that have any type of life- crippling setbacks or experienced any number of unpleasant chain of events which wreak havoc in their lives. Those with mental or physical disabilities, others who grow up in horrid environments causing deleterious outcomes in their life, or basically any negative factor that prevents some humans from living a stable and exultant life. Any type of hindrance that makes standard living harder to cope with than the many more fortunate human inhabitants out there; one's who only need to put forth an average amount of effort into this world and things usually work out fine for them.

To all who live within a vortex of irrepressible misfortunes;

the outcasts, the unfortunate, the completely fucked...my jimmy hat's off to you!

I also give praise to the non-conformist outcasts of the world. Any outside the box thinker or social pariahs out there who never get much chance to shine or fit in with cultural standards by taking the more unorthodox, riskier path out there, this book most certainly signifies a reflection of your life too.

And let's give kudos to all street performers of the world. Whether it's juggling a bunch of flame-lit dildos in front of a Sunday crowd eating ice cream or basking away on a street corner with any musical instrument or noise-making device, you rock! Just taking the time to load up your vehicle, drive, park, unload, set up, and perform live at any random destination to give the public some free entertainment is quite a feat. And it's usually a solo mission with no help, companionship, or even time for a bathroom break. Just you and the instrument(s) or toy(s) of choice doing your thing. \m/

Also let it be known this book writing process has been anything but easy or "naturally flowy" for me. I've had to update/upgrade/transfer files so many times along this journey and re-convert/re-save this book numerous times from Pages to PDF to Word and whatever the fuck else so the format is correct for online publishing. To then have my Word document go corrupt; right as I was finishing the final bits of edits and about to upload this god damned book into the Internet world for sale. Again after almost TWO DECADES in the making already!

I was forced to delete then re-install my Microsoft Office package and go through the entire tech-nerd bullshit process again; spending HOURS trying to get my one book file re-loaded and up to par for publishing!

Anyhoo, (lame term) this is my memoir and it's kinda perfect that the formatting is a bit tweaked throughout the pages within, as so is my brain. Just been such an arduous process!

Next book will be written by hammer and chisel on slabs of stone. Without any "help" from any type of shit-ass lame-gay digital technology that hinders the natural flow of analog brilliance.

Lastly, I'm super visual. The thought of this book being published without including any photos is killing me. I appreciate the addition of any visuals that are incorporated within any publication, acting as a significant enhancement to the written content along the way. I have albums and computer files filled with photos I've taken over the years and they act as a big part of my life's story. It's a bit concerning for me at this point but just keep an eye out for a *Visuals of the Spin Cycle* follow up book soon…

Authors Note:

About me and this crazy ass book

Before one makes the decision to lunge into the unruly depths of the autobiographical delineations of my life, it's only fair I give a brief synapse of who I am and what I stand for; summing up the basis of my existence and reasonings for this eccentric life I live.

Much of what you will read throughout *Life in the Spin Cycle* is very idiosyncratic and includes some darker subject matter that's hard to fathom, yet it's all so god damned entertaining to read! There will be many interesting things shared and analyzed to the hilt. I will go about this as if I have an angel who has been with me throughout my life; one that has an unbiased, truthful perspective on who I am and could validate all the examples, scenarios, and such I write about that make my living much more laborious than the average chump.

I apologize to the many of you that will have a hard time reading through the first half of this book, which contains a tremendous amount of griping, moaning, wailing about from so many odd circumstances that have presented too many imbalanced outcomes during my life.

Please try and absorb all that is being written about and don't be so biased or judgemental. Again I can only promise it's all very entertaining material for y'all to read. And the brighter more succulent stuff comes forth during the second half of reading. So stick it out and be glad you haven't been tormented throughout your life in as many ways as I have. Many millions out there have been through "worse" but the number of setbacks and amount of bullshit I've endured throughout four decades of my life so far is absolutely mesmerizing.

I really am a good guy with good intentions, high ambitions, unbiased, wholesome perspectives in life, yet also have a confused, frustrated, frenzied mindset. I've come to describe myself as possessing a jock physique, hippie heart, and a punk rock soul. I'm a very resilient, sincere person who respects life, likes people, loves animals, and rebels against the vanilla-coated, cookie cutter ideologies of the world. I never hesitate to embark on any endeavor and will accept any challenge; the hardest challenge entailing the interminable battles inside my own head! (And more so in recent years these screwy-stressful times we all battle day to day; much more than during previous eras of more fairness and bliss in our beloved country or world in general.)

I have always been very affable and easy to get along with; absorbing any moment with open heart and mind and I never show disrespect or mess with anyone's mojo. I've always been truthful, sincere, and have a commendable track record overall. I give everyone the benefit of the doubt and end up walking on eggshells more than I wish because many people and situations don't allow for a person to "be themselves". And with my neurotic anxiety and inner sensitivity I can't handle drama or stressful situations much at all. I tend to clam up and falsify a state of unperturbed mannerisms in certain predicaments in order to avoid further anxiety or inevitable conflict.

I was fortunate to be raised by very genuine, nurturing parents in pleasantly safe, middle class suburbs. And this is certainly a contributing factor for a more favored outcome in life (one would speculate). I possess many unique talents and abilities beyond anyone I know, and most all these talents and abilities came naturally to me with little effort. I excel at most all sports and recreational activities, as well as very artistic and musically inclined. I perform stand-up comedy at open mics on occasion, been hosting an internet radio show for the past decade, and have many creative works in progress revolving around music, film, and animation. I also have a comprehensive list of around fifty product inventions, some that easily could/should exist if I had adequate funding to pay for the help that's needed to properly launch an idea. (Luckily I have something in the making that can help people launch their ideas and bypass the old school process that involves way too much time and money.)

Hardly anyone I know can ski moguls at all, let alone good, and then switch over to snowboard and conquer any terrain on that device as well. At one point in time when I was playing little league baseball my coach was fed up with both our pitchers during a game and yelled out to the team, "Anyone else wanna try?" And me being usually passive and shy held up my hand and volunteered to leave my usual position at third base for a trial at the mound. Having never pitched before I ended up with eight strikeouts and became the starting pitcher for the remaining seasons of my little league career.

This is all just who I am; very nice, genuine, down to earth, naturally athletic, creative, and enough vigor to persevere and conquer almost anything. It's extremely rare to find people that possess all these traits within one entity, but aside from these fine qualities comes a whole other set of disconcerting issues I constantly face.

How many people do you know have the courage to talk in front of a crowd? Or even more daunting try to be funny and witty in front of a room full of strangers; on an open mic stage, standing under a spotlight and only seeing numerous silhouettes staring in your direction all expecting to laugh. I've done it numerous times with minimal preparation and never once "bombed."

All the videos and photos I take are always complimented with high regards and some people wonder if I'm a professional. I'm not a "professional" at all, yet even John Fielder commended some of my photos I submitted to him via email, when all my still photos are taken with a pocket camera or smart phone and only *appear* as very professional. It's all in the eye of the beholder. (Great Metallica song!)

I've never cheated on any girl I've dated. This is the inherited and indoctrinated morals I was raised with. It's unmannerly to cheat on someone within a serious relationship of any kind. I'm too neurotic and overly proper to ever fabricate a crippling situation for anyone else anyway. *However, I do believe that humans have animalistic tendencies so I get the idea of "reasonable cheating" but will hopefully never partake.*

I feel very fortunate and privileged to have my amazing family and all these wonderful traits and such, it's just too bad I'm not living a life nearly to my acceptance and capabilities. The term "starving artist" is almost an understatement, and living life with such a mix of ambitious creative talents and none of them providing me much credibility or financial reward after so many years effort is asinine. If I was succeeding in just one or a few of these crafts or "avocations" I enjoy and am naturally good at I could be living on top of the world. Unfortunately this is not the case by any means.

My mindset is too busy, unorganized, and distraught. I have some form of ADD and/or Bi-Polar disorder and been on medications for a good portion of my life. Sometimes I can barely function or carry out basic tasks that we all face daily in life. I refer to my ailment as "ADDepression";

which is ADD that accentuates symptoms of depression with a nice, sincere coating of neurosis, anxiety, OCD, and even PTSD. It's "tolerable insanity" of sorts. (Much more on this shit later.)

My many great traits and talents are genuine yet toilsome to live with. I include many examples in the *Spin Cycle* where I've blown important opportunities in the past and nearly drive myself into insanity while trying to cope with all of life's insanity. How could I allow myself to go through such imbecilic phases in my life? Read on and find out.

It's easy to say that attitude and perseverance are the keys to success, but when your mind is in permanent disarray and we're all dealing with these harder than ever times to achieve a fair, balanced lifestyle, how the fuck can you achieve much or maintain enough stability to get by adequately in life at all? My unstable, manic mindset combined with modern trends, hardships, and certain inclinations within our society is too overwhelming. Life in general is becoming more demanding, competitive, expensive, and unpredictable. Society has become very capricious, unreliable, and self-absorbed within this confusing, oversaturated circus of a world anymore. There's more stress, divorce, depression, even suicides and many other negative factors that weren't so prevalent in our world for countless decades prior to the 21st Century.

I'm sure many of you readers will be rolling your eyes quite often with that "Can't this guy just shut up, chill out, except what is and be satisfied?" Don't I wish, but I am a special strain that has a lot to share, accomplish, and vent about for good reasoning and you will learn plenty about me and my take on reality soon enough.

Let's face it, there's WAY TOO MUCH inexcusable bullshit produced by humans more and more these days, as more and more of these humans and their fucked-up ideologies inhabit the lands of this beautiful Earth. I can't help but call out lots of this gratuitous crapola that unfortunately does exist at unprecedented levels and needs to be flushed from the world in which we live. However, according to the standard masses of arrogant, dumbass individuals, calling out the truth (using any adverse means to do so) only comes across as senseless ranting, rather than obvious truth, by smartass individuals such as me.

So let it be known, as many of you are rolling your naïve eyes while reading through any of my doleful grievances to come throughout the *Spin Cycle,* you're secretly being flipped off by me. Imagine the scornful words on the page which are bugging you coming together as a big middle-finger, saying "Up yours ignorant fool. It's negative *truthful* bantering against wrongful actualities that exist in our society and seem to affect many good people with too many negative scenarios far too often." (As if Socrates, George Carlin, and many other brilliant philosophers and entertainers throughout history haven't justified the truth, or validated this type of "truthful bantering" enough over time, I must continue to do so as well. *Until more of humanity ever--never, not a fucking chance--gets it!*

I also seem to mention poop a lot throughout this book. Why? Beats the shit out of me.

And so derives the title of my book; *Life in the Spin Cycle.* Like that of a washing machine that goes through all the cycles until it reaches that final *spin cycle,* my life reflects that same pattern. I've experienced and been through a lot and put forth tremendous efforts towards my goals for success in life but can't seem to ever get to where I belong! I've made it through all the washing cycles in this "life machine" but remain stuck in that final spin cycle. All I want is the spinning to stop so I can enter the warmth of the dryer already for fuck's sake! No need for any fabric softener; just let me in, close the door, and hit START.

You can look at this like I'm in a giant room with all these locked doors. Each door represents a different gateway I can take towards my calling but I can't find any keys to unlock these fricking doors! Or maybe I have the one right key but people and differing circumstances or situations keep giving me the runaround and directing me to the wrong doors.

I might not ever find the correct door to open and obtain the life I was meant to live; mostly because of my own debilitating mindset and continuing mistakes, as well as the growing difficulty to advance properly in these current times, and of course douchebag people and their deceitful undertakings.

I do have to proclaim that although there will be hostile criticism and deleterious ridiculing towards society and certain situations I've endured, I really do love life! I take the most boring moments and turn them into silver. (Fuck gold.) I make anyone in my presence welcome to be who they are with no judgment at all. I'm a sincere, unbiased, empathetic mofo living in my own twisted reality, while trying to make legit connections and progress in a world gone batshit crazy.

I'm a "glass could/should be 80% full" realist. Could be worse? Yes, but also so many things could be better. We as a nation, and the planet in general, never progress to our full potential. Instead of uniting and striving for better ways to make things more balanced and honorable in this world, most humans just ride the wave of conformity and chill in the hammock of mediocrity (i.e. glass *half* full). While the powerful, avaricious individuals who are running the whole shit show keep laughing all the way to the bank.

As much as I hate the greed and hypocrisy that's so prevalent amongst the politics and corporate swine in this country, I believe the middle-class majority is also to blame for so much gone to shit in the 21st Century. (Thanks to an abundance of digital technology, consumer product saturation overload, countless new-age trends gone berserk, and other nonsense that seems to be the real cause of the human race roiling themselves into herds of braindead sheep anymore.)

Screw the 1%? Sure, but how about the 70% as well? Vanilla-coated, self-absorbed, middle-class imbeciles. It's a whacky combo of greedy extremists and run-of-the-mill conformists who have ruined what could/should be a more sensible world to live in. To the 71%; please eat shit, move on, and let the rest of us (the 29%) live in coherent peace and happiness we deserve.

Okay, it's now come time for you readers to take the *RGH Challenge* and try to make it through this entire book. Who knows what's all to derive from many more pages of interesting tales to be shared.

As I desperately want out of my "spin cycle lifestyle", you all are now about to enter *Life in the Spin Cycle.*

PRELUDE/PROLOGUE/PITSWEAT

First written journal entry that gave birth to *Life in the Spin Cycle:*

It's just past midnight as I sit here in my Boulder, CO home with a scented candle lit on what is now May 4, 1999. The thunderous overture of *Force Ten* by Rush kicks in on my headphones and the salty, refreshing taste of a rarely eaten tuna sandwich is being washed down with a Mountain Breeze soda.

Here I sit, about to begin writing this book, or manifest, reminiscing over the many experiences, adventures, and tribulations throughout the years I've been alive so far. Also included in the *Spin Cycle* will be a spewing showcase of alluring ideas, thoughts, analogies, and other unhinged randomness that my frenzied brain conceives, just for entertainment sake and a diversion away from so much of my inundated reality.

As the song *Time Stand Still* ends, I'm thinking how it is the perfect affirmation for one of the things I've dwelled upon throughout my life. I feel that time really needs to stand still sometimes in order to fulfill our desires, or at least allow us to relish longer within those blissful moments we experience. Time seems to pass by so rapidly we can't fully captivate on the great moments or achieve many aspirations in this one lifetime. As we get older the precious times we share with our friends and families seem to fade into memory as the clock's hands continue rotating and the pages of calendars are flipping forward. Time does *not* stand still.

The Internet and advancing technology is allowing for limitless opportunities, enabling humans to get anything they want by clicking a mouse or tapping on a screen rather than knocking on a door. This phenomenon is creating a world of digitally absorbed laziness in which the human spirit and any valid, personable connection is becoming obsolete. We are so brainwashed with constant distractions and unnecessary clutter we obtain from looking at multiple screens every day that we have forgotten about the sole purpose of why we are here in the first place. Humans were meant to interact with one another, experience more reality outside of these digital domains and make the most of this one life we live without the need for so much of this 21st Century technological nonsense.

Albert Einstein stated: “I fear the day that technology will surpass our human interaction. The world will become a generation of idiots.” And whether he actually said this or not is not the point. The rapid advances in technology *are* bringing about this exact consequence within our beloved human race.

Nothing is objectively certain about life except death, but each individual carries with them an opinion, belief, or faith of why we exist and what our purpose is during this one lifetime. Look at the dinosaurs, what the fuck were they doing here? And did they have their own God and/or fabricated Heaven? The Universe is infinite and it’s very hard to comprehend or put any valid “reasoning” for our existence we have on this one tiny planet amongst the endless vastness of space beyond.

Aside from what scientists and astronomers discover we don't know enough to say anything about any meaning or purpose for human existence, and we don't have a clue what really happens after we die. There could be a "God" or "Heaven" but until we die we will never know for sure. And if there is a god-like entity he/she/it has *nothing* to do with what's going on down here! Pray away, hope for the best, think what you want, but life on Earth is all moment to moment randomness and will throw anything at us at any time it wants.

Anyway, here's an item I'd like to share with you before I take us into the first chapter. This sample of writing is an amalgamation of how much I believe in myself and my desperation to manifest what I represent to those who don't know squat about me:

RAW Artists (talent bio)

This opportunity to be included as a performer in the RAW Artists "Menagerie" event represents a few pieces of the convoluted puzzle that make up the intuitively intrinsic, artistic world I live. I just hope that this event will help promote my creative talents and vibrant personality enough to justify what I'm capable of the outer world; that wonderful world outside of conformity and redundant nonsense.

During my childhood I spent countless hours in my room pretending to be a radio DJ and recording my self-produced music programs to tape using my boom box. On a visual level I was acting as "producer" for mock rock concerts I put on with my stuffed animals. I was the puppeteer and lighting director while the show's music was playing through my twenty-pound Panasonic boom box. Sometimes I would force my two sisters and a couple neighbor friends to join me for lip sync concerts, or better yet put on my director's hat to create our own movie scenes outside around the property.

After working my first official summer job as a dishwasher at age 15, I was able to save enough money and upgrade from pots, pans and Tupperware into owning a real drum set. Playing along to various tapes on my Walkman I gained proficiency on the drums in a short amount of time. I also took up an interest in photography and began documenting various excursions on camera. I, like my parents, have filled numerous photo albums with pictures that represent the experiences I've happily indulged in over the years.

After graduating college I began to implement the power of video and captured hours of footage on various camcorders. I also conceived the idea of the helmet cam long before it's true existence by duct taping a small camcorder to my bike helmet in order to capture the rider's perspective. (Slick Rock Trail. Moab, UT 2003)

Now, at middle age, I'm more ambitious than ever and continue to indulge in all these fun, time consuming "avocations". I continue to write, document, create, produce and perform, while my laptop files overflow with countless numbers of photos, videos, and written works in progress that remain on the back burners of multiple stoves.

Gunnar (aka "Scarpie" or "Cygnus", depending on which

persona I choose to go by.)

https://youtu.be/KRYusjvOXkA (RAW Artists video intro)

A couple other attempts I made with hope to achieve television fame was during the late 90s. I submitted a homemade video to MTV and VH1 of me pretending to be a VJ, but nothing came of it.

A few years later while living in Santa Barbara, CA, I filled out the forms and submitted another video to MTV with intent to make it on The Real World or Road Rules.

I actually drove the tape up to MTV headquarters in Van Nuys, CA myself to ensure it got in the right hands; the hands of a scrawny college intern who can't do shit for me except tell me, "Good luck."

To this day I'm still surfing the web for any connections and opportunities that can help my aptitudes gain some exposure and launch me into the right sectors of the arts & entertainment world I belong in; doing what I enjoy and have put forth tremendous efforts into for over many years during my life with marginal success. It's a glass half empty, unforgiving industry to say the least.

Enough of this "INTRO" bantering, let's finally move into the actual *Spin Cycle...*

SPERM TO HUMAN

EARLY YEARS (East Coast/West Coast)

I was born into this lovely world on July 23, 1971. It was a hot, humid day and the busiest ever on record for Georgetown Hospital, Washington D.C. I was the first born and only boy of three that were fashioned to be the Hauge siblings. Oddly enough the nurse brought me out wrapped in a pink blanket, as they were out of blue ones, which gave my dad the impression that his first born was a girl and not the boy he was expecting. Then the nurse lifted the pink blanket and surprised daddy with my tiny pink missile to clarify. I think it was from this perplexing moment that would be the precursor for me to end up living such an unconventional life as it stands to this day.

Just out from under the blanket, my parents and I only spent a couple short years in the D.C. area until my dad was transferred to San Francisco, CA. We resided in Concord, CA, which is a better alternative than living in the city by avoiding expensive living costs mixed with the smell of sea harbors and cold, foggy weather. Living in the East Bay we became supporters of the Oakland A's and Raiders as opposed to San Francisco Giants and 49ers. I remember one time heading to a Raiders game on BART with my dad and there was a delay so the packed mob of us watched the opening quarter of the game off some guy holding up a small portable television he had with him.

Within the next few years both my sisters, Kathryn and Ingrid, were born in Walnut Creek, CA and we now had our nice, quaint suburban family. Our family of five, plus addition of our first black lab, Skipper, lived together in Concord about six years. While I was too young to really reminisce about my first eight years on Earth, I will quickly sum up a few of the more memorable times I can remember in one fragmented chunk of a paragraph:

The first school I attended was Silverwood Elementary, we lived near Cowel Pool that had a dark and scary 15ft deep end. I spent most days riding my bike, plastic skateboard, and Green Machine around the neighborhood. I loved to throw rocks and burn things with the guys in our cul-de-sac and play doctor with the neighbor girl. I also distinctly remember the last time I officially dropped a load of shit in my pants while crouched down by the side of the house one afternoon. My first official boner I recall *popped up* while waiting in line at school and the wind blew this girl's skirt up. My final days in Concord were spent gazing out my bedroom window at Mt. Diablo, which ended up catching ablaze just before we moved to Colorado.

Chronic Nightmare

While living in California I began having a reoccurring nightmare. It consisted of these small creatures that mimicked white porcelain toilets and would march along through the gutters of the streets. I have no idea what provoked this bizarre dream but they were marching to get at me! The worst part about this dream is that it continued after our move to Colorado, and each time the dream took place I thought the toilet creatures were getting closer to me.

Funny thing is I know now that the marching portion of the dream was caused by my heartbeat that I heard while my head was on the pillow; that constant pulsating in my ears created the marching sounds of these toilet creatures.

Ants

Since I was a child I've had a fascination with ants. All throughout my life I've been known to play with their nests and watch them at work. Some of my favorite shows on TV are those that feature creepy crawly critters, especially ants. The most intense of all are most certainly the Driver Ants. (i.e. Siafu) These satanic bastards are found in Africa and can nest 20 million inhabitants! They burrow in caverns deep within the Earth's soil and spill out of the nest on mass raids on the jungle floor. Check them out!

And you know how so many people have aquariums in their home? Well I plan to have a giant ant farm in mine. I'll have people over and put on ant battles and such, party on!

ADOLESCENT YEARS (Evergreen, CO)

The LOOGIE Era:

During our final days in California my dad bought a 1974 Suburban. This thing was classic! A 2-wheel-drive model, faded sunset gold in color, vinyl interior, and no air conditioning. The great thing about this ugly school bus was my dad took us on many epic excursions across the country in it. We had that thing stuffed with all five family members, our necessities, and our black lab, Skipper, in the back. My two sisters and I were allowed to bring one stuffed animal and a tote box full of reading books, coloring books, toys, and sometimes homework. Yep that's right, a couple of these road trip vacations required us siblings to add extra days to our spring break and do a little homework while cruising the country. We were also only allowed one juice in the morning and a soda in the afternoon. We ate sandwiches every day at little rest area pull- offs and if we were lucky we'd be treated to McDonald's on occasion, and maybe even get to stay in a hotel with a pool once or twice during these many weeks on the road. But usually we roughed it out in tents the entire time, rain or shine.

We took three cross country expeditions in our Suburban during the summertime seasons. One was from California all the way to New York to visit relatives. The other two were from Colorado (where we had moved to in the fall of 1978) to various other areas in the country, even tapping into parts of Canada and Mexico.

I will never forget that nice, hot burrow ride from Texas into Mexico where each of us were rewarded with the most refreshing 16oz bottle of Coke I have ever enjoyed in my life! Or better yet the time crossing through Death Valley in the middle of the summer at 120 degrees; again with no air conditioning or tinted windows. Rock on!

We were troopers at the highest level possible compared to any other traveling family who were equipped with Winnebagos and such. One time while camping at Indian Trees in Oregon it was wet and murky with no other campers around. Our entertainment consisted of a game my sister's and I made up throwing rocks into cow pies for points.

While on the road dad would complain numerous times about slow pokes getting in our way, especially during the two-lane scenic drives. During a trip out east we made signs with big drawing paper and markers and wrote phrases like, "Out of the way POKE" and I made a "Raiders Rule!" sign and put it up in the window as we were driving around D.C. just after the Raiders beat the Redskins in the Superbowl. Silly kids, if we did that sort of thing today it would cause road rage no question.

My dad showed us every major city, historic site, and national park in the U.S. I can't give my dad enough praise or regards for educating us about our native land and all the amazing things we saw and learned about during my adolescent years. The only problem was at the time us kids didn't give a hoot about many of these historical stops we made and rather focused all hope for a stop at McDonald's or a stay in a hotel with a pool.

Thankfully my dad was a photo taking maniac and documented everywhere we went during all these years of travel.

We live in an amazing country that's full of beauty and interesting sites to see. Like the centralized theme in the animated movie *Cars* points out, you must check out the scenery along the way and not just rush to your destination.

Years later I wish for nothing else but being able to embark on many of these same adventures again. (Except maybe this time experience all this as a traveling writer/musician on a pimped-out tour bus with air conditioning and tinted windows!)

My dad also took me to hundreds of sporting events over

the years. He is so dedicated to supporting his teams and is never late or leaves early for any game he attends. The one big regret I have was the time when he scored box seat tickets for the NBA All Star game back in 1986. This game featured all the legendary players from that era, and instead of attending the game I went skiing. To make the story more painful I chose a cruddy little ski resort located just outside of Denver, Arapahoe East, and was stuck on the lift for over an hour at the end of the day!

After I was rescued off the chairlift I saw my dad who was there to pick me up and tell me about all the highlights of the amazing game I missed.

So how did our Suburban become known as the Loogie? One day a friend and I were sitting on the swing set in my yard and saw my mom driving the Suburban down the hill towards our house. My friend blurted out the comment, "It looks like a big yellow loogie". And so the name stuck. (Funny enough that my family and select friends still use the term "Loogie" to refer to Suburbans out on the road, no matter what color.)

Appaloosa Drive (A 30-year legacy)

We Hauges lived in a basic two-story house in Evergreen, CO with an unfinished, walkout basement that soon became my personal space of refuge. The house had shag carpeting and was decorated with our redwood furniture and ugly as hell puke orange itchy furniture pads to sit on. I had my own room and across the hall my sisters shared theirs. My room contained blue carpeting that reminded me of ocean water so much that I had nightmares about being stranded in the ocean floating on my bed with sharks amongst me. (Thankfully the toilet creature freaks had given up trying to find me.)

Being that the Colorado school systems were different than in California I started in 3rd grade rather than 2nd, which made me the younger kid in that class. Oddly enough I would end up repeating 9th grade some years later. (More on this to come.)

I did well all through my grade school years, good enough that my dad bought me a gift after I finished 6th grade; a black and white checkered O.P. Velcro wallet. I used this wallet all the way through college, only to lose it soon after graduating when a friend and I hit Carl's Jr. for lunch after a round of disc golf. I was so devastated that I went back to the burger joint two more times in the days following and looked around the entire lot in case someone just took the cash and chucked the wallet somewhere. Thankfully I took a picture of this wallet for memory's sake.

The neighborhood we lived in was known as El Pinal, or the "Radiation Pit", as it was referred to because it was the only place in Evergreen where hardly any trees existed. For the first few years we lived there all the roads were dirt so that made it fun for me and the neighborhood kids to ride our bikes around the hilly streets and see how far we could skid down the dirt roads. Me and my awesome Diamondback could get up to 30 yards skidding distance on the inclined street. (No photo captured of this mighty Diamondback ☹)

As skateboarding was making its second phase of popularity into the public during the mid-80s (the first phase being the Dogtown era in the mid-70s) we all bought these wide ramp boards that had become the new industry token. Our neighborhood streets had been paved by this time and we always walked our boards up to the small neighborhood gas station, Wilco, located at the top of El Pinal Drive. We would butt-board all the way to the rodeo grounds located about a mile down the road. What a fast-paced rush, especially on my colorful Jeff Phillips ramp board.

The Bears (Matola, Matalita, Matoog, Matook)

No teddy bears in the history of the world have anything on our family of bears. Matola, Indian term for "she bear", was the first bear to enter our family; a gift to my mom from one of her friends. As my sisters and I took a liking to Matola we all got our own bears soon after; Matalita the "little she bear" and the twin sisters, Matook and Matoog. These bears have been in our family for years now and traveled all over the country with us. They are so soft, fluffy, and loved by all!

Classic Times of the 80s

Len Jovi

My first and forever best friend is Leigh, who's name would be changed to Len after another friend and I decided to combine his official first name, Ben, and middle name, Leigh. How clever. So many events and stories came from both our upbringings in Evergreen and my years spent with Len.

Early on we had a tradition of taking my Panasonic boom box "ghetto blaster" on walks to various stores where we would buy a soda then proceed to the Safeway shopping center and play a few video games, or skateboard around the hood.

As years past it turned into bike riding adventures; sometimes for the three-mile journey to catch a movie at the local theater. We saw some epic movies together: *Ferris Beuller's Day Off, Silverado, Top Gun, Hot Dog, Sheena, Yellow Submarine...*

Mall Cruising

Embarrassingly enough one of our favorite past times was catching a ride with our moms to one of a few malls they would shop at on weekends. Len and I would enjoy the two or three hours of walking the mall corridors; checking out Spenser's Gifts, the music stores, arcades, and stalking chicks.

Southwest Plaza was our all-time favorite. It was fairly new, had the most adventurous layout, and hottest teen girls abundant during the mid/late 80s. Another frequented mall was Villa Italia. This mall became a bit more hardcore during the last of its remaining years and I will always remember one incident where Len almost got in a fight with this leather jacket bad ass guy. We crossed paths in the mall and he blurted out, "Pretty boy". So Len turned around with a "what the fuck" look on his face and the guy came back and started threatening him with pleasant lines such as, "What the fuck you lookin' at? I will take you out to the parking garage and kick your teeth in!"

I think that was our last trip to Villa Italia.

Caving

Another activity we participated in was caving. Len's dad discovered a liking to it and invited us on some expeditions during our teenage years.

I remember the very first cave we explored located in Golden, CO. It was Fault Cave, and the name sure made a statement as it was full of tight, dark, rocky passage ways to conquer.

Since we were all amateurs and totally unprepared, we crawled around these dark caverns holding flashlights while bumping our heads on rocks. Len even left a tuft of his hair on a rock. *Rock* on!

After a few more expeditions in various caves we were coined the "Bitch and Moan Crew" by Len's dad, as we were always complaining about something during the journey. But overall we were privileged to have partaken in so many interesting caving adventures during this era of our lives.

Perfect Days

The Perfect Day events took place on my birthday and consisted of me and Len engaging in three fun activities that filled up an entire day and into the night. Throughout most of our teenage years we would indulge in this epic day ritual consisting of nine holes of golf in the early morning, then proceeding to Elitch Gardens amusement park for a full day of rides and cruising chicks. We'd close out the Perfect Day by attending a double feature drive-in movie. The best drive-in movie I remember seeing was *Aliens* followed by *The Money Pit*. (Underrated movie!) Watching these contrasting films back to back was quite entertaining and amusing; all taking place in the Loogie of course.

These really were the "perfect days" for us as teenagers and became some of the most memorable birthdays I've ever had.

Erik

Erik stepped into my life early on as well. I can't remember how we originally hit it off but we certainly generated a very fun, fulfilling childhood together. Erik's dad was a computer programmer for IBM during the 1980s computer boom, so I always loved staying the night at his house since it was big and full of things to do.

Outdoor activities usually included tossing a nerf football over his gigantic swing set structure and making a game out of it with certain points earned for catches and such. But the most epic of all activities had to be building Stomper tracks. Anyone who was a child from the 1980s certainly remembers these small battery powered mechanisms that resembled 4X4 vehicles offered in various models to choose from. The real cool thing about Stompers was they had working headlights and interchangeable tires for indoor and outdoor purposes. We would spend hours digging these long tracks in the dirt complete with bridges, berms, and whatever else that would be found on a real 4X4 dirt track.

Craig

As Len, Erik, and I continued our fun times together another pal, Craig, entered my life. His mom had come over to hang some homemade drapes in our house and Craig was with her so we road bikes together around the neighborhood. These were the times of my adolescence entering junior high and we bonded in a different sort of way, as troublemakers.

Just like the earlier days hanging with Erik, staying the night at Craig's house was nothing short of awesome. He had an Atari game box with all the essential games that we would play for hours. Then we always had two exciting movie rentals to watch during the night hours. Being that his parents were very liberal and hip, we were allowed to watch any movie we chose, and this included R-rated movies. Each time I stayed overnight we would make sure to have our two good movies of choice ready; a freaky, slasher horror film followed by a comedy which usually contained some bonus nude scenes as well. (got Porky's?)

Craig's house was located on top of a rocky cliff that dropped a few hundred feet down onto the canyon road below. Well it didn't take us long to realize that chucking things off the cliff onto this road below would make for amusing entertainment. We found that raw eggs made the best weapon of choice and I'm sure we ruined a lot of people's days as an egg or two would splatter on their windshield.

What a fucked-up thing to do, maybe not as bad as

chucking rocks at cars like I did with Len's younger brother, but still an awful, ignorant thing to do.

Bryan

Straight out of Long Island Bryan G. enters my life. We really clicked well throughout the remainder of our school years together in Evergreen. I remember one crazy incident on the bus during a field trip to Denver where this guy in a pickup truck pulled up next to the school bus in the middle of the highway going 60mph. He asked me and Bryan to roll down our window and proceeded to hand over a zip lock bag full of reefer. Bryan reached out, grabbed it, and put it in his backpack.

Bryan's dad was a big-time accountant for major corporations and the house was ample in size and full of entertaining things to play with. We would spend time on Nintendo, jump on the trampoline, shoot hoops, roam around the golf course at night and fuck with the tee boxes and sand traps, or just sit in his room and listen to music and talk life. The most fun of all was jamming on his drum kit which he had bought off a local drum hero. The coolest thing about this 5-piece black Ludwig kit was that it came with three roto toms!

Bryan was also the persuasive friend who first introduced me to alcohol and marijuana. One time he brought over a six pack and some hard liquor and we drank most of it as my parents were out. I remember the funny feeling I got with this new buzz I had never experienced and running around my parent's property for about ten minutes laughing and yelling. It was only after Bryan left that I was puking my guts out in the garage, fixing the mess by rinsing out the garage with a hose.

Sean

I met Sean through Bryan in junior high, or unofficially on a whim when we sat next to each other in gym class and he made a remark about my Adidas shoes that had "U2 Unforgettable Fire" written on them with pen. He said, "Boy is a great album as well." Sean was a little guy, about the size of Michael J. Fox, but he was a funny dude and full of energy.

A gathering of the now "Main Four" (Me, Len, Bryan, Sean) took place some months later in the school year when everyone spent the night at my house. We planned to sneak out during the night and drink a bunch of beers in the field across the street. We brought my infamous Panasonic boom box and recorded the expedition throughout the entire evening.

The first landmark we crossed through was a large concrete tunnel that led to the open property across the highway. This tunnel had a lot of graffiti spray painted all over it, including some nice "poetry" that me and Len added to these walls.

We reached a spot in the field across the way and set up camp for the remainder of the evening. This was Len's first time drinking booze so we were all anxious to see him get faded. Bryan had been known to projectile vomit while drinking and was referred to as "Niagara Falls". After a number of beers were consumed he forewarned us that

Niagara was about to commence. I cued up the tape on my boom box and recorded the sound of the largest projectile vomit spill I've ever witnessed! And not too soon after Len started puking a bunch in little spurts, so we named him "Evergreen Falls". (Referring to the small falls that spilled out from Evergreen Lake).

The night was so classic, and my mom only "heard" about it all when she discovered the tape we made throughout that evening. Oh well, what a tape of entertaining craziness it is, and I still have it in my cassette collection!

Ramtrack

During junior high the school granted us five days off each year, allowing us to pick one of many activities offered to partake in. These escapes were called Ramtrack, as we were the Evergreen Junior High Rams. Bryan and I always picked skiing at Loveland Ski Area and ended the year at Celebrity, a fun center with bowling, putt-putt golf, arcade, swimming pool, and the works. It was very gratifying to have these days off during the school year rather than stuck in a classroom.

For the ski trips a group of us would board onto a Greyhound bus which took us up to Loveland. Bryan and I were always the nutty entertainment during the hour-long haul, as well as a couple of the better skiers in the group. All the more advanced skiers would follow each other to the steeper runs and eventually across the highway to where the chutes were. It was a great feeling flying off the cliffs that led into the chutes and being able to show off in front of some girls that were good enough to ski with us.

The rules inevitably changed and the last couple years of my Ramtrack experiences were cut to only three days a year. I experienced four years of Ramtrack as I stayed back and repeated 9th grade; a decision not made due to bad grades or anything, but rather a choice I made with the influential help of Bryan.

Four Years of Junior High? Why not.

Bryan was staying back in 9th grade due to bad grades so he convinced me to join him in another year of junior high experiences; as he stated we were "too immature" to handle high school anyway. With many days spent in deep thought and discussion regarding this crazy idea I decided to go for it. (A decision that most any sane person would never consider.)

Oddly enough our school system had us in junior high for three years and then high school for the remaining three, and here I am experiencing four years of junior high when most others experience two! Although the whole notion seems ludicrous for some honor student like me to take a step back instead of forward, it ended up being one of the best decisions of my life.

I always got along more with the kids in the class a year behind me, and being that Len was two grades behind me it would bump me closer to him and the others in his class. It turned out to be such a great year because I enrolled in the most ridiculous class schedule: I had two PE classes, art class, and worked as a custodial assistant to earn a free lunch every day. The only real class I took was Geometry, which was ironic as math has always been my worst subject and I was now in an advanced math class, and would remain so all throughout the early part of college.

Minimal Days

The occasional half days, or "Minimal Days", that were offered during each school year were fantastic. Not only was it a day cut in half from school but a large gang of us would bring our skateboards and make a half hour trek through the neighborhoods of Hiwan and end up at the local Pizza Hut. We would invade the booths, fill up the jukebox with our favorite tunes, and proceed to devour a ton of pizza. Many people would skip on the bill and bail while the rest of us would head next door to Village Inn where the advanced skateboarders would ride through the parking lot and drop-jump off the Village Inn sign. Fun, adolescent insanity at its finest!

3/3 Days

As I've always had a fixation for the number 3, I came up with the idea to start celebrating 3/3 Day during each school year. Len, Bryan and I would all wear our large, baggy army fatigue pants and some sports jersey. That was it. We would just dress weird on 3/3 Day each year and go to classes as usual.

During high school we took it to another level, focusing our efforts on pre-class alcohol consumption rather than wearing goofy outfits. I would pick up Bryan and Chris (a new member in our clan) in the Loogie, we would park somewhere secluded and proceed to slam beers before first period class began. It was a trip being in class while sporting a huge liquor buzz. All homage to the 3/3 days!

Grand Slam Contests (featuring Howard Jones)

Bryan and I started a trend in junior high where after school we would head down the hill to Bergen Elementary and have slam dunk contests on their eight-foot rims. If this wasn't cheating enough, we also used the smaller children's basketballs as well. And for some reason it became tradition to sing along to various Howard Jones songs on the way down to the elementary playground. These were the days of Dominique Wilkins, Rick Stansbury, Spud Webb, and of course Michael Jordan, so we had plenty of dunking madmen to try and emulate during our contests.

We even got Len involved, and as he was uncoordinated in sports the only dunk he could do was a goofy style dunk that he made happen by launching off his right foot! Everyone knows in basketball that if you shoot right-handed you take off with your left foot, but Len made this dunk happen every time with the right foot launch and hooking the ball through the hoop as he passed under the rim. Wow.

Next in line were Chris, Sean, and other new arrivals in our gang; Rylan, Bruce, and Heath. These chaps became the next batch of close friends that I would continue to hang out with for the remainder of high school and after college as well.

Ski Trips with Chris

Perfect blend of great tunes and epic skiing!

Every winter season my favorite activity was ski trips up to the mountains. Thanks hugely in part to my dad's intern at the time, Chris. We would meet up at exactly 7:15am at El Rancho parking lot in Evergreen for many weekend ski adventures that continued for years before I could drive myself. It was some of the most gratifying and influential times in my life. Because of these ski trips with Chris in the mid/late 80s I not only became a good skier but also discovered some great music.

Chris would stick a cassette tape into the stereo and give me a quick analysis of why a certain band and particular album was so great. The choice bands we listened to over the years included: Yes, Scorpions, Def Leppard, Moody Blues, and Pink Floyd. Scorpions was usually listened to on the drive up to get us psyched for a full day of aggressive skiing, and Yes *90125* was put in the tape deck every time we headed up to Copper Mountain. As the song "Hold On" would play it would give us the blessing of a great ski day. "Sunshine, shine on, shine on through. Sunshine, shine on, shine on you…"

We were usually one of the first to arrive in the parking lot of whatever resort we were skiing at that day; Copper, Keystone, or Mary Jane being our top three choices. I remember it always being very cold on those first couple lift rides up the mountain and we would take a warm up blue cruiser run before hitting the mighty black diamond moguls for the rest of the day. Chris was already a good skier and he took me down some of the more difficult runs at each ski area, which I loved because it increased my level of performance quickly.

From these beneficial times with Chris I began to ski many times a season with friends during high school. We were all at the same level by this point, and invading all the mogul runs became the main ritual, especially blazing through the many perfect bumps at Mary Jane!

Mary Jane consists of about 85% black diamond runs and was my go to ski area for years. Mary Jane was the area of choice for most Evergreen skiers as half the freestyle ski team was from my home turf. You can still see "EVERGREEN" scraped into many of the chairs on the Challenger lift; which caters to all black diamond bump runs. My only regret was never joining the Winter Park Freestyle ski team myself to see how far I could take my bump skiing abilities, as you never know.

After so many years of skiing moguls I finally learned to snowboard in the mid-90s. I now must bring both my skis and board to each area I venture to so I can switch it up at lunch. And for the record I call it "skiing" no matter which activity I choose. I hate using the term "riding" for snowboarding. Sorry, I'm not that hipster or "slangy". However it is fun when asked if I ski or snowboard I get to respond with, "I go both ways."

I've made a decision that after I'm cremated I want my ashes spread at the top of Phantom Bridge at Mary Jane. Actually, I want my ashes split up and spread in three different places; the top of Mary Jane, behind the stage at Red Rocks, and at the top of the Great Sand Dunes.

Ah fuck it, just sprinkle my dusty remains onto a big poop log and flush me down a toilet.

HIGH SCHOOL DAYS

Summer of '88: Time of Revival

As my life was entering a darker period during my mid-teens I needed a fresh reboot to help bring back more joyfulness into my life. I was losing interest in sports and not enjoying much of anything overall. I called this period my "curse years". I didn't know what to think of myself or my surroundings and felt I was somehow actually cursed.

I proceeded to see a therapist for a couple months, and the most concerning moment from all these sessions was when he asked if I needed help with my confidence, especially with girls. I told him no, even though I really did want to work on these things that hindered me in life. Because of my "fuck it" attitude during this time and rejecting the counselors offer to work on my confidence and social skills, I still have problems to this day dealing with girls and certain social situations.

After living through a couple years of this dark "curse years" phase a revelation struck. I met the owner of a local sporting goods store, Ben, who also happened to be heavily involved with various youth group activities around the Evergreen community. As "fate" would have it there was an opportunity to go away on a weeklong retreat with a group of other teenagers. This week would not only end up being one of the best experiences of my life, but also a saving grace for my tormented mindset and soul.

Young Life Chronicles

Frontier Ranch

Frontier Ranch is an awesome Young Life compound located at the base of Mt. Princeton near Buena Vista, CO. It is constructed on a huge plot of land and consists of various structures used to house all the staff and campers. There's a multitude of activities that take place, and there's every type of accommodation imaginable to keep you occupied, as you hope to find Jesus of course. Activities included basketball, volleyball, swimming, horseback riding, repelling, a challenging ropes course, a dirt track with Honda Odysseys to ride, and a 9-hole disc golf course.

Our small group from Evergreen met at the Sports Mine parking lot, the large sporting goods store Ben owned, and loaded into a van to make the drive out to Frontier Ranch. I was in charge of the music on the way out, which consisted of Rush, Yes, U2, and the Pretty in Pink soundtrack.

After a few hours of driving we pulled into the entrance gate and were approached by some guys dressed as cowboys. They pretended to hold us up like bank robbers and demanded to see a guy named Brian. They "kidnapped" Brian and the rest of us drove into the camp where soon after Brian and a few others came ripping down the dirt road in go-carts.

Our group took refuge in a cabin set-up full of bunk beds known as Cochise. We staked claim on our bunks then proceeded to cruise around the compound to check things out. Me and a different Brian buddied up at first and he happened to have a bottle of liquor with him so we thought it would be fun to include a nice head buzz as we ventured around. We hid in the woods and took shots from the bottle, only to then bump into a couple alternative goth-like girls in our group who happened to be tripping on acid! Here we were at a religious camp for youths to become better people in life and four of us are already intoxicated from the start. God help us!

Each day began with breakfast, and on the first morning our group walked over to check out the ropes course before eating. One guy in our group was taking many photos, and as we passed by a girl's cabin another character in our posse yelled out, "Nice bras!" (As these girls had hung their wet bikinis on a surrounding fence to dry.)

From here on out everyone in our group had a nickname all conceived from me and the go-cart Brian. We had Cameraman, Bra, Oreo, our leader Ben was QG (Quotes Galore), Brian became Sarcastic and I was Original.

After partaking in various activities each day all the campers ended up in the Kiva, where we had a time of worship and participated in singing some great songs. The Kiva nights were always the perfect way to wrap up a fulfilling day of activities and whatnot, and we were shown a slide show of photos that were taken during the daily activities as well.

On one of the last days of the week the entire camp climbed

to the top of Mt. Princeton. As most of the campers were from out of state and grew up in lower altitudes it became a major challenge for many. After a long haul to the top our Colorado group hiked back down a few hundred yards and ended up acting as "Sherpa Guides", aiding others who were having difficulty breathing and keeping their footing under control. That's when I noticed Len on the way down with two girls clinching onto his arms, so I of course decided to help him out.

Both girls were part of a group from Texas and I took over helping this cute skinny blonde named Becca. She was so thankful for my help and gave me a nice shoulder massage on the bus ride back to camp. From this connection with Becca she became my "girlfriend" I hung with for the last couple days at camp.

During the final evening all the campers were loading into vans and buses to begin the journey back home. Brian, Len, and I were so upset about the week's ending and having to say goodbye to all our new friends we decided to play the entire U2 *Unforgettable Fire* album two times in a row on the way home, as it has the elements of a spiritual vibe.

After Len and I were dropped off at the top of our driveways in the late-night hours we stood there for a while reminiscing about all the recent events we just experienced. It was such a gratifying week for us all; a time so magnificent it gave me the focus and energy I really needed to get my life flowing positively again, and it would indeed as the duration of 1988 became one of the best years of my life thus far.

The Breakfast Club

The Breakfast Club was another great Young Life concept derived out of the heart and mind of our leader Ben. It was a brilliant movie that was written and directed by John Hughes and…wait, sorry, our Breakfast Club was a weekly gathering which took place every Wednesday morning before school started. As Len was my next-door neighbor and Brian was growing in friendship, he would pick me and Len up every Wednesday morning in the cold, dark hours at 6am and drive us to each Breakfast Club, which was located in a church near our high school. Brian owned a Ford Galaxy and I remember one of the windows was always cracked open enough to freeze out whoever was fortunate enough to ride in the back seat.

We were fed breakfast each time then the songs would kick off, followed by the sermon, and concluding with a guest speaker would share stories. (A great concept and perfect jolt of spiritual energy to begin our hump day each week.)

The Breakfast Club didn't end after the school year ended, it would continue on throughout the summer break, on top of a mountain at Ben's private residence. It was still held each Wednesday and it was still called the Breakfast Club. The only difference was that it took place during warm summer afternoons and there was a huge plot of land to screw around on. The family even owned a buffalo that roamed around in a large, fenced in portion of the property.

One afternoon it was my turn to speak, and I did so by setting up my enormous double- bass drum kit on the back porch of the house and performed a ten-minute solo in front of the group. Doin' it for Jesus! (Unfortunately there's no documentation of any kind from this event taking place, but I promise you I did "speak" that afternoon.)

The Link

The Link came into existence after Ben bought out a space in a small strip mall near downtown Evergreen. He fixed it up and made it into an after school fun center for teens. There was a stage for performance, fuzz ball and pool tables, and most importantly the interaction and shared spirit between great people. The most classic event that took place at The Link was when we had an all-night slumber party there. It was a group of about twenty in total and I was the only one who made it through the entire night without dozing off once. (And I can still pull an all-nighter with no problem to this day. Wanna party?)

Monday Night Movies

Another fine ritual me and Len participated in during the summer of '88 was Monday Night Movies. Len and I began this tradition of going to a movie every Monday night throughout the summer, just to get our week rolling on the right track. It was usually just us two best buds partaking in this activity but sometimes others joined the cause.

On one occasion these two metal heads approached us for a ride to a nearby party. They hopped in the backseat of my dad's new Chevy Celebrity, and as we drove them around they insisted we put a cassette of Slayer in the stereo. As my heaviest taste in music at this time was still Van Halen and Scorpions, Slayer was shock rock for me to hear for the first time. These two guys were getting us lost, smoking cigarettes, weed, all the elements that stirred up my emotions to a very uncomfortable level. I finally had to boot them out so Len and I could make it back to Evergreen before we broke curfew. (During our late teens we had to drive to Denver to see movies, as the one theatre in Evergreen had shut down.)

There was also a growing popularity in dollar movie cinemas during the late 80s, so in the years following the summer of Monday Night Movies many of us would drive to Denver and catch the dollar movies. These were great times as it was usually a carload of drinking maniacs and we would sneak beers into the theater and roll our bottles down under the rows of seats. We almost always drank bottles as the cheapest beer deal during these times was a twelve pack of Olympia 11oz bottles.

The weird thing about these dollar movie theaters was for some reason the bathrooms were all painted black in color. Even the sinks and urinals were that of black porcelain.

JeffCo Open Space

After years of household chores for pocket change, some casual landscaping gigs, and one horrendous dishwashing job, I finally landed my first good job in the summer of '88. I was selected to work as a trail maintenance employee for JeffCo Open Space. This was a blessing as so many teenagers apply for this job every summer and only a select number are hired.

This job kept me in shape and paid us enough to where we could live well as wild teenagers all summer long. Even better was I got on the crew with the coolest foreman of the entire bunch. He was a mellow outdoor mountain hippie type and very easy to work with. Our entire crew was fun in general. We were the Gray Crew, as each crew had the ends of their tools painted a certain color to keep everything in order and accountable.

On the very last day of the Open Space trail job, a few coworkers from my crew treated me to Elitch Gardens amusement park to celebrate my birthday. It turned into a very late evening after many great amusement rides, then I made it to bed for some much needed sleep, as my adventures continued the next morning...

Return of Becca

The morning after Elitch's I had to get up early to pick Becca up at the airport. She was flying in from El Paso, TX to visit me for a week. With her coming out on the same day as the Monsters of Rock music festival I could hardly contain my excitement. I had to rush down to the airport to pick her up then drive back up to Evergreen, let her regroup a bit and head right back down to the concert. Me, Becca, and Len hopped in the Loogie, picked up one more friend on the way, and we were off to the all-day event.

The line to get into Mile High Stadium seemed like a mile long! Imagine a huge line full of impatient metal heads waiting to get into an all-day concert, right as some jackass chucked a glass beer bottle from the front of the line into the area where we were standing, and that sure stirred up some major commotion.

We got through the entrance gates and proceeded past the stage to our floor seats in the far back. The guitarist for the opening band, Kingdom Come, was in the middle of his solo and I now realized we were in for hours of hard rocking metalized entertainment.

It was a very hot day, about 95 degrees, so the crowd was being dowsed with fire hoses to save everyone from heat stroke. It was so hot and draining that by the time Metallica took stage I was the only one in our foursome who stood for the entire set.

When nightfall set in the Scorpions took stage, followed by headliners Van Halen. Eddie and Alex performing a couple long flamboyant solos of course, but what a great fulfilling day of metal, I must say.

We then proceeded home to Evergreen where Becca and I continued with another very fond memory: I was devirginized by her that very night on my waterbed. Those fifteen to twenty seconds sure was a wavy ride of pleasure I had never yet experienced.

During the remaining days of Becca's visit I took her to Water World and showed her Red Rocks as well. At night we would sneak out of my parent's house and take walks, set up a blanket, and check out the stars. One day we drove to Ft. Collins, CO to visit Chris and Jane. (Yes, the skiing Chris, now married.) They weren't home so we drove around the town cranking Guns n Roses *Appetite for Destruction* and The Cure *Singles* on the stereo in my dad's Chevy Celebrity.

Matt

Growing up in the Bay Area my parents became friends

with a few families that also had kids my age. Years later one of these friends, Matt, came out to visit me. It was perfect timing as Becca had just gone home the week prior, so I welcomed another friendly visit.

I remember opening my first official checking account at the Credit Union of Denver on 8-8-88, and I'm still a member all these years later! After the bank stop I drove out to the airport once again to pick up Matt. His dad and my dad worked together for EPA so this gave way for Matt and I to become close buddies who also happened to share very similar interests in life like most other guys; sports, music, and girls. Like me Matt was also a drummer so when he saw my drum kit in the Evergreen home basement he sat down and played away before I even showed him the guest room.

Like the previous week with Becca, Matt and I indulged in many adventures together. We also hit Water World and Red Rocks, and one evening got busted at a fun center place called Funplex. We were slamming beers in the parking lot and the ticket window people would not let us in to take a quick piss, so I decided to get on my knees and let loose in the grass by the car. During mid-stream a spotlight beamed into my eyes, turning out to be a security officer in a golf cart. They searched our car, emptied out the remainder of the beer, and took us into a back room for "interrogation".

CONCERTS

As like the Monday Night Movies many epic concerts were attended in 1988. The most anticipated and memorable was

Monsters of Rock at Mile High Stadium, but there were many more, like my very first Red Rocks experience seeing Robert Plant. I also saw Yes for the first time live at McNichol's. My only regrets was missing Aerosmith and Pink Floyd, otherwise I conquered every good show imaginable during my epic year of 1988.

EHS

Most people say they hated high school and couldn't wait to graduate, I on the other hand loved high school and experienced some of the best years of my life during these times. In fact, it's hard to say if I would rather live through my high school years again or college.

There were about 1200 of us roaming the halls of one of the ugliest schools in the district; which is ironic as we were one of the wealthiest towns in the district. Although we had the usual clicks like every high school, we all got along pretty well. Yes there were plenty of fights and whatnot but for the most part all the assortment of various factions of students knew each other from growing up together in a smaller town.

As there was a lot of wealth throughout Evergreen the house parties were off the hook! Every weekend there would be parents out of town on some vacation so a number of houses would be invaded by dozens of us hyperactive teens. To this day it amazes me how many parties we had in our three years during school and how much booze was consumed. Obviously I can't share stories about all of them but I remember one time we convinced a girl that she had swallowed a dose of acid we put in her beer. We told her the only way to avoid tripping was to drink a glass of vinegar. Wow did she puke her guts out the rest of that night.

Our card game of choice was Asshole. Not only did we play this game religiously but we had certain rules that no other high school or anyone in college ever used. And believe me, our rules made the most sense dammit.

During my senior year both guys and girls soccer teams took home state championships. These games were awesome to attend. It was a ritual of pounding beers and toking weed on the way down to the game, raising hell in the stands, and partying afterward. I remember one classic trip traveling down to a night game in a minivan with a couple friends, one who had a girlfriend who drove so us guys could party. We drank and smoked a ton of weed and as I was standing in line to get into the game, a friend ran up to me and yelled out, "Dude you are so stoned! Holy shit look at your eyes!". This was fantastic as many other eyes gazed in my direction, most of them parents.

When the game was over we all piled in the minivan and headed back up to Evergreen. The funniest thing happened during the drive back as me and one other guy were sitting in the very back seats, comatose from all the substances we put into our systems. This orange rolled out from nowhere into the middle of the floor of the van and just sat there. My friend and I looked down at it, stared at each other, and just cracked up. It was so random.

Another funny moment I recall in high school was during

math one day the hottest girls in our entire senior class sneezed and farted at the same time; with the fart amplified loud being projected off the plastic seat. I coined a phrase for this incident, calling a sneeze- fart a "Farfegnugan". Even though this is already the name of a VW sports car I thought it was appropriate enough to use the same name in describing a sneeze-fart.

Unfortunately sneeze-farts occur so seldomly that I never get to use the phrase for fuck's sake. Would someone Fargegnugan already! (Oh wait, I better change the spelling as to not get into a lawsuit with VW.)

Bruce

Bruce moved in town from New Jersey during my sophomore year. His dad was some big-wig for AT&T so he was transferred to a nice big home in Evergreen. Bruce was an awesome companion as he was into skiing, golf, tennis, and hoops. I introduced him to Rush and *Exit...Stage Left* became the main album cranked on the way up to the slopes.

For some reason Bruce and I began a custom of eating cinnamon donut holes during the drive up skiing. (This was a change from my day's skiing with Bryan where our snack of choice was orange slices candy.) We referred to the donut holes as testicles, as they were the exact size and shape of human balls. (Because we're so clever and funny.)

I spent New Year's 1990 with Bruce's family at Copper Mountain. This was a memorable New Year's as not only did a new decade enter our world, but somehow we got away with having drinks in the bar that evening. The bar staff passed out leis and kazoos to all the patrons, and as Bruce and I got our buzz rolling I used the kazoo to play along to the Rolling Stones "Symphony for the Devil". Anyone who knows this tune well can appreciate the perfect roll the kazoo played into this scenario during the "woo-woo" parts. It was a packed bar and we eventually had everyone joining in with their kazoos.

Hat Gang

I was part of the "Hat Gang", or "Cap Gang", during high school. This "gang" consisted of about a dozen members that were predominately sport-a-holics and would almost always wear a baseball cap every day during the school year. Most all my best friends were Cap Gang members but I also had connections with the stoner crowd and some nerds as well, cause I'm like that.

Another activity me and some of the Cap Gang indulged in was taking Chevy Chase movie quizzes after school. We had an infatuation with Chevy Chase movies so a couple guys would make up a list of questions from a variety of his movies and the rest of us would spread out on the gym floor and see who could answer the most questions correctly. Really? Yep.

Case Day

Our most esteemed fabrication during high school was Case Day. This day was inaugurated on the 4th of July and took place during all three summers of high school. The idea of Case Day was to engulf an entire case of beer during the hours of twelve noon until twelve midnight on July 4th. That's two beers every hour, and although it was easy to accomplish during the first twelve pack or so, it was an almost impossible task to consume all twenty-four beers in that time frame, puking or not. The first summer I made it through twenty-one beers, and the next summer I "only" put down around eighteen, but all without puking.

Case Day always ended with us joining a large gathering of other EHS students at the local public golf course where the fireworks display took place over Evergreen Lake.

P.E. classes were the greatest thing ever during high school. There was every single activity to indulge in imaginable. We had basketball, flag football, soccer, softball, floor hockey and more. All my best friends were in the same P.E. class as me so that made it all the more fun. The instructor was a character named Mr. Henley. He was point guard for the Kansas Jayhawks at one time so he would take us on at H.O.R.S.E and destroy us every time. He had the energy of a child and would heckle us as we tried to make each basket.

Our senior year softball team was the most notable of all. Again all my friends were on this team and the greatest moment ever was on the very last day of school when Mr. Henley set up a game between both P.E. classes in the afternoon. I hit my 12th home run of the "season" on this day and we took this big group photo at the end of the game. (This photo would mark the end of our high school career.)

Pranks

Our senior pranks were also some of the best that EHS had ever witnessed in the history of this school. We covered the entire flagpole with car tires, filled the school pond with golf balls, took off all the license plates of the underclassmen's vehicles and hung them in the senior hallway. A group of us even stole a life-sized plastic horse off the roof of a restaurant and placed it in the courtyard, along with a bunch of road signs and our stuffed cougar mascot! (If I only had my camera on hand to document this shit.)

During the last few days of school, we indulged in a bunch of other mischief as well. Someone made a collage of porn pictures and printed a bunch of copies to stick all around the school. The best part about these pictures was the face of our campus security cop was cropped onto the head of each porn star in the collage! His name was Mr. Batie but with our immature ingenuity he became known as "Master Batie". It was priceless to see Master Batie trying to scrape off one of these collages that was glued onto the main stop sign as you exited the school parking lots.

We also reserved a night were everyone drove their cars down onto the football field and engaged in actual races around the running track. Of those fortunate enough to own trucks, they were off-roading all along the hillsides of the school while the rest of us were circling the track.

Graduation

During our graduation ceremony we had the popular high

school rock band, Symposium, play a song or two while the rest of us 365 graduates were tossing around beach balls, blow up dolls, and spraying crazy string all over each other. Many of the Cap Gang wore their baseball hats rather than traditional graduation caps, and one guy even skated up to the podium on rollerblades.

The grand finale was when I decided to pull what we called "A Chevy". As Chevy Chase was our hero and the king of prat falls we would try to emulate his dorky actions from time to time. I decided that I would pull "A Chevy" during graduation on the way up to the podium when receiving my diploma. As they were calling the names just before mine I just stood there as casual as can be, with the entire Cap Gang looking on as they anticipated my scheme. They called my name and I proceeded to trip on my way up the ramp to the podium. I received high fives from some of the graduates as I wandered back to my seat, as I'm sure many adult spectators in the stands felt so bad for me yet wondered why I was getting praised by my peers.

Lotto

This idiomatic phrase was coined by me and Brian during the summer after we graduated. We were dining together at the local Pizza Hut and went off on a tangent of weird thoughts. There was an advertisement sitting on the table for Lotto and we were saying how funny it would be if your name was Lotto. Then we took it to a more extreme level and said that Lotto was dead and his body would be on display in the ice of the salad bar. And from this day we became the weirdest duo in Evergreen's history.

We spent one night in my room reenacting movie quotes

and citing random poetic nonsense into my Panasonic boom box. One act was to recreate the opening scene from *Full Metal Jacket*, where Brian was the infamous drill sergeant and I played all the various platoon characters. Anyone that has seen that movie knows how epic that opening sequence is and we did a pretty good job rehashing the entire thing!

Brian then read through an entire children's book about a worm's adventure. Then we had a list of made-up words that came to our minds and read it off onto the tape. It opened with "Scow Ertal Mor Swap", and these four words are still the foundation of our outlandish language that we speak, now known as "Scow". All thanks to "Lotto".

COLLEGE DAYS

FRESHMAN YEAR: Ft. Lewis College

I had the most classic introduction into college. I was awoken by my sister who reminded me I had a huge shiner on my face from a fight I got in the night before. I spent the entire nine-hour drive from Evergreen to Durango battling the pain of a wicked hangover and a bruised, swollen face.

As I was unloading my belongings into my dorm room I never took my sunglasses off in order to hide my enormous black eye. The funniest thing was all the guys in my dorm avoided me during the first couple weeks of school as I was presumed to be the fighter guy; walking around with my black eye accompanied with Georgetown Hoyas tank top and Coors Light hat.

Tim

My hippie dippy roommate was Tim. I really lucked out being set up with him as we both shared interest in music, partying, and staying up mega late each night causing mischief.

Jon

My suite mates were an unusual duo to say the least. They were both engineering majors yet one was small, skinny, and completely nerdy and the other was a huge, long-haired metal head. I remember Jon, the metal head, coming over to our room and the first thing he asked Tim and I was what kind of music we were into. I responded with a list compromising of Rush, Metallica, Beatles, or something of that sort and he was very thankful that at least we all had similar tastes in music.

Jon turned out to be way cool and fun to hang with. We would not hit the same parties together but we sure partied hard in our dorm rooms. His drink of choice was always Captain Morgan's and Pepsi, not Coke, which I always gave him shit about because I like Coke and that's the proper way to mix that certain drink.

KDUR

During my first collegiate semester I got involved with the campus radio station. I signed up for a class to learn about the main operations of radio; production, programming, and hosting. In order to earn our own weekly show we had to first host an early morning jazz show.

It turns out that hosting this morning jazz show was an inspirational experience. I've never been a morning person so each week I would enter the station, turn on the board, stick on a record or CD, then take a cat nap under the consul. A nap for me usually consists of just lying there and thinking about a million things, but being that I love music I would listen to these great jazz albums and got to know some amazing artists over the semester. One in particular was Dave Weckl, who had just released his first solo album, *Master Plan*, and this album introduced me to electric jazz and fusion. From this I discovered other artists like Chick Corea, John Patitucci, and of course Miles Davis.

I must pay homage to this morning jazz show for expanding my horizons further into music beyond rock and roll.

First Party

TOGA! Yep that's right, it happens to be that my very first college party experience was a huge toga party, located in this house with the local band Pink Sprinkler playing. I dressed up with my sheet and got very drunk.

First *Trip*

A bunch of us in the dorms wanted to try mushrooms for the first time and Milan was our go to guy. He was of German descent but grew up in Chili so he could speak three languages. Milan obtained some mushrooms for a small group of us so we ate the shit and proceeded into town on a nightlong adventure.

This trip was one of my all-time most enjoyable that I've experienced in my life by far. Unlike the first time getting laid where it's over in seconds, this adventure lasted *hours*. As our buzzes settled in we proceeded to walk down a nature trail that led from campus into town. Milan was going nuts and running through the bushes during the descent like a wild deer while the rest of us walked, talked, and giggled.

As we entered town we first came across (gross) a McDonald's that we decided would be great to invade first. A few of us ended up in the play land area where you can climb through all those hamster tubes and jump in the pool of balls. Believe it or not we were allowed to carry on for about a half hour before the manager on duty told us it was enough.

We then moved onward to a historic hotel and engaged in a game of hide and seek throughout the hallways, as well as getting into a major ice fight. Then venturing on to a playground that had a skateboard ramp where we all tried to "fake skate" all over the ramp that was made of metal.

The trip concluded at the local Denny's. As Durango is a smaller town this was the only place that was open late enough for people to grub and hang out at, and it was crowded. We were sat at a large, circular table right in the middle of the back area of the restaurant. Our buzzes were still rolling strong and we made a scene. Our laughter was at full force and I was so out of my mind and paranoid I poked two holes into a napkin and used it as a mask to hide from the public view. I don't remember the remaining details of the evening but the whole adventure was worth every minute.

Big Accident

A group of us decided to attend a huge party being held up in Wildcat Canyon. A girl in our resident hall agreed to be the sober driver so a bunch of us piled into this guy's Toyota pickup. The passengers consisted of the one female driver and owner of the pickup in shotgun, me and Tim crammed behind them in the extra cab, and six others in the back.

The party took place in a warehouse with another local band jamming and kegs galore. We all proceeded to get wasted beyond walking ability knowing that we wouldn't have to drive or have any cares in the world, right?

When the party was over the entire group of us piled back into the same Toyota pickup and our female driver proceeded to take us back down to town. We thought our driver was sober but it turned out she had a few drinks during the evening. We were stuck behind a slower vehicle on this windy, canyon road and all the guys in the back of the pickup started chanting for her to pass the other car. After about a minute of this taunting she succumbed to the pressure and gunned it. As we passed the other car the pickup began to fish tale violently due to all the extra weight in the back. We rolled twice and everyone was flung out of the truck and the driver and passenger crashed through the front windshield.

As we rolled I remember hearing the scraping and crunching of the truck's frame making contact with the ground, and glass breaking right by my head. During the second roll I looked over to see Tim's boot coming right at my head. His boot connected with my face and knocked me out.

I came to moments later, lying in a pile of glass over dirt where the pickup had finished its final roll. I was still wedged in behind the passenger seat, the engine was on, and no one else was left in the vehicle. I was stunned to be the only person left inside the pickup and had blood gushing from my face, dripping onto the broken glass, making for beautiful art.

The most classic part of this whole scene was Tim's Grateful Dead mix still jamming on the stereo playing "Franklin's Tower", featuring lyrics such as "Roll away..."

I reached up, turned off the ignition and crawled out the front windshield where a couple of people were startled to see that I was still in the pickup. I remember seeing bodies spread all over the grassy knoll where they were flung from the pickup. Amazingly no one died or was seriously hurt. One guy had a broken back and others were cut up and in pain but that was it. I only had the bleeding to deal with and felt some pain in my hip area from being twisted in the extra cab during the violent rolls.

The paramedics took all of us to the local hospital and examined every one of us. I was the last to be checked out and was so annoyed sitting in that hospital waiting room that I was purposely letting out all these loud beer farts onto the reverberating plastic seats for all others to enjoy. Because we were all so drunk I think that helped prevent any of us from going into shock or being more freaked out by the event than we were. See kids, alcohol is our friend!

That accident made the front page of the local paper and was talked about for years after, as the infamous Wildcat Canyon wreck. (Interestingly enough was a couple other friends that didn't partake in the party with us that evening were instead involved in a road rage fight.)

Skiing, Biking, Humping

Durango had such an array of awesome mountain biking trails and a great ski area, Purgatory, located just twenty miles off campus. We were spoiled to have these trails and skiing so close to campus, and more fortunate to witness the world mountain biking championships that were held in Durango during my freshman year, 1990.

On one occasion a group of us decided to take a moonlight ride on one of these trails. Of course we all had many drinks before we took off and only a few of us had headlamps that were efficient for night riding. I was taking up the tail end of the group, and as I was crossing over a dried-up river section I hit the embankment on the other side and proceeded to rack myself on the frame of my bike! I fell in pain as the others rode on not knowing that I had fallen. I looked up and saw their headlamps cruising up the trial in the distance as I lay there, drunk and moaning.

Overall the skiing and mountain biking I experienced

during my freshman year was priceless, and I rode all these trails on a heavy, steel bike with no suspension.

Humping?

Mud Football

Another fun event to briefly discuss was the mud football tournament. This took place during parent's weekend so my mom and dad were privileged to witness this spectacle. My dorm formed a team and we got our asses whooped by the other teams that were made up of testosterone driven jock fuckwads.

However we did have the best team name of the tournament, The NADS. Our team captain made the point that all the spectators could cheer for us and yell, "GO NADS!"

Navajo Reservoir

The grand finale of stories to share during my freshman year has to be my experience at Navajo Reservoir. A group of us from the dorms, and my good friend Brian from the Young Life days, drove out to the reservoir one sunny weekend.

We arrived and walked out to the reservoir, set up our day camp and proceeded to scope out the options. Turns out that Navajo Reservoir did have an array of cliffs to jump off, ranging in many different heights.

We warmed up on the smaller drops located by our "camp". These cliffs ranged from 15- 40 feet high. From here it didn't take long for our group to venture up towards the bigger drops, ranging from about 60-80 feet high! A few plunged off the 60-foot slab and decided to hit the 80 footer next. (It was actually 78 feet high, as we had our engineering students calculate the drop time of a stone into the water.)

I hesitated to make the 60-foot jump for a while and after I finally did I was last up to conquer the 78-foot beast. It was very intimidating as the upper ten feet of the cliff was a huge bolder that you stood on and had to get a running start to clear the edge below. I remember taking off and free falling for at least three seconds, then plunging into the water, sinking about twenty feet under the surface. The only injury sustained from my jump was the slap of the water against my neck and chin, otherwise it was quite a rush.

Speaking of *rush*, one other interesting moment to share from my freshman year was just after a bunch of us finished our final exam for Astronomy. We gathered in a dorm room with beer to celebrate and I played "Cygnus X-1" by Rush on a stereo as a salute to the power of black holes and space. Lo and behold once the song was near end and Geddy starts shrieking the lyrics: SPINNING, WHIRLING...one of the girls said, "What is this? It's awful turn it off!" Most people, especially women, just don't get it.

SOPHOMORE YEAR: Ft. Lewis cont.

Like my freshman year my sophomore of college was also a winner. I landed a spot in a two-bedroom apartment with three other friends I had met and got to know during my freshman year in the dorms. One of these friends was my original sweet mate, Jon, and the other two were Josh and Louie.

We had the perfect apartment on campus; a top floor looking right out into the main quadrant for our viewing pleasure. Our decor consisted of a small black and white television and a bunch of cut out articles from the Weekly World News I pasted all over the living room walls. Our tradition was cooking Hamburger Helper meals for dinner and we started to cut out the helper hands logo and paste them all over the cabinets in the kitchen. What freaks we were. (Or just me as I instigated all this random behavior.)

My other new friend, Tom, also had an apartment nearby and we began a tradition of cooking Totino's Party Pizzas and watching any number of Rush videos we owned. A funny thing would persist in the late hours of the night as we would cook a Totino's and pass out drunk in front of his television. The pizza would overcook and burn to a crisp; in that of a flattened hockey puck. What art.

A group of us that lived in these apartments would gather and watch football games together on Sundays. During halftime at one of these gatherings Jon offered me $50 to chew on a used band aid we found on the ground. I complied and received a check written out for $50.

I guess I can also share with you a game that my sophomore roomies and I came up with. From the brilliant creators that brought you Lotto and the language of Scow comes a new game, Paken. Brian and I derived the concept and rules for the game of Paken one day in our apartment, which was equipped with a nerf hoop and a few nerf balls. And now let's have a look at the rules: (As written out in a mix of English and Scow)

PAKEN

The initial five hapless members of Paken included Rolf the "Zike Master", Jon "Captain Morgan Man", Josh "What's going on?", Louie "Time for a nap", and Brian "Don't argue with".

(These nicknames sounded better with last names included but I don't want to hassle with permission issues and crap.)

RULES: The object of the game is to shoot the blue ball into the hoop while your opponent tries to deflect your shot with the green ball. The first player to get nine points, as well as the bonus orange ball in the hoop, is declared the winner.

Time limit = 17 min, 33 sec

Bakey- offensive player (blue ball) allowed to make a drink
Vis- defensive player (green ball) allowed to take a drink
Naffel- game judge
Staker- when a player takes a drink while handling the wrong ball, or no ball at all
***3 Stakers = Grom** (penalty of 11 pushups)
Zike- when the offensive player scores any points in 3s (3, 6, 9) they must spin on one leg and yell "ZIKE" (Zike 1

after 3 points, Zike 2 after 6 points, Zike 3 after 9 points) After Zike 3 the offensive player shoots the orange bonus ball from the couch (3 tries)

Zont- a missed shot
Hord- shooting with the wrong ball
Krot- when a judge fucks up
Jaypar- when a ball hits a window
Trame- when a ball hits the wall or ceiling
Fakel- when a ball lands in someone's drink
Qual- interference or hindrance of play
Wako- a tie in competition

And there you have it, the game of Paken. Wanna play?

G.O.C.

Me, Brian, and Tom derived this term from the fact that we were a few dudes that would never get into a legit relationship or last with a girl. G.O.C. is the acronym for "Ghost of a Chance", a song by Rush describing how it's nearly impossible to find love and make it last. I became "Ghost", Tom was "of a", and Brian was "Chance".

"Lob" was also a term made up by us in relation to that of acting like a dork. We not only use this term to describe ourselves to this day but we made a rule that when bowling if you leave the middle pin standing you must partake in the "Lob Dance" before you roll the next ball, hopefully knocking down the "Lob Pin", or else…

How did I originally meet Tom? It was unofficially during my freshman year while playing hacky sack with my roommate in the dorms. We were listening to *Exit…Stage*

Left by Rush and Tom walked by and made a comment about the music. At the beginning of my sophomore year I was officially introduced to Tom after mentioning Rush to a mutual acquaintance. We have been good friends ever since and will forever share our admiration for Rush! There you have it.

What else can I share from this sophomore year? A lot but it's time to write about other events during my later college years, the years spent in another fort; Ft. Collins.

CSU

I transferred to Colorado State University and became a Ram for my third year of college. It was time for a change and a few other friends from Ft. Lewis transferred to CSU as well. I moved into the perfect apartment once again, Rams Village, a new establishment that was built right by campus. It was me, Brian, another Brian, and Nathan. (Nathan, or "Beef", who was another good friend from Evergreen)

Nathan and I moved into the apartment first, and during that evening we set up the television and sat there most of the night watching MTV 120 Minutes while eating salads with crumbled Ritz crackers and psychedelic mushrooms added on top.

My good friend Len joined us and lived in the main floor closet under the stairs for a while. No shit, we had him pay for the utilities as "rent". It was awful in the fact that this space under the stairs was where we stored our beer cans and other recycled materials, but he couldn't pass up the price and toughed it out.

There were many memorable times experienced while living in Rams Village. "101 Club" night was a doozy. This is a game where you must take a shot of beer every minute until you have surpassed 100 total. (This is sometimes referred to as "Century Club" but like the game of Asshole, we from Evergreen made it into our own thing.) Nathan and I made it past 200 shots on this occasion; 205 and 233.

As the first day of classes commenced we all rode our bikes together with a mob of other students to campus. I remember noticing how many more students were present compared to Ft. Lewis, as well as the number of hot girls that were riding along with us in their Daisy Duke jean shorts. Welcome to the big leagues Rolf Gunnar Hauge!

Disc Golf

During the first week of classes Brian and I were strolling through the main campus quad area and noticed these guys throwing Frisbees at chained baskets. We were caught off guard until we realized they were playing Frisbee golf. We hadn't ever played on a real course since Frontier Ranch and were intrigued right away. My roommates and I bought some discs and proceeded to play the campus course an uncountable number of times for the remainder of our collegiate years at CSU. It was a fantastic leisure activity to engage in after classes were out for the day, or during the weekends to rid ourselves of the brutal hangovers we endured.

I still play rounds of disc golf to this day; participated in two tournaments over the years, taking 2nd place in one. Fantastic leisure activity, especially for slacking stoners.

Frat Boy

I will try almost anything once and was convinced to join a fraternity. Brian's older brother and one of our other friends was already a member of Sigma Chi. The rush week was a blast! Being that David Letterman was a former Sigma Chi we had a "David Letterman Party", consisting of chucking large items of furniture, a toilet, and other stuff off the roof of the house. That same evening we also got to use baseball bats and beat the shit out of an old car they had placed in the back parking lot.

You're not allowed to share some of the secrets revolving around the fraternity life but I can at least share a bit of the tales during our pledging semester. The twelve of us that became the group of Sigma Chi pledges in 1992 were referred to as the Dirty Dozen. Not too creative of a title but it sure related to all the boundaries we pushed during that one semester. Everyone in our pledge class were pretty good guys, and even the active members commented that we were the best group the house had seen in a while.

There would be parties every weekend of course and our jobs were to be back at the house each morning after and clean up the mayhem leftover from the night before. This would also be interesting as many girls had to partake in the "walk of shame" when they left the house after a one night stand with one of the members while us pledges were cleaning away.

Pledges were also in charge of setting up the tailgaters for each football game, which included saving a section of seats for the active members inside the stadium. The tailgaters were so much fun as anyone can imagine.

Derby Days was weeklong event that took place in the spring and consisted of all the sororities competing for points with Sigma Chi. These points were earned by pulling pranks on us. I was kidnapped one day and duct taped to a light pole near campus. The girls stuck maxi pads with Taco Bell sauce all over me! Luckily this was in front of the dorms so some guy came out and cut me loose with a pair of scissors. Another time I was blindfolded, stuck in a van, and drove to a sorority house. One of the girls rubbed Ben Gay on my balls. OUCH!

Initiation Week was the final chapter as a pledge. It consisted of each pledge having to spend the week in the house and engage in various rituals to finalize our fate. Just hours before the week began Brian and I went to the local movie theater and watched *Last of the Mohicans*. It was such a great film and our anxiety became prevalent after the movie ended and we made our way to the fraternity house, knowing we would be prisoners for the reminder of the week.

After becoming an official member of Sigma Chi I remained active in the fraternity for about another year. The parties and activities were dwindling down and I was getting sick of paying the monthly dues that were required. I had enough but don't regret partaking in the Greek scene and all the great experiences it brought into my life.

Spring Breaks

Many college students spend their spring break at Daytona Beach, South Padre Island, or Cancun, yet me and my gang of friends went to Lake Havasu. CSU's spring break was one week earlier than most other big universities so there was little action to be found.

We were all on a tight budget and our crew couldn't afford to go in on a house boat which would have enabled us to venture out onto Lake Havasu. Copper Canyon is infamous as the area of the lake where all the debauchery takes place. It's where everyone connects their boats together and it's a free for all event.

Because we did not get out onto the lake we were stuck on the beach drinking in our own social circle on the patio of the only bar accessible. The highlight of our days spent on this patio was drinking green beer on St. Patrick's Day and the bartender allowing me to play my mix tapes on the sound system. Otherwise we were all in envy of the other college students who were out on the lake really partying it up hard while we sat around.

The second spring break during CSU times included a group of us skiing at Mary Jane resort for the day then packing up and driving towards Arizona to relive more of Lake Havasu once again. There was an incident where I lost all my friends after spending some time at a nightclub. I ended up inland at some campground and recall being kicked out of someone's tent. I was taking a nap in one of their sleeping bags. I was so drunk, disoriented, and jogged my way through some vacant fields towards where the beach area was about a mile or two away. I was wobbling along and at one point tripped on some barbed wire and cut my leg open. I found a hotel and asked them to get me a cab back to the beach. I had no money on me and offered the driver a small bag of potato chips I had in my pocket. He was cool enough to bring me back to base without charging me for the ride, even rejecting my awesome chips.

Take note that during both these spring break ventures to Lake Havasu we stopped in Las Vegas on the way out and way home each time.

What happens in Vegas…should happen more often!!!

Final Collegiate Years

A group of us moved into a large house during our final two years as students at CSU. There were seven bedrooms throughout the three levels of this house. The house was located right off the huge oval quadrant in party ally. There were many other houses within a two-block radius all loaded with college student tenants and it turned into Marti Gras every weekend. We were infamous for throwing some big ragers to the point where the campus television station conducted an interview with us just before another one of our massive parties commenced, covering the topic of noise complaints after having been busted twice within the first few weeks of the school year.

You'll have to take my word for it that all my experiences; the booze, drugs, parties, girls, music gigs, spring breaks, taking final exams while hungover…all this reckless debauchery mixed in with some valuable education I acquired over my 5.5 years of collegiate life was all worthy of praise.

However, the most brutal onslaught of realism struck me on the day of graduation. As I sat amongst the many other Liberal Arts majors in the large basketball gymnasium, I had a panic attack. My heart rate increased and I was almost hyperventilating as the thoughts of "Now what?" crossed my mind. I remember this vividly; the notion of my college years coming to a close and having to dip into the real world and work a full-time job suddenly petrified me.

I happened to be sitting next to someone I went to high school with and asked him what he was going to do. He responded with, "Fuck it, I'm moving out to Squaw Valley to be a ski bum for a while." Not only did this sound more gratifying than any desk job option for me but coincidentally I too worked a season as a ski bum as one of my first official post-collegiate jobs.

THE STING OF REALITY

The Sting of Reality is a metaphorical idealism of sorts which signifies all the unfortunate happenings in our realities that clogs the flow of the many efforts we put into our endeavors in life. Life is an ongoing battle; we have goals, make plans of action, put our heart, soul, efforts, and money into these ambitions, then something or someone will divert our objectives, making for a calamitous outcome.

For example, you sign a friend up for an event you both want to attend and have planned for and they back out at the last minute, creating more frustration for you to take more time and energy to fill their spot or pay for their spot and go alone. This is a weak yet common example of the many "stings" we take in our lives, and there's other examples from numerous circumstances we all encounter which can be much more enervating.

Instead of an actual sting from a bee, it's a metaphorical *sting of reality*. Which in my case I seem to be continually attacked by a swarm of tenacious bees.

You think Africanized killer bees are scary? Look up the Japanese Giant Hornet!

ME, MYSELF & AYE?

It's not easy being me. (As sung by Robin Williams in the movie *Popeye*). This is the opening statement I choose to kick off this arduous chapter. I was pondering what to use as a title for this first section and as I exited the shower one morning this cheesy, forthright song sprung up in my head.

Life sure can be a bitch, we can all agree on this perception, but for me life can be a fowl cunt. Everyone is born with certain genes they acquire after their parent's sperm and egg have a party together. You exit your mother and splat into the nurse's arms to then have your original lifeline clipped away. You are now part of the real world. Good luck.

As time ticks onward you begin to show similar

characteristics that both your parents “handed down to you”. You’ve inherited traits that match certain components of each of them. How you were brought up can most certainly conjure up what your persona becomes but there is the DNA from both your parents that created who you are.

My parents are the two greatest anyone could ask for. They both have heart, intelligence, are full of life, and are very devoted to family and everything good they stand for. Although I too possess many of my parent’s whimsical traits, I also have my internal demons to cope with.

The problem with me, and this skewed artistic mindset I possess, is that nothing is ever concrete with any thought or action I take. My mental intellect runs so deep yet is so chaotic at the same time. If you take my musical interests and ideas alone you would run into a huge fork in the road within my brain that gives you dozens of options on where to take the ideas and aspirations that dwell within.

It’s hard enough just to play a musical instrument, let alone take the craft to exciting new levels by learning and mastering the fundamentals, meshing various styles, or even playing multiple instruments. Then with me it becomes a nerve-racking endeavor of not only building up the ultimate drum kit or composing the ultimate musical parts, but how to incorporate all these pieces of the puzzle into different songs and projects I’m in. Each band I’m involved with writes, learns, performs different genres of music. Then I deal with varying artistic personalities and conflicts within each band, and must factor in drumming on different set ups in every project. A love and passion for me becomes more of a pain-staking nuisance when you add in all the elements involved.

People wonder why artists, especially musicians, are so dark and cynical. This is because the mindset of an artistic thinker is not wired properly. Properly as in just good enough to handle all that is necessary to achieve and live life within a basic, standard means of stability, success, and happiness. To have a mind that is constantly shifting from thought to thought and is layered with too many interests and ideas while also in a state of darkness and confusion just doesn't cut it within the conventional flow of the world we live. This is tough for artistic people to cope with when trying to persevere in their crafts *and* keep up with the changing trends and demands of the real world that everyone must face. All while trying to maintain sanity along the way.

Majority rules. And most people possess a healthier, calmer, more rudimentary mindset which "allows" them to mesh within the confines of conformity and function within the means of basic wants and needs of the world. Most humans have more balance in life without the mental anguish or time consuming hassles pursuing creative endeavors like us "artistic minorities". That's the fact jack(asses).

While most people come home from a hectic day at the office and running errands afterward, they hit the couch for Netflix time. We artists are back out hitting the pavement.

With the mindset I possess it would take me five lifetimes to achieve all that I have locked up in the mental vault. Everyone says this about themselves and it's true that every human dies with many unaccomplished goals and undiscovered aptitudes, but with me it goes beyond just one lifetime and a list of could of/should of regrets or what could/should be in my life that demoralizes me.

A perfect example of how my brain operates was when I was watching a comedian at a small club one night. I was with a couple friends in the front row and during the middle of this guy's routine I tuned everything out around me and began to re-write his routine as he was performing! My mind went into a hyper-focus/psycho creative mode within a certain instant and I was editing his routine and visualizing him performing this alternate routine I was "writing for him". Sure I had some 420 incentive but what a trip! How did this happen? (Don't ask me, ask my brain.)

The hardest part about being me is a reflection from this example and more innovative tendencies that are constantly being generated and recycled within seconds of my thoughts every fucking day. Yet I must work dull, pointless jobs to survive and spend so much frustrating time and energy trying to make something out of all my ideas, talents, and being part of any number of great music projects getting nowhere.

I will be thinking of an idea for a movie and my mind will begin writing the script, music score, casting the characters, figuring out the props, location setting, camera angles…you name it and I've already got it figured out within minutes. The problem is it's all in my head, and trying to get so many ideas and visions to turn into reality is the hard part of this infuriating realism.

It's my lack of effort or bad attitude to blame for such miniscule success in my life? FUCK NO. It's lack of money, the times, trends, and especially other people and their lame-duck mannerisms that act as the true culprits for so many possible things not coming to life that easily could. Simple plans, agreements, and other standards that go nowhere these days, when for *centuries* prior there was rarely such a thing as being flaky, irresponsible, non-committal, and other nonsensical human behaviors that are so prevalent in today's world. (Like the song by Slipknot, people really can = shit.)

Just like writing this dog gamed book, it's a never-ending process of thinking, writing, organizing, editing, then debating what will work and what is expected from myself and others who will be reading it. I dwell over the proper use of grammar; First person? Third person? Present tense? Past tense? I don't know, fuck off, just let me write and someone else take care of all this tedious nonsense. An editor, agent, manager, mortician…But this extra help all takes money to pay for these services offered, acting as the icing on the many cakes I'm baking. (Icing ain't cheap!)

All this mental chaos within a single mindset, on top of also having to manage the numerous other realities/stresses in life that every person deals with day to day? It's a grueling lifestyle to say the least. Being an artist really is a 24/7 job. We never "relax" in this lifetime; we're always "working". Our brain's RPMs are constantly redlining with ideas to pursue and agendas at hand. (And you wonder why Van Gogh cut off his ear, or how Sid Barrett ended up in a mental ward?)

At this point in my life, and spending so many frustrating years being flung around in a continuous hurricane, I would love to witness another human adopt my brain and live my life for a few months. Fuck it, just a few weeks would be sufficient enough to enable any person to realize the tormenting chaos that dwells within my reality that be. I've had a few friends tell me they would never want my life after witnessing some of my nightmarish scenarios.

However, during my rare golden moments of magical bliss, there's nothing better for a person to experience with a mind like I have. (Too bad the rare blissful times are usually overshadowed by the more prominent realities of darkness.)

I have concluded that only the homeless, paraplegics, people born with diseases like cerebral palsy and terminal patients have it worse than us with mental disorders. Yet many homeless and paraplegics say they are happy enough in their minds to carry on! Many would argue that war veterans have it the worst with PTSD and all the shit they went through, and I would agree, except most of them signed up for the duties and hardships that come with being in the armed forces! You must know you're signing up to enter Hell. I never signed up for this uncontrollable mental insanity that acts as a malicious tenant I can't ever evict out of my brain's "apartment complex". So eat me!

These sound like bold and arrogant statements but if you've lived my life in its entirety then you would know how I can make such accusations. I would rather have drug and alcohol struggles any day than deal with mental issues. And again, eat me if your predictable comeback is, "You don't know that for certain it's all relative, subjective, they suffer just as much." Please.

I don't know it firsthand what many other's go through but I know how people with substance abuse issues can get through it and *move on*. Sure it's a disease and painful living in it for however long the phase lasts but if you have a functioning mind and will power you can get through almost anything bad or disheartening.

There's plenty of alcoholics in my family tree and I see

many of the struggles first hand, but their lives are mostly fine and their drinking problems only screw with other loved- ones who have to live with them. Mental people are harmless, empathetic softies and only fuck themselves, not other fuckers.

One uncle quit drinking years ago, yet he's still referred to as an alcoholic? Even though he's been completely sober all these years since, he's still an "alcoholic" because it's a "disease"? Weird.

Makes about as much sense as getting a DUI when you're drunk but not even driving a vehicle at the time. Maybe you're taking a nap in your vehicle until you sober up enough to drive. You're not actually driving or any threat to society during this time, yet an officer can issue a citation for DUI? Or there's reports of people having their keys on them within fifty feet of their vehicle and if drunk they can get a DUI from some sort of bullshit "intent to drive" rule. Awesome. Suck a big sweaty dick USgAy legal system!

It's like this: Almost anyone can work a job, get a college degree, or do whatever it takes to "earn" their status in this world. Heck anyone has the backbone to strive far in whatever they want with attitude, focus, hard work and all. (Except those oddly unfortunate like me.)

If someone works hard to get their master's degree or doctorate then they are usually rewarded for their advanced accomplishments. Does an athlete that works his entire life and makes it into the pros deserve his net worth? In a morally logic world, FUCK NO! Even though that person worked hard to get to where they are no one deserves a minimum of six figures to sit on a bench as a third string quarterback or a backup kicker, let alone a big seven or eight figure contract deal for all the starters on the field of play.

What I'm getting at is with the world of the arts *nothing* is guaranteed. No matter how hard an artist works at their craft; factoring in all their abilities, determination, efforts…they might not ever earn shit for this. An athlete gets millions and an artist who is on the same level as "deserved status" gets the shaft most of the time. And I know there's thousands of athletes that work their butts off and never earn income of any kind as well, but I hope you get my point that overall artists have the toughest odds against them for making any kind of healthy living within their craft over most any other pursuance of so many other achievable endeavors in the world.

Artists are best off accepting their interests and abilities as hobbies or avocations at best, and are usually forced to take another income route in that other "real world" to compensate. But after a certain amount of time living this lifestyle it can drive that creative individual into severe depression or literal insanity.

If the average person wants to play the violin and tell me to quit whining about us poor artists and our issues then I ask of them to run a 10K race while they have a strong head cold. Go out and work on the roof or finish building that fence while fighting the flu. See, you can't because you are temporarily hindered by a virus that drains all your energy and focus, so you can't accomplish normal functioning tasks while sick. This is very similar in relation to a person with an artistic mindset or certainly a mental disorder, except our symptoms are not just impeding phases to get through, but instead PERMANENT.

This is why I must constantly defend myself and all the thousands/millions of others who have to live a life with any debilitating hindrance, against the *many more* millions that are fortunate to have very little or no issues to deal with at all. So play the violin for me you ignorant conformists, as I will retaliate by pounding some lurid drum and percussion pandemonium into your calm, simplistic, underachieving, boring world. Deal?

This really takes on a new perspective to the "life is what you make of it" theory doesn't it? If you're disabled in any way there are things you just can't accomplish in life no matter what your attitude, determination, or belief. You make the most of it, but "it" is much harsher bitch to deal with when plagued by anything debilitating.

If an artistic person does get a lucky break into the industry and finally gets to live in all the hype and benefits that come with that new fame, there are a couple artistic careers I must mention that are highly overrated with status and pay; TV advertising and modeling.

TV commercial actors get paid top dollar to memorize very few lines for a commercial spot on TV. They can make more than a teacher's yearly salary in one shoot! A shoot that lasts a few days at most, then you factor in residuals and all else that comes with the package. Who in what fucking world created this idealism that after an actor makes a national television commercial they get more money in their pocket every time it airs?

They already made more than they deserve to be showcased on TV in the first place, why do they get more money just because that ad is shown numerous times?

These actors should be happy enough that they get to brag to their family and friends about being on television, for free even, but not over-compensated and spoiled to the extent as they are for such an easy task. *Can you hear me now?*

As for models, are you kidding? Many get paid huge amounts of money to pose in front of a camera. Yes it's a form of "art" but you basically just have to look pretty and pose. Most women still have no idea the power they have with good looks alone. Sex sells and any attractive female should jump all over any opportunity to make good money doing nothing more than posing for some douche photographer; representing whatever brand by wearing various outfits required or no clothes at all.

Fuck, sign me up! I'll book an appointment right now in Trinidad, CO for that "cock-to- cunt" transformation; add in some silicone chest enhancements, and be jumping into any easy, money-making opportunity out there that only requires some T&A.

With the new trends and hype in transgenderism, this will go over even better! Fuck my natural talents and abilities, just look good and get a bit freaky in order to make quick easy money; a sexy female package being controlled by cogent male brain power. Perfect.

Other benefits included in the modeling package aside from the ridiculous amounts of money earned for such derisory "work", is the hotel and travel packages included and obtaining a vast collection of free clothing from top of the line designers. All this hype, fame, and reward just for having a certain look and moving around a bit in front of a camera. Fucking really???

Seriously, it's this type of illogical nonsense within our legal system, entertainment industry, and so much else in this great yet extremely retarded country of ours that makes me wonder what the true values are in this world anymore.

A teacher's yearly salary earned for a few day's work? You have a certain look and can make more money than a majority of the other 7 billion inhabitants on this planet? Most who usually have more to offer with actual skills and perseverance than just "lucking out" with certain inherited biological looks? Holy shit. Suck on this notion, fuck this world. Kill me!

Wait, before you pull that trigger, one more subject of concern regarding people of fame and all this over-hyped praising that comes with it. I have never *agreed with the notion that once a person becomes famous that everything they do from that point on is "brilliant".*

For example, if Picasso blew his nose onto a sheet of paper it could be sold for $10,000, just because it's Picasso's snot. This is complete rubbish! Just because someone like him might very well be "gifted" doesn't validate everything *he does from then on is suddenly "priceless." It's sNOT. Quit worshipping people of fame!!!*

If a 3rd grader made the same "art" out of his snot and hung it on the wall of the school halls, all the other students and parents would say, "Gross! That's stupid, he's a weirdo anyways." Yet maybe he gets a "lucky break" down the road and all those students and parents are regretting tearing down and burning his original work of art, because years later this freak kid has an established name and credibility in the arts world now.

Anyway, I sincerely hope many of you outcast "snot-heads" out there do indeed get that lucky break, and laugh all the way to the bank! You'll be blowing your nose in satin tissues from then on.

Overachieving Perfectionist/Neurotic Slacker

Since my transition out of college and into the real world I somehow lost my focus, drive, and momentum needed to maintain basic stability to be able to strive forward like most everyone else. I can't seem to employ my natural skills properly or accomplish certain things that could boost my overall wellbeing. I employed too much vitality at a younger age living as such a persistent, striving, overachiever when most adolescents and teens are screwing off and not caring about things to the level I did. I burned too much fuel during the times when things don't matter so much and didn't leave enough in the tank to keep the vehicle of determination driving forward steadily into adulthood.

For years I applied so much time and precision to perfect any project or craft I became involved in. After so many years of this process I lost the momentum and drive to continue. My "edge" has diminished and nowadays I'm ready to leap off an edge!

A strange coincidence of verification how my mental affliction hinders my life is one of my sisters has gone through similar changes and struggles in her adult life. She too was a golden child; scholastic student, star athlete all through her younger years, then took a 180 for the worse after college and into middle-age adulthood like me as well.

It's actually not a coincidence at all, as we're both exhibiting the same behavior patterns and struggles from biologically inherited mental issues mixed with overachieving burnout from our younger years that now makes for disheartening outcomes in our more important adult years of life.

To the majority in this world who played their cards in an opposite manor; lucky you, you did it right.

Procrastinative Tendencies

Funny scenario how so much time had passed just to set up my damn computer and begin writing this book in the first place. All I needed was an adapter plug to compensate for my outdated, two-hole outlets prevalent in the house's ancient walls. It took me days just to get motivated enough to go to the hardware store and spend a dollar on one fucking adapter. Even my cashless ass has that kind of change floating around in my car ashtray, yet it still took me days to accomplish this simple task.

Using this one example out of hundreds of other predicaments I put myself in, the main reason for taking so much time to get this book translated from pondering thoughts within my manic mind and onto the computer screen is my dilemma with procrastination.
Analyze, debate, procrastinate!

After months of thought and anticipation I finally printed a t-shirt that says *Procrastinative Tendencies*. Of course the font is that of the same as the band `Suicidal`

`Tendencies.` (Which is ironic that I really have those tendencies as well, yikes.)

Warning: I not only tend to drift from subject to subject, or thought to thought as I interrupt myself throughout every subject in this book, but I also have a **tendency** *to become very desultory and drift way too deep into many extraneous subjects within this written manifesto.*

Where was I? Ah whatever. Give me some lotion and tissues, I'm off to procrasturbate! (Kudos to Chad for thinking up this one.)

Anticipatory Anxiety

The ill-fated existence of anxiety can be a killer in anyone's life. Then you add in the anticipation of an upcoming event or situation that you are feeling uncomfortable about and this can escalate the anxiety to new levels.

I can't tell you how many times I have dwelled over certain upcoming events I must face, just out of the anticipation of what's to come before it even happens. Hours of sleep lost the night before I was to start another dead-end job, or the minutes counting down before arguing a case of defense to a boss or someone of power can bring about this anticipatory anxiety.

It's that pre-conceived trepidation for any upcoming event you're not looking forward to that makes up anticipatory anxiety. Something you are almost certain will make for a troublesome outcome so panic sets in before the occurrence takes place. Usually the event turns out not as bad as you anticipated, but trying to convince my brain of this never does justice. It's still always, "Fuck I don't want to do this! I have so much else to offer that isn't so typical or only semi-emblematic!"

It's never fun to be anywhere we don't want to be, and being that most humans spend most of their lives working forty hours a week at a place they don't want to be at is fucking sad. I can only anticipate the best to work out for me at some point, sooner than fucking later, and not have to live the rest of my life facing anymore anxiety-induced scenarios or unfortunate dilemmas like I already have for YEARS.

Do You Play Pinball? My brain does.

I'd like to cut right to the chase and describe an example of a neurotic debate gone haywire. This scenario came about some years back and it's unreal even to me how much I put myself through. Someone keeps putting quarters in my pinball machine and ricocheting my round, silver ass all over the place! Okay here we go…

"Just got into Vail. Apparently we're throwing raging pre and post parties, place is enormous!" This is the text message I received from a friend while I made my descent down Loveland Pass and homebound from skiing at Copper Mountain Resort. I decided that after 3.5 hours sleep and an impressive day of skiing (conquering eleven runs in four hours) that I would have to officially bypass the day's final option; to drive a bit further west and join five hyper Bostonians for a night of fun in a penthouse suite located in the middle of Vail Village. Or wait, do it? Don't do it?

The debating began as I was pulling out of the parking lot at the base of Copper. I hit a red light just before the ramp that leads onto I-70 and that had me make a right turn into the gas station complex that had a Seattle's Best coffee shop attached to it. I figured I could get a coffee to help revive my energy and maybe hang out there for a short while and make calls, texts, check emails and all that would allow me just enough time to see if my friend convinces me to get my ass to the condo. Or I just head home and be happy with a great day of skiing.

Well the girl behind the counter was very cute and had a fun personality. She was a dancer, singer, artist and appeared so wholesome. She was fun to flirt with so now I was able to use this influence as an excuse to linger around a bit longer and continue onward to a level of "advanced debating".

I lingered for a half hour then got in my trusty 4Runner and exited onto I-70...EAST. I decided to just get home as I figured the 3.5 hours sleep and long ski day would ruin any attempt at a fun, social evening in Vail. But as I passed the Frisco exit a new subject of debate entered my mind; the barista girl! Screw the Vail condo option at this point when I had just met a cute, fun girl who lived in Leadville and might be bored and want to hang out for the evening.

As I approached the town of Silverthorne I was about to exit the highway and turn around but was cut off from the exit ramp and stuck on the highway up the long, steep hill to the summit of Eisenhower Tunnel. I was livid at this point as I had conjured up this new plan to "work the girl" and even added in the notion that it was a full moon and everyone's auras are sprouting with vibrant energy. But I was also pissed that I didn't try to close any deal with her just minutes earlier when I was there in the first place!

I then passed the Loveland exit while debating again whether to turn around and finally had to exit at Georgetown to take a piss and regroup my thoughts. I called a friend and explained my predicament and he said, "Fuck it, turn around and go back, what's 15-20 minutes of driving? Just stick in some tunes and fucking go." (Thanks Chad.)

Let it be known that Chad is an altered name but he has become one of my best friends in recent years. I've known him since junior high but we never hung out much until after I was out of college. He's a great guy with a twisted sense of humor, and a fellow Leo like me. There's a lot that could/should be written about him for sure.

I arrived back at the gas station complex about 15-20 minutes later only to find that the coffee place had just closed five minutes earlier. Luckily the gas station side was still open so I cruised in and took another piss, as some guy was releasing the most wretched smelling shit in history, enough to make me dry heave as I urinated. (You see, this detail was in honor of Chad and our love of "poop talk".)

I knocked on the glass door to Seattle's Best and the girl came right over and unlocked it. I made up a quick story that I drove to Vail, checked my emails, and had received a message from my friend about skiing Loveland Pass during the full moon. I told her I was heading back that way when I realized I left a ski coupon at the coffee shop(?)

Of course I didn't take Chad's advice to be straight up and just ask her out, so I beat around the bush a little and passively asked what she was up to for the evening. As she had a 3-year-old son her plan was to just go home and chill with him, whereas my final attempt to dial her in consisted of, "Oh come on it's a full moon we're supposed to get rowdy!" And her response of, "That's why I want to stay in and chill because of the full moon." Okay.

My journey slowly progressed back east towards Denver and I was still battling my racing thoughts and frolicking about the Vail opportunity. I pulled off I-70 a couple more times during this prolonged debacle just to stop and debate some more, never trusting any ideal conclusion I came up with. It was unbelievable, and when I was finally good with just going home after the midnight hour I realized that I really do have a huge problem with neurosis! I can't manage my life, make adequate decisions in any kind or timely manner, or even progress fashionably in life without diving myself fucking nuts!

I ended up driving over Loveland Pass on my second trip towards Denver and after hanging out on the pass for a while I began texting girls I knew that were single and might be ready to party in Denver. I had to once again turn to pussy as my new motivator in order to stop overanalyzing my options and thinking about some amazing times, and pussy, I could be missing out on in Vail.

Is my age truly becoming a factor, or am I just burnt out and too paranoid of an event not ending up as good as I expect it to be in my mind? It's a mix of both. I've experienced a lot in life and maybe some of this burnout feeling comes from the "been there done that" brashness, but come on, what am I thinking here?

Impossible Persuasiveness to the Masses

God is it hard to persuade anyone of anything anymore; unless you're already established in life, have a respectable status, or a lot of fucking money to "buy people's attention".

Hardly anyone gives you the benefit of the doubt these days. Unlike me and a handful of humans who always give others the benefit of the doubt. Far too often in fact, that it gets me in predicaments I don't deserve because too many people are heartless, soulless fucks; without a doubt.

I believe a lot of this is due to the "rotten apple" theory where enough people in the past have bragged about something they deem worthy, when really it isn't worthy at all. So the rest of us up and comers who really are legit and worthy get screwed by the "heard that before" skeptics, who now won't budge because of all the moronic idiots that talked smack in the past!

The only gratification us starving artists receive is when an already rich and famous figure gives us kudos that there are many of us out there trying to break ground and make it to the level they have. They understand the agony of working diligently at a skill and trying to promote our abilities and usually get nowhere with it all. If we don't personally know a famous person or a have close significant other with a generous cash flow, we most likely be forever fucked in the world of arts and entertainment.

Like everything I love to gripe about in life there are so many factors that sum up the reasoning behind all this misfortune, but again it's so much worse in this current state of our society and nation in general. People say it's all attitude but I call bullshit on that. A good attitude is healthy but can only do so much against the random curveballs life throws at you whenever it wants. It's mostly who you know, luck and timing, or again "buying your way into success". (Unless you're a conformist cookie cutter then just think positive and do your job! Bitches.)

With enough money or the right connections you can accomplish ANYTHING. Otherwise you end up like the thousands of other talented artists, innovators, and "dreamers" that work a bill-paying job for life and only have the satisfaction of part-time artistic release for little reward. While the millions of others out there only need to input some hard work, maintain a good (i.e. "realistic") attitude, and kiss some ass to get by adequately in life.

Some are fine with this, but not me. I need money so I can fund my endeavors; "buy" the proper help needed for advancement, then utilize these connections to help "sell" my ideas, creations, and thrive in life within the multitude of interests and talents I possess! All this amazing shit that will otherwise go forever unrecognized to the world. And that's that.

Poor me? FUCK YOU!

Sodomized by Unruly Standards

No one likes to get it in the ass. (Aside from gay people and a small number of women who prefer the exit tunnel from time to time.) I can't stand certain people, or rules formed by people, that screw your world within unnecessary means. Anyone who treats another human unfairly to the extent that it messes with that person's spirit deserves to get a big one in the ass. You don't screw with other people or their belongings, period. Go ahead and vandalize or steal but do it to corporate property and not private citizens!

I hate to focus on so much negativity surrounding our realities but it's all these disputes I have with society that keep me on the rampage of wanting to be the ultimate revolutionary against this crap. Too many indiscriminate circumstances and forlorn outcomes exist in our one lifetime. Even when we're destined to try and make for the best and succeed, something or someone will inevitably fuck you in the ass!

I can't begin to tell you the list of places I would love to shit-bomb with a bag of bloody dog poop that have fucked me during a time of desperation in my life. Usually within an endeavor where I belong and deserved to succeed in after figuring, "This is finally it!" To then have everything crumble because of their false promise or stubborn, greedy principles. It fills your soul with anger and permanent skepticism. "Society-induced PTSD".

WAY too much inexcusable bullshit in this world! Humans are **so** *capable of better than what is and what's become.*

Undiscovered Intellectuals

Being an unknown intellectual myself I can fully contend that it's unfortunate only a select number of brilliant people ever get discovered. I'm not calling myself brilliant per se but I do fit into the mold of the small percentage of humans that has that "make or break" scenario in life. So many creative, talented minds get overlooked in this world and remain undiscovered. We as a society overpraise and worship people of fame yet look down upon the majority of artistic brilliance who have the same abilities and wonderful shit to offer but can't get a lucky, deserved break. It's this simple, and unfortunate painful reality for so many.

Since I'm a right-brained, intuitive creative type (that make up 15-20% of the world's population) I look up to scientists, engineers, doctors, and the likes as some of the most intelligent and important professions on the planet. Without these folks the human race would dissolve into dust. Interestingly most people look up to the entertainers and athletes as the worthiest of praise. Entertainers are commendable for the success they've obtained but they are way overpraised and overcompensated for what they do in general.

Like the central theme within the Rush album, *Roll the Bones:* "Fate is just the weight of circumstances." So fucking true; keep plugging along, roll the dice, and hope. And that's exactly what almost everyone does in life, just that in the artistic world the Craps Table consists of players trying to work against us and not team up for the common win like all the other tables in the casino.

I know, boo-hoo, play the violin again but most people just don't possess the formula in their thought process to comprehend the ongoing draining efforts and all the twists and turns it takes to pursue these creative vocations and get anywhere past a "good job" comment, or a weak-ass, teasing "Like" on social media. Like, fuck you very much!

An average person's hobby can be an artist's avocation. Meaning most people can enjoy the pleasure of some creative outlet for fun, as the true artist will drive themselves mad trying to make something of this outlet and turn it into something more than a basic hobby. No one is better than the other, it's just much more frustrating being naturally artistic and wanting to make some type of living at it and not just enjoy it leisurely. Capisce?

All we artists want is a bit more understanding and credibility, maybe a sprinkle of empathy too. I need people to really listen to me; my ideas, analogies, and validations for my many worthy concepts and complaints, rather than only focusing on the whining or negative wording.

I'm always trying to validate the truth, and always speak the truth. It's not hard. I can't stand when so many people can't see the obvious difference between right or wrong. Sometimes it's 100% right or wrong, other times it's a bit subjective, but overall I'm very unimpressed with so many humans inability to be more rational and unbiased about certain things that all 7 billion people could/should agree on in so many instances.

I have a great track record in life with perceptive intelligence, binding credibility, unbiased honesty, good heart, fine character...there's no reason for people to blow off my magnanimity because of "negative ranting". (Huh-Huh, I said "off".)

AFTER THE FACT: Killer Regrets

This is a subject that has scarred me beyond belief. I know, you shouldn't live life dwelling on past regrets, it's water under the bridge, move on…but my copious amount of regrets have been so injurious to my livelihood. Sometimes I can dwell on a regretful situation for days, weeks, months, or YEARS! I might leave a situation and within days, hours, or sometimes moments later I am re-assessing the scenario; recognizing the mistake I made to not close a deal of some kind or whatever, and now that chance is lost and forever gone.

I realize there's always more opportunities around each corner but with my extreme ADD and neurosis it's inevitable that I have plenty more "after the fact regrets" awaiting and ready to haunt me around each of these upcoming corners along the sidewalk of shame.

So, allow me to raise my glass to those also unfortunate enough to have a streak of painful, self-sabotaging disillusionments like I have over the years. I know there's more of you out there and this arduous chapter is dedicated to you. Ladies first:

Burning Man Babes

I came up with the term "after the fact" while attending the Burning Man festival in 2009 with my friend Nate. This story is the kickoff of many others I will share that have left permanent scars on my already messed up brain and intermittent soul.

The very first night upon arrival at Burning Man, me and Nate ate some mushrooms, took about two hours to set up camp in the dark, then set out on foot to cruise the action on the playa. This all occurred after hours of driving, making multiple stops gathering supplies along the way, getting a flat tire, and waiting in a huge line of cars to get through the main gate.

Within the first hour of wandering we stumbled upon two cruiser bikes that we could use to ride and cover more ground. Minutes after we obtained these bikes we crossed paths with two hot, younger girls that were taking a breather from the massive techno-rave dome that was booming with loud music and packed with people. The brunette was cute as ever and her blonde friend was wearing a mesh shirt with no bra!

The usual small talk commenced for a bit and the brunette mentioned it was her birthday, which happened to be the exact birthday of the Burning Man himself. It was also all our first times attending this event.

We asked what area they were camping at for the week, they gave us the coordinates and my brain comprehended absolutely nothing of what they told us. So instead of continuing with more conversation and maybe joining these girls in the techno-rave dome for some dancing fun, I told them we were going to check out more of the playa action and we took off.

As we rode off my friend Nate was like, "What are you doing man, they were into us. We could've hung out with them for the next few days or something." And that was when my heart sank and I realized I did not take proper action in the moment that was right in front of our boners. I was immediately enraged at myself, turned around on my bike to find them but they had already disappeared back into the dome.

Hence the regret of not seizing a great opportunity that could've led to a great time during our first experience at Burning Man. The pain of this missed opportunity dwelled in me for the rest of the festival, but not enough to ruin our adventurous times of course. Two hot girls dressed all seductively sexy, vulnerable, they were first-timers like us, it was one's birthday, and we bailed the scene?

This lost opportunity officially coined the phrase "after the fact" from that point on. All my regrets from the past are now referred to by this axiom.

Oddly enough I recently attended the Desert Rocks festival and a similar regret was staged to that of the Burning Man torture. A very sexy, bohemian, hippie girl offered me a hit of acid on a sugar cube. We had a beer back at my camp and she was all excited and holding my hand on the way back into the festival area.

Along the way random guys kept interrupting our flow to flirt with her. As we spoke with a couple of these vultures she eventually became too impatient and took off into the concert crowd alone.

Why didn't I just grab her hand and say, "Nice to meet you gentlemen, now fuck off we're outta here!"

Girls admire that type of aggressive confidence without any room for neurotic hesitation. I'm so passive and slow at seizing moments with girls, and it's been a killer all my life!

Fran

Fran was hands down the most attractive girl I ever got close to dialing in. I first crossed paths with her as my friend Joe and I attended this hip jazz club in the Gaslamp District in downtown San Diego. She was our server and had the sexiest presence ever. As she served us our first round of drinks I could not make eye contact with her and just kept my focus on the acid jazz band that was playing, The Price of Dope.

To my surprise Joe said she gave me a nice long look as she was putting our drinks on the table. I thought nothing of this leading to anything and just enjoyed the music for the remainder of the night.

Some days later I attended the same club with a couple other friends. As we sat in a circle around a small table I spotted this sexy waitress again. She was checking me out from across the room and even nudged her coworker to take a look as well. With this inviting body language I had no excuse to hesitate and got up to seize the opportunity.

I walked over and introduced myself and asked for her number. She complied and wrote her name and number on a napkin. (Oh such were the times when cell phones were not quite the thing yet. I kinda miss the name-and-number-on-a-napkin days.)

Hey, that brings up an idea for an app that makes for a fun way one can save a name and contact info, while also keeping things foolproof and safe. (Wouldn't you like to know.)

Okay, here's another idea I will *share that can make texting more interesting. Have a program one could install where your phone would showcase a couple cartoon-like Indians on each side of the screen; holding a blanket over a campfire, which of course causes a cloud of smoke to accumulate under the blanket. The texter would then type their message (displayed in the smoke cloud) then tap* SEND, *where the Indians then move the blanket away to allow the smoke cloud to float upward and vanish from the screen.*

The other person, the receiver, would then get a notification beep, and upon checking their new message, POOF, *a cloud of smoke would appear on their phone screen and reveal the message within. If a response is needed then the text receiver would tap* REPLY, *in which a campfire would ignite on the bottom of their phone screen and the two Indians would walk into the scene and assume their positions; standing on each side of the fire while holding a blanket overhead to accumulate another smoke signal message.*

"Smoke Signal App". *Not really an app but an optional program of sorts that can be included with any phone plan. Maybe include another option to release the scent of campfire smoke! Yes, another brilliantly pointless idea to keep the world staring down at a tiny screen even more; the ability to upload and exchange various scents to one another. Text a fart to a friend!*

If we're going to continue living and interacting exclusively through our digital devices, why not keep making things more interesting? (And perhaps cause an uproar from politically correct nimrods that don't want Native Americans associated with a custom of their culture that's centuries old, and now being used predominantly by goofy Caucasian Americans via digital devices for giggling purposes only. Perfect.)

Being that I only had a pager at the time I called Fran from a pay phone a few days later, and had to leave a message. (Leaving messages always seems to be a curse with a minimal chance for any response or connection to happen in reality. If you try for another attempt and get voicemail again, FORGET IT. Let it go and be pissed about it.)

From this message Fran now knew where I worked and came to visit me with her wild, drunken friends. This is when I realized she was really a party brat rather than the sophisticated glamour girl that I pegged her as from observing her at the jazz club.

I next met her for what was supposed to be a first date of sorts at a trendy place called Open Bar. It was a crowded night, she was drunk, and had a friend with her.

We were all lingering outside at the end of the night and she proceeded to hail a cab and yelled out that they were going back to her place for bong hits. Being the passive guy I am I just stood there and watched as they climbed into this cab and took off. Meanwhile my mind was informing me of the opportunity I passed up to jump into the cab with them for an evening of amazing possibilities! Holy shit Rolf Gunnar, you fucking fool!

The idea that she was a stoner party girl drove me nuts in the fact that when I first asked for her number that night at the jazz club my friends and I were working out a big drug deal revolving around marijuana. Had she known I also possessed a snippet of bad boy tendencies we might have clicked that evening and bonded over the green into finer pastures from there.

I'm proud of myself for approaching her but that was only because she showed definite signs of interest. I'm way too neurotic and shy to approach any attractive girl on most occasions, but overall this Fran debacle was a killer for me to experience.

Jamie

I was out in Las Vegas once again for a reunion with a few college buddies. It was late at night in the MGM casino and I was the solo straggler roaming the floor as the others gambled. I saw this sexy girl next door type who was on a cell phone call but also took notice of me. I awaited the ending of her call and approached her.

We hit it off and within minutes I was up in her hotel room suite snorting cocaine with her, as her male friend was passed out on the bed in the same room! This was a bit uncomfortable as she was talking loud and kept waking this poor guy up, but things were happening and we carried on.

My friends and I were departing the next day but I kept in touch with Jamie for weeks after this Vegas meeting. We finally decided to make arrangements to spend New Year's together out in Colorado; get a condo up in the mountains and romance the shit out of each other.

After we made this decision I decided to back out on an opportunity to play a big New Year's show with my band

Slugworth; opening for an 80's metal band who were on a reunion tour. After so many times ruining certain occasions by putting my hopes in a girl, I did it once again. I let my bandmates down and passed up an opportunity to play a huge show with money, backstage mayhem, and all the elements musicians live for. Worst part besides not playing a huge New Year's show was me and Jamie cancelled our New Year's plans anyway. Jesus H Fuckhell Christ.

However, we decided to meet in Vegas again, as she lived in California and could take a quick drive or cheap flight out to meet me. I booked a room at Hard Rock Casino figuring it would be the perfect setting for the likes of us.

Jamie snuck a small chunk of rock in her panties during the short flight. This turned me on and we proceeded to snort and drink a bunch then head down to the late-night club. I was on sinus medication at the time and didn't factor in the mixing of substances with the prescribed meds, and this created a disaster.

While in the long line for the club entrance I became nauseous and had to bail outside to sit down and get some fresh air. Minutes later she came out to rescue me and dragged me into the club. She was so pumped up on coke and booze and I was a mess. She was grinding on the dance floor with other guys as I just leaned against the wall. Next thing I know I'm being escorted out of the club by a group of bouncers. I was so lost in a hazy zone by this point and wandered all alone back up to the room and passed out in bed.

Not too long after Jamie enters the room with two guys who had some weed. We all smoked some but I was so agitated by this point with the mix of all these substances in my system I threatened these guys to get them out of the room so I could finally have time with Jamie. It never happened. Jamie was freaked out by my actions and we both just passed out.

Back home days later I had to email her explaining that it was the sinus medication that tweaked my behavior. She said it was all okay but I know deep down that she was so over me and figured it was just a lame excuse coming from my end. But as I've had plenty of experiences mixing substances and having fun with it all I can conclude that it was the sinus meds that tweaked the scene.

It's so annoying after all the time between us since the first Vegas meeting, canceling a huge music performance opportunity, and spending so much on the room for the second Vegas adventure that nothing came of it. Awesome.

Tina

One of the marketing companies that I work promotions for had me drive a big box truck full of supplies from Denver to Seattle.

On the way I gassed up in a small town in Oregon. The girl who worked at the gas station was pretty cute. I bought snacks and beer I decided to give her my number in case something was happening in town later on.

She did call later that night and invited me to Denny's for some food with her friends. Turns out they looked up my name on MySpace and couldn't believe how old I was. Oh well, they dug me and we had a great time at Denny's.

Tina decided to hang out with me in the hotel for a bit after our late dinner. We drank "red beers" which were a favorite of hers; a mix of cheap beer and tomato juice. As we drank and talked she proceeded to lay back on the hotel bed with the most seductive look on her face. Although she had a boyfriend it was obvious they were on the verge of break up and it was basically over. I sat in the chair across the way looking at her with intent to jump her bones but just couldn't get it out of my head that she has a boyfriend and I should hold back from making any move on her. Dammit!

She eventually had to leave so I walked her out, gave her a hug, and that was it.

I realize most people, especially you ladies, would say I made the right choice being a gentleman and all, but here we are years later and she insists that I should have made a move on her. BE THE BAD BOY!!!

Me and most morally efficient people are proven too nice, weak, and lose out once again. God DAMMIT.

Judith

I met this tight little blonde during a weekend church getaway in high school. Her friends insisted I give her a back rub during the bus ride to camp and I complied. Turns out she had just broken up with a controlling boyfriend and we planned to go out together after the church retreat.

On our first date, while in line at the McDonald's drive thru, we debated what to do. Judith blurted out, "Let's go park."

I complied, thinking we would hang somewhere and talk. We got up to this high point on a mountain that overlooked the Denver lights and hopped in the back seat of my Nissan hatchback. She was all over me; kissing, grabbing my crotch...but what do I do? I stop her and say the classic "Wait, maybe we shouldn't do this" line. What am I living in the fucking 1950s?

Another killer for me because it was a prime moment to just go at it in a car with a girl who was all about me. And from that moment on she never let loose again, even after dating her for a few months. Fuck shit fuck.

You must seize any good opportunity that crosses your path, strike while the iron is hot. Unfortunately I've had so many of these demoralizing moments in my life with girls it hurts beyond any mental repair. Don't worry, there's more opportunities out there? Yes I know, more opportunities most likely to be sabotaged by my neurosis and poor "game strategy" with girls to cum.

The game has become much harder in general over time. Back in the day you might screw up a moment for a hookup or even a good make-out session, but if you got the phone number it was very probable you'd have a second chance. Nowadays, forget it. Once the moment is gone in these times, it's 100% GAME OVER.

Enough reminiscing on my regrets from the state of Virgina, here's some examples of painstaking regrets I've chalked up that were potential advancements into succulent careers!

Symposium Drummer (EHS)

During my second 9th grade school year a few friends of mine were putting together a band and looking for a drummer. Bryan and I "auditioned" for this drummer spot via phone! We took turns playing drum beats over the phone that was placed down on a nearby shelf. After a few quick minutes of this process Bryan got back on the receiver and said, "Rolf's a better drummer isn't he." He then handed me the phone and Jim, bassist, in return said, "Yeah, you're better than Bryan, what do you say?" And my only response was that I would like to join the band but didn't have any drums of my own. Jim closed the conversation by insisting that I get some drums and start making music with them.

Not only but a couple weeks had passed and Symposium already recruited a drummer they knew from the school jazz band. I was not too disappointed in this due to the fact I had just began playing the drums and was more focused on school activities, drinking, and skiing bumps on the weekends anyway. No loss right? WRONG.

Turns out Symposium grew quickly into a great trio (after having dropped bassist Jim) and playing as an ELP/Doors kind of lineup with just guitar, keys, and drums. They played a near sold out show at the Paramount Theater during my senior year, they played on graduation day, and each member went on to fairly successful musical careers of some sort just after high school.

The drummer and keyboardist of Symposium soon joined

with up and coming local band, Psychedelic Zombiez. The Zombiez had a great run for a number of years playing all over Colorado, the west coast, and opening for national acts like Fishbone, Primus, and Red Hot Chili Peppers. No Doubt actually opened for the Zombiez one time at the Mercury Café in Denver!

It wasn't until years later that I realized the unfortunate timing of not owning drums at a time where I could have dove head first into a world of music and never turned back. It all came down to me not having $433 to purchase the drums off Bryan. That's a lot of money to come up with for a 16-year-old, and since I was just getting my feet wet as a drummer and occupied enough in other activities, me nor my parents could validate getting these drums.

At the time none of us knew how significant drumming was to become in my life or what would come of Symposium. Opportunity knocked and I couldn't answer the door in time. FUCK_ME.

With my love of music, drums, and traveling, this missed opportunity stands as number one on the list of my unfortunate letdowns in life, no question. It's not that I deserved the drum spot more than who ended up getting it, and it's not a "regret" so much but rather an extremely bad timing scenario that seems to have fucked my fate ever since. (Or put my calling on hold for a LONG FUCKING TIME...and counting.)

Had I joined the band at such a ripe age with my drumming skills progressing rapidly and the industry amidst a peak of awesomeness as well, this situation was primo to launch me into the world of music and entertainment (where I fucking belong anyway) no question.

Radio DJ (Casper, WY)

When the VP of Clear Channel in Denver offers you a position as a legit DJ at a rock station, you fucking take it! You go for it when one of your first dreams as a kid was becoming a radio DJ.

My sister had played on the same soccer team for years with these twin girls whose dad was the General Manager at KOA, Denver's #1 AM station. At the time I would attend games on the weekends just to be out and subconsciously flirt with some of the team members.

I finished college with a degree in Liberal Arts and no intentions for any type of "standard career". I soon met a popular local DJ, Uncle Nasty, who worked at Denver's premier metal station KBPI. This was the station I grew up listening to in my room as a kid when we first moved to Colorado in the early 80s. (Although back then the station was all classic rock, by the late 80s it changed to a heavy metal format. I will never forget the hours I spent listening to Pete McKay's nostalgic rock show on KBPI in my bedroom back in the day, but anyway...)

Meeting Uncle Nasty backstage at an Iron Maiden concert brought me back to the realization that I wanted to work in radio, television, or some similar medium. I contacted KOA to explain my situation and he set me up with a trial phase of learning about programming and possibly working the board for late night AM shows at the studios.

I sat through one session and was overwhelmed by the intensity of all that was involved and let KOA know that I couldn't hang with this methodology. He then offered to have me work promotional events at concerts for pocket change and I denied this opportunity as well, focusing my energy on a "real-ish career".

A couple more years past and I once again contacted KOA (now VP of Clear Channel) and he proposed a great opportunity for me to work at an FM rock station in Casper, WY. I pondered this idea for only a couple days and again turned down the opportunity. My excuse this time around was not wanting to live in a small, secluded town like Casper. (Nice one RGH)

Lesson learned: Being that music and hosting a radio show, or being involved within any type of music-based career, was my dream since childhood, I completely overlooked the big picture potential having taken this opportunity. All I could think about was how lame Casper would be to live in, rather than accepting the opportunity and expanding to bigger markets in radio elsewhere after proving my talents worthy at a smaller station. Plus I could have been the rock star of Casper! I would have been the rock DJ/Drummer guy from Colorado getting all the attention in a small town.

Too bad I didn't realize this aspect of it all until years later, AFTER THE FACT.

Pool Cleaning (Malibu, CA)

My sister's college roommate's dad owned his own pool cleaning business, based in Malibu, CA. During my second phase living in southern California I organized a dinner meeting with the pool cleaning guru. I was staying in San

Diego by this time and took a quick road trip up to Hollywood to spend time with a couple friends I hadn't seen in years, as well as try my stab at some networking into the Hollywood scene.

After spending most of my last day in LA driving around and dealing with the stresses of Hollywood on a sleep deprived hangover, I began to head up north for this big dinner meeting. As darkness was settling in during the drive and my grumpy state was at full force I pulled over at a gas station to call and see what was up. After a brief conversation from this pay phone we both concluded that the best choice was to cancel our meeting, as from his perspective, "You don't want to do this shit anyway. You moved out here to be in music and film and not clean pools."

From this I was relieved and proceeded to drive all the way back to San Diego that night.

Only a short time later I realized the opportunity I had passed up. Because of my sleep deprivation, hangover, and passive neurotic contemplating state of mind I let him "convince me" to give up on this pool cleaning endeavor. The fact is this hip, partying dad was willing to show me the ropes of the business and allow me to live in the basement of their home for free until I had income rolling in and could move on…all the while I would be cleaning pools for the rich and famous in Malibu and bound to cross paths with various powerful people who have all succeeded within my exact realms of interests; within the heart of the entertainment industry!

This would be the ultimate of epic networking opportunities I could ever ask for! Worst case I might have engaged in a few "fantasy style" hookups from lonely rich women or college girls home for the summers, but really the connections I could have made in that environment would have been priceless. SHIT ON MY FACE, PISS ON MY BRAIN.

What a regret not having been in a more focused mindset or looking at the big picture of what this opportunity could have led to. And I would most likely have stayed out in Hollywood for years after, succeeding at one of my passions within entertainment!

Although with my issues who really knows what would've come of it, but that infamous phone call was the basis for a tremendously painful outcome any way you look at it. And nothing close to this type of opportunistic "in" has presented itself to me for nearly two decades since. FUUUUUUUUUCK.

Seattle (w/Len)

My best buddy and I were burnt out on jobs and Colorado in general, so in the summer proceeding our jobs as lift operators at Copper Mountain Resort we planned a northwest "business trip". We were determined to find our new calling and residing somewhere between Lake Tahoe, CA and Seattle, WA. It was such an easy trip to plan as we had both traveled these parts of the country before, plus the fact that each city within our path offered a lifestyle that would be perfectly suited for me and Len.

Our first stop was Lake Tahoe, which was Len's first choice since they have the casino culture there which offers tons of service industry job opportunities. Plus I could dig further into the ski industry and work marketing or something at one of the big resorts around the area. I could also get in a local working band at night for extra income.

Next we headed up to San Francisco and immediately agreed it was just too much for us. Even though I grew up there and know it has one of the best music and art cultures in the country, it's just too big and expensive for our chump asses. (Although we did have fun checking out Fisherman's Warf, Alcatraz Island, an Oakland A's game, and bars at night.)

Our next stop was Portland, OR, the city I was offered an account management position for Great Expectations dating service back when I had just graduated college. We really liked the city but only spent one afternoon there on the Henry Weinhardts underground tour, where we proceeded to get really drunk on unlimited beer in the basement sampling room. Luckily we had a place to crash that night in Vancouver, WA with another high school buddy that was managing a couple restaurants in that area.

We reached our final destination, Seattle, my first choice and the city that we both agreed was the ideal place for our likings. We stayed with another of my sister's childhood friends. She drove us into the city the next morning and gave us a tour of Ride Snowboards factory where she worked. I had almost forgotten that I was trying to get a job there through some supervisor she worked for. He ended up blowing me off so when we were introduced in person I had to act out the "it's all good bro" snowboarder vibe.

For the rest of the day me and Len just walked all over the city and I was determined to find the OK Hotel; the location of the diner scene that includes the shot of Matt Dillon and Pearl Jam in the movie *Singles*. We found it and had a couple drinks there, right in the presence of Ben Shepard, bassist for Soundgarden, who was now part owner of the establishment. I remember my one shining moment was getting a quick picture of this sexy, hip, punk rock girl sitting solo at the bar wearing these mega platform boots, skirt, fish net stockings, and colored dreads flowing. It was a perfect postcard scene: "Welcome to Seattle, from the OK Hotel".

We hit the infamous Pioneer Square district that night. For some reason I sunk into one of my random dark funks and sat there like a loaf, remaining mute and watching everyone else play pool. I think I was pissed that we weren't checking out some live music in the city at any of the venues that put the 90s grunge music on the map.

Later that night, still drunk and back at the house with everyone else passed out, I proceeded to call some dating site numbers out of the *Seattle Stranger* weekly magazine. I left a voicemail on a girl's machine who seemed exactly my type. She was looking for a surfer boy with lots of interest in the arts and high energy for adventures in life, etc.

The next morning we were all so hungover we sat in front of the television watching kung fu movies. Len was totally into it but I sat there grazing the pages of the *Stranger* hoping to find a place to live, as this was our intent of the trip in the first place!

I came across one ad that was ideal: "Two girls, early 20s, looking for a couple more to share house, hot tub included." I called the number in the ad and a girl answered and said it was still available for rent and we could come check it out that day! But somehow the day passed on and nothing happened.

We packed up and drove out of Seattle the next morning, and for a solid hour I was only thinking about this place and why we blew off the notion to at least check it out. Our "excuse" this time was we needed to get back home and regroup.

Only a day had passed since we were back in Colorado and I couldn't stand it. I called the number again to say hello and remind the tenants who we were and they said it was still available! I remember closing the conversation with something like, "Well we screwed up by leaving town before checking it out but we are here to regroup and intend on going back out there as soon as possible." I hung up the phone and lay back on my bed in the room I grew up in most of my adolescent life, staring out the window with the thoughts of how we just missed out on a great opportunity. Our mission would've been complete, with a better than expected living situation to top it off-uck!

On another note, me and Len had fun during our last day driving back home. We wore Burger King crowns upside down on our heads and got off on the reactions from people passing by in their vehicles. Yippie.

Grad School? Film School? Fuck School.

After working with so many therapists and career coaches over the years I've had plenty of opportunity to step up to the plate and take their advice of getting further education to better my life. Although I am all about it there's still that proud artist in me that wants to "make my life" by means of my own natural abilities and desires.

During my undergrad years, I was a partier and didn't take full advantage of joining campus programs where others like me would collaborate on fun artistic endeavors. It's never too late but I'm not in a zone where focusing and achieving further in the education world seems like a good fit anymore. I wasted a full decade of debating more school as a healthy option and now I'm just not into the idea of studying and paying back more loans. Fuck it.

I've been leaning towards a teaching degree or better yet a psychology degree with an emphasis in counseling. I don't know if I could handle all the pressure for a private practice in counseling but working at a high school would be a good option. Holidays and summers off with pay is a HUGE incentive, and I haven't ruled this option out yet. I just need another decade to think it over.

As for film school; I researched, applied, and was accepted into Vancouver Film School. I had a phone interview with one of the program specialists and was on my way, until I read a review posted by filmmaker Kevin Smith. Kevin attended VFS and dropped out after one semester stating: "Why spend thousands of dollars on a program when you can buy a camera and make your own movie."

From this I took on a different perspective, and at the last minute backed out of the agreement to attend. I figured my lack of technical abilities would most likely get me thrown out of the program anyway, and I didn't want to rack up more debt after taking eleven years paying off my undergraduate loans. However, just a few years later I changed my perception again and thought how I might have connected with some key filmmaker students, or worst case at least experienced a couple years learning more about film while living in an awesome city; Vancouver, the Hollywood of Canada.

And that sums up some of the biggest regrets in my life; crucial moments where I could have seized an opportunity if my mind was focused and willing. This all just pains my authenticity so much more than it already is with all my other ongoing dilemmas and shit I withstand.

Oh wait, let's rehash one more topic of regret: During high school my mom offered to put me on the Winter Park freestyle ski team. Being self-taught and having the endurance and ability to rip through moguls, this opportunity might have launched me into a possible short career in freestyle skiing! I was already skiing better than most of my friends with no lessons under my belt and they all started skiing about 6-7 years earlier than I did.

All the recognition, sponsorship, traveling...all that could have come with a practical decision to go for it in freestyle skiing. In fact, one of my dreams was to partake in the 1994 Lillehammer Olympics. A fellow skier from Evergreen made it onto the US Freestyle team and skied in these Olympics! I was crushed as I imagined what it would be like to represent my country in an Olympic event, plus the games were being held in a country where much of my heritage is from, Norway.

Shit, even this girl in my dorms told her friends how watching me ski gets her wet. Hummm, glad I didn't capitalize on that.

Oh well we all move on, right into…

ANALYTICAL INSANITY

THE 21ST CENTURY

Why it sucks to be middle-age amidst these times

Here's one of my more memorable expressions I've come up with in recent years regarding the consternation of this reality we live in today:

"Experience life! Flush your iSHIT down the toilet."

This idiom sums up one of the main reasons for society losing their grip on reality; digital technology. Let's dive further into this topic as the chapter progresses. (Or digresses, like most standards of practical living are anymore).

I must give a short analysis of why my constant griping about the 21st Century is plausible. If you have lived on this planet long enough you know as well as I that the latter half of the 20th Century was superior to the 21st Century overall, so far. Even more unfortunate are these 2010s, which are becoming more and more of a *complete* shit show of a decade in general.

I seriously do not understand why our society and the systems that keep this country rolling have become so corrupt since the turn of the century. It's so ridiculous that it pains me to have to write about this shit. Many people think it's all a result of 9/11 and the war that came after, yet this is just the icing on the cake. (The cake itself had already been baked and was turning moldy since the late 90s.)

Higher education? An undergraduate degree serves as more of a high school diploma anymore, and even graduate students are struggling to jump into their anticipated careers as well. (At least the marijuana industry is rolling strong, so go get yourself a true *higher* education, fuck-os.)

I believe the university system is more irrelevant for any type of respectable living outcome than ever before. Why spend those young adult years of your life racking up thousands of dollars in debt that you will be paying back for more years to come? Sure the experience is fun and makes anyone a more well-rounded individual, but for the most part you don't get much out of earning a basic degree as you did for decades prior to this 2010s lame, stale, shit-pile era.

If I became a motivational speaker I would stress the importance for high school grads to avoid an overrated, overpriced university institution and enroll in a more focused program that helps them implement their true purpose in life. Tuition keeps rising, jobs opportunities are declining. And the campus scene is fucking dead anymore, compared to what it was when movies like *Animal House* told a not-so-exaggerated truth of the collegiate lifestyle. Let's go to college! (Sure, anytime *before* the Shit Show era began.)

Next we move into the social issues of our country. We are living in a time where people are so consumed with digital devices and other realms of technological distractions we're losing touch with one another. Human interaction outside of the expanding digital world is practically nonexistent anymore. For some reason meeting people and keeping a worthy connection with them has become nearly impossible in recent years. At least back in the day you would meet someone, hit it off, and maintain a connection. Now you meet someone, hit it off, and all goes nowhere.

I can't handle this lack of commitment from people in our society. Everyone is full of false promises and this screws anyone else who was depending on another for a helping hand to get through the door into a laudable venture. We've defeated the whole purpose of "who you know" anymore, because mostly all that's out there are fickle, flaky, fair-weather fucks!

I've had to become my own best friend; a frustrated, solo wanderer who wants to be out there socializing and connecting with others but the odds of it being a dead-end cause from any efforts are so high that I just continue onward with my own adventures. I usually prefer going at my own pace anyway but once in a while it's nice to have a network of others to bond with for fuck's sake. The problem is not only that society is more distracted and stressed, but older generations, including my own, are over the hump in life and have families and other obligations to keep them busy so they can't commit to much outside of the home.

Millennials are the worst! So young and prosperous yet only give a shit about technology, digital gadgets, and have such selectively poor taste in music it's sickening. Millennials are completely worthless to establish connections with because they're happiest befriending any number of non-human devices they carry around and stare at throughout most of every day!

It's not necessarily their "fault", as Millennials were born into this digital age shit show, but their weak, flaky-sissy personalities, metro-sexual vibes, and horrible taste in fashion is astonishing. (Guys for sure, not girls. Them Millennial chicks are hot as fuck! Sexy-artsy yoga pants, Daisy Dukes showing more and more cheek-age while sporting Chuck Taylor's or ankle boots into the mix…nice going, keep it up ladies!)

However, the most appalling thing about Millennials is their musical preferences are god awful. There's more stuff to choose from than ever before; a lot more musical genres and sub-genres out there than just DJs, hip hop, and electronica. The next generation behind them is fine; they are learning and adapting from their Gen-X parents and still accepting some of the more tolerable Millennial music out there. But Millennials themselves cannot get outside their musical box full of weak, redundant shit. They can't get enough of all this stale, over-saturated hip hop, tranced-out electronic madness, and constantly supporting them kinked-neck, button pushing, arm flailing DJs out there!

Expand your horizons you hipster-douche freakoids, before I cut off that man bun and stuff it down your scrawny throat!

Baby Boomers, these bastards had it made! They grew up in the right era, during mostly thriving times in our country that haven't been matched since. So much was handed to them from the previous generation that did all the real work building this country's infrastructure. The Boomers were born right into the golden era of America and thrived with rudimentary efforts and got to indulge in the authentic times of sex, drugs, rock & roll; no bullshit, no questions asked.

And now they're all retired and don't have to deal with modern day digital nonsense and so many other obnoxious stresses us younger generations encounter. Honest work, honest pay? Job security? Retirement packages? One parent worked and covered all expenses? A handshake meant something? Neighborhoods had gatherings? Computers didn't matter? Condomless sex? Wow, rough times for those Boomers.

Christ, how has society lost their grip such as it has? Without much genuine human interaction or any type of legit follow-through anymore? Guess I'll have to start a campaign for "Operation Commit-a-Bit"; rallying people together again and re-training the human race to obligate to agreements made and stick to their word.

Meetup groups exist entirely for this purpose, but lo and behold even this strategy is becoming an over-saturated mess; with entirely too many options of groups to choose from that try to appease to every type of individual on the fucking planet. Where everyone involved joins multiple Meetup groups with good intentions but rarely ***meets up*** *for any of the group functions!*

I do believe most people are genuinely good and mean well but just aren't worth a shit anymore when it comes to the follow-through after any plan or agreement is discussed. Everything genuine and what seems to be real is in the moment, then it's usually gone.

And then there's all the health concerns in this country. Even with endless, salubrious options available and many new programs for exercise and diet, so many more humans are obese as ever. Two thirds of the country is overweight, and many are to the level of obese! These stats are horrendous when you look at the plethora of options we can choose from that help keep us in better shape. And knowing that a balanced, healthy diet and a bit of exercise is all we need to improve our unhealthy lifestyles, what's the fucking problem America?

I have lived nearby college towns for many years, and back in the day I would almost crash my vehicle or bike being distracted by so many hot, tight coeds roaming around. Now all these coeds are chunking out at astonishing rates and turning the "Freshman Fifteen" into the "Freshman Twenty-Five". Women in their late 30s and 40s are in better shape than these young twenty-somethings nowadays.

A lot of this reasoning again is technology. So much information can be downloaded off the internet so there's no reason to walk to the library to get what you need. Plus, there is so much online social networking and more shows than ever offered on television and this keeps people's asses stuck to a chair or couch far too often.

Oh, and don't forget about those delicious calorie-filled, sugary Starbucks drinks that usually have a sixteen-syllable name associated with them. The muffin top "Starbucks Chunk" is a huge concern for Americans these days. Chill out, save money and just get a basic latte, or a drip coffee with cream and a sprinkle of sugar is all that's needed. (Chalk up *another* brilliant, metaphorical phrase thought of by my good friend and fellow Leo-freak, Chad. "Starbucks Chunk", too epic!)

You know, people like Hunter S. Thompson, George Carlin, (and in some ways the Mafia, without the murdering factored in) really lived the American dream. They did what they wanted by having a "fuck the bullshit" attitude, bending the rules, and were rewarded for their unconventional actions. They lived in the era where their talents were more easily recognized and they had people dialed in to their rhetoric, as well as stirred up some commotion within the more conservative times of the country, which was desperately needed. They achieved success by being themselves and avoiding conformity. They lived a long, fulfilling life and have departed from this world right when so many things are becoming less idealistic or worthy to live for anymore anyway. I'm sure many who grew up and lived during the golden era of America died proud and knew they had done what was needed during the greatest era since this country's existence; the latter half of the 20th Century. Lucky bastards. (While the rest of us still living are forced to carry on and continue to swim laps in the 21st Century pool of piss.)

One of my analytical comparisons between dissimilar thinkers is: "An ***optimist*** *sweeps the dirt and grime under the couch and moves on. A* ***realist*** *sweeps the dirt and grime into a dustpan and throws it away."*

Basically I'm poking fun at that typical, weak, middle-class attitude of, "Glass half full, good enough, move on." When really we need to *fix* the glitch *then* move on, not just set things aside or keep the remains hidden and only ignore the glitch. FIX IT!

I get so frustrated with how many things are dealt with, or never dealt with, and want to be part of a "fix-it revolution" of sorts. I have more heart, empathy, energy, and intuitive common sense than most people, so of course I'm a frustrated realist and pissed off about many things that could and should be *fixed*; and this fixing of so many glitches would benefit hundreds, thousands, or millions of people!

One of my biggest problems is listening too much. I take in and overanalyze so much information and advice from others. I believe in the perception to follow your heart, go with your gut and all, yet *still* haven't learned to live by these standards. I always seek advice from others to make more adequate decisions to better my life's progression. Problem is much of this advice comes from these hypocritical, cookie cutter optimists that say things like, "Reach for the stars, follow your dreams…", and then when stating I wish to be a rock star, inventor, or famous writer/entertainer, they come right back with, "Be realistic, lower your expectations…" and crap like that. I get it, but when will the majority ever GET ME? (And when will I ever stop listening to all these stupid, proud, conformist, advice-giving nimrods?)

Karma? Fate? Fuck off.

Like hand sanitizer, I'm 99.99% positive that karma and fate do not exist; as some people get handed a silver spoon in life and others get a splintery wooden stake up the ass. Even people who commit immoral acts of unkindness will sometimes never see this "karma" bite back at them. Life is all moment to moment chance, nothing is planned or makes practical sense for any karma to exist when you factor in so many depraved outcomes we endure in our one lifetime.

As I was watching this documentary based on the wrongful incarceration of so many people within the American prison system, the basis for the entire show was: You're better off being rich and guilty than poor and innocent. Sw(h)ell.

If there was fate then life would be nearly perfect for everyone, right? We would have no divorce, as almost every couple credits "fate" that they were destined to meet and get married. Yet we have a near 60% divorce rate in this country. No fate, no soulmate.

There's *hundreds* maybe *thousands* of other humans on the planet that are perfectly suited for each of us to settle with, not just one. Chances are you will meet one of these many out there that are compatible for you; settle down, get married, go through a divorce, and move on. That's true "fate".

It's not magical fate or destiny folks, it's random chance. Get out and find out.

Another similar topic to analyze is the bullshit perception of "everything happens for a reason". Well maybe, just maybe there's some reasoning for our life's path to turn out such as it does, but mostly I say NOPE. Most of us are good people just trying to make life worth living, but there's no definitive rhyme or reason for anything that comes in and out of our lives throughout this mysterious process of life as we know it.

I also love how some people believe that prayer controls their "fate", especially when there's a dying loved one in the hospital and everyone is optimistic and praying for their recovery, then they die. What's the usual cover up? "It was meant to be. God wanted them." Sure, after days of agonizing stress hoping this loved one will survive by any means possible, (with God's help), now it's suddenly fine that they're gone because it was their time to go? For God? No fucking way. "God" gave us a life to enjoy and relish into older age, *then* die peacefully, not check out early because of "his orders". (Damn you believer fucktards!)

Everything happens for a reason, it was meant to be, good things come to those who wait...so many speculations we live by with the notion that certain thoughts and beliefs induce better outcomes in our lives. Like when people say "It was meant to be" all due to a band's success; selling millions of albums and inspiring so many people and other up and coming musicians globally, when really it was only a product of being a good musician in the right band at the right time and nothing derailed their course of action into success.

Look at Ozzy, in an interview he talked about getting in with Black Sabbath, and the reason being? He was the only bloke on the block who owned a PA. He said, "You kidding, I wasn't a singer with any qualifications for this band, I just had a PA…" So here's Ozzy, who became the Prince of Darkness in the band that's considered to be the Godfather's of Metal, stating the humbling truth that it was all luck, timing, and a bit of hard work and perseverance to follow that created their success. Then you have Tony Iommi, who accidently sliced off the tips of his middle and ring fingers on his right hand, which as a lefty made it difficult to fret chords like most other guitarists out there. He had to "re-invent" his own way to play, and this "created" what became heavy metal. It was a random miraculous outcome to say the least, but never "meant to be"! Yet almost everyone in the world does say it was meant to be due to how it all turned out for Ozzy, Tony, and Black Sabbath.

No one wants to lose their finger tips or any body part from an accidental cause, yet once in a blue moon an accident becomes a miracle. (Because "God wanted it that way, it was meant to be." Sure, like for hundreds, thousands, or millions of others who suffer from accidental causes that fucks their life completely with no positive, miraculous outcome of it all.)

Notice we only say "meant to be" when there's positive results in this world? Whenever things go wrong we never say "meant to be", only because it's a sad situational outcome or devastatingly bad news. NOTHING is meant to be, dipshits! Things just are; some things work out, others do not.

Sorry, one more example of something that was "meant to be" going AWOL:

For many years I had a vision and tried to put together the ultimate 90's tribute band; featuring all the best alternative, grunge, and metal music from that decade. I spent so much time posting ads, playing message tag with potential musicians, had a few sporadic jams, and nothing came of it all.

Then, after a few years of discouraging failures, a singer from an established cover band responded to one of my ads and we exchanged many emails between us the following days. The outcome being they liked at least 80% of all the songs I had listed as potentials to perform, they had a rehearsal space with drums provided, they had local connections established, bass player came from money and could fund our progress, etc. I was peeing my pants with excitement! After all my anticipation and efforts it was *finally* going to happen! All the prior years of constant letdowns can now be forgotten, because this opportunity can't be beat. It was meant to be!

NOPE. Just after our first rehearsal was scheduled I lost touch with the singer. I emailed him a couple more times, no response.

A week later he gets back to me stating the band is no longer. He had a breakup with a long-term girlfriend, (proposing to her but she said "no" and left him on the spot), so he took off to the mountains and camped alone for the remainder of that week, dwelling in his sorrows. When he came back he had a huge argument with the band and they split up. Even with me just about to enter the ring and take the fight to new levels, not one fucking jam could take place. Everyone was too emotional and enraged to let things settle and keep at it.

I felt so bad for this singer, but also felt cheated out of my "destiny in life" once again. Where after many previous years of failures from efforts within something I love so much and am 100% qualified for, the planets and stars finally aligned, to then only let me down with *another* evil-teasing circumstantial outcome that once again fucked my "fate-meant-to-be-destiny" in life; with something that is very attainable and deserved for me!

Thirty years on the drums; with eligible skills to play in almost any type of musical project, my love for 70s prog and especially 90s alt/grunge/metal, all my attempts in making a 90s tribute happen over many years…this project was *it.*

Honestly, I've been living a respectable, morally efficient life since birth, and I'm always waiting for good things to present themselves to me. (Especially after all my respectable, kind-hearted, understandable patience and efforts are incorporated into *anything* or *anyone* I deal with in life.) Sometimes I do get rewarded out there, but for the most part I'm not getting the proper respect, reciprocation, or "karma" that I deserve from all my years of genuinely positive, persevering energies inputted within so many endeavors I pursue.

I would expect to have "karma" give me a pat on the back or kiss on the cheek more often, rather than continually slapping me aside the head or kicking me in the fucking balls!

I *pray* things work out for me. (Hopefully right about the time I'm too old to pop a worthy boner anymore. That would be nice; because of course, everything happens for a reason and good things come to those who wait. Right on, can't wait!)

DRUGS (Short & Sweet)

I love drugs, but not excessively. I've never been a druggie, or even a "stoner" for that matter. I've experimented with about every drug known to man at one point in time, and not only do I enjoy altering my mind from time to time but I can also tolerate most all drugs with no impediments. Anything in moderation is a good thing, and most drugs work for me; in moderation.

Hunter S. Thompson said it perfectly, “I don’t recommend a life of drugs and debauchery, but it sure works for me.”

Five in One

One evening, while tailgating before a Jane’s Addiction concert, I mixed five different drugs into my system. Can you guess which five? It’s not that hard. Obviously alcohol and weed began the night, but then as we all sat there in the parking lot we indulged in some coke and then ate some mushrooms and took ecstasy. I ended up with the bag of shrooms and proceeded to eat more and more during the concert, alone.

What a show it was; full of theatrical bliss and included many erotic women dressed up in white lingerie swinging from ropes over the stage. It couldn’t have been a better concert to mix all those substances at. Plus it was Jane’s Addiction’s first reunion show in a decade, so party on! (It was also the same night as the Oysterhead performance and I remember having trouble deciding which show to attend. I think I picked the right one, all things considered.)

After the Jane’s show ended I was too messed up to function or drive a vehicle, so I slept a few hours in my car at a Denny’s parking lot and had to go right to work the following morning.

*Oddly enough Jane's Addiction is playing in Denver tonight (12/28/17) while my punk band has a gig in Boulder.

(I'M STILL WORKING ON THIS FUCKING BOOK?)

I know this is not the chapter for discussing my job history but I must explain the reason behind me getting into the floral delivery business.

I had just moved back from California during summer 2001 and was very distraught. I spent the night at my sister's place and watched the movie Singles. In this film Matt Dillon plays the role of a struggling musician who works a job as a floral delivery guy. From this I decided it would be the perfect job for me, applied, and worked for a pregnancy term amount of time within the floral delivery industry.

This job even got me laid! As being a bad-ass musician and intellectual artist with a vibrant persona never gets me any action, it took flowers instead. Okay then, such is "how it is".

Crack, really?

Yep. While living out of my car in San Diego I was fed up with the isolated loneliness and drove around the downtown area looking for action. What I found was what I assumed to be a hooker and let her into my car. I didn't give a fuck, and wasn't going to pay her to fuck, I was just desperate for human interaction honestly.

We went on a run to get some crack, found a cheap, seedy

hotel room, and I spent a short while smoking crack with this street hooker in the room. Really? Yes, and that was that.

The very next night I was at a Primus concert with three good friends.

Heroin

Okay I've never shot the shit but I did at one point take an ecstasy pill that had heroin in it; Green Nipple. It was probably the best buzz I've ever experienced, and now realize why so many people do heroin. Or do I?

Abortion, Religion

Both these subjects are always under constant debate and have been for centuries. I'm here to elucidate the only rational, conclusive analysis of these two subjects once and for all.

Abortion: Morally abortion is wrong, period. You don't purposely kill something that has been conceived, just like you don't take bread out of the oven before it's finished baking. On the contrary you must look at the logical side of abortion being legal. The world is becoming overpopulated and there's a lot of poverty and starvation issues at hand. If abortion was illegal and almost every pregnancy resulted in a birth then we would have even bigger issues with overcrowding, poverty, and starvation. (Not to mention a more strenuous job market to compete in, and other negative outcomes thrown into the mix.) The world would be a congested disaster and ironically more people would commit heinous crimes, like murder, to survive amongst the mass of masses.

Imagine if hunting became illegal. The outcome would be having too many deer and other herbivores roaming around starving and getting hit by cars.

I hate to say that in our modern society I feel abortion is pretty much warranted a lot like hunting. It sucks to go against morals but the logical reasoning in keeping abortion legal is it "benefits" the masses of humans that are already alive. A fetus is not nearly as significant compared to anything that exists outside of the womb and has an actual life, so we must help and protect the already living first, well before we put so much attention and strain into a soon-to-be living blob floating in embryonic fluid.

None of us remember shit about our lives before the age of two really, so dying any time before age two is not a big deal. It's very sad for the living who knew the infant and wanted to see it grow up and all, but the infant itself has no clue, cares, or genuine emotions within the first couple years of life. All we can recollect from our lives before age two is lying on our backs under dangling toys and seeing big, smiley-faced humans looking down at us talking in weird, annoying voices.

And let's not start adding in the typical abridgments such as, "What if that fetus grew up to be the next Steve Jobs or Dalai Lama?" Then my response to this is always, "Well that fetus could of also have been the next Charles Manson or Jeffrey Dahmer." But most likely the unborn fetus that got murdered would've become another average person with an average life. So in this case it makes most sense to focus more on the *living*, rather than dwell on a tiny entity that is not really "living" yet at all.

I just ask that Mormons, Catholics, lower income families, and third world countries chill out on how many kids they keep bringing into the world. Think before you fuck, fucking people!

Religion: Are you religious or just spiritual? Whatever. Be what you want, believe what you want, just don't be fucking ridiculous.

So many people, so many religions, all causing so many problems within our world. Argue your opinion to the hilt with any references you can dig up, but remember no matter how educated or smart you are or how much you believe in the premise of your particular religion as being the truth, it's really mostly all fantasy. Even with the Bible and all the historical teachings over the centuries since, there's really NOTHING that fully validates a "God" that exists or any one religion to be fully correct with their views.

Man wrote the Bible out of boredom. There wasn't much entertainment to keep human minds occupied some 2000+ years ago. Instead their minds wandered into fantasy land and they came up with many amazing stories and tales of how this amazing Earth came to be. Back then there was not enough science or technology to know exactly what the Earth or Universe was, so it had to be a supernatural power or "god" that made all this come into existence. And is one god in charge of Earth, the galaxy, or the entire Universe?

As for the Universe, it's so massive, infinite, and full of breathtaking amazingness that I do believe there's a minute chance some godly force might have created all this infinite subsistence. If there was this "Big Bang" that created our Universe, then what caused this bang 15 billion years ago? Maybe some supreme being caused the Big Bang and said, "I've done my part, now let this new Universe I created fend for itself. I'll now kick back and be entertained observing all that happens in this infinite wonderland for eternity."

But wait, how and when did God appear in the first place? Pre-bang or post-bang? It's impossible to know how he/she/it came to be or how any of all this began. Five words sum up pretty much everything about all religions, theories, and the Universe in general: NO ONE KNOWS FOR SURE.

Previous life? Afterlife? Heaven? Hell? Again, NO ONE KNOWS. We shall find out what's beyond this life on Earth after we die. There's a chance that some beautiful eternal afterlife exists, as well as a good chance we just vanish into nothing. I'm not ruling out some type of "Heaven" after we die, it's possible-ish. Hell, not so sure about that place. It really doesn't make sense that there could be a place that exists like Hell. Maybe rather a "Heaven Prison" where people must stay and make up for their wrongdoings during their time on Earth, but not an actual Hell.

What the hell, what do I know? Like all the billions of other humans that have inhabited this world for centuries now, and the dinosaurs before us, it's still one big mystery of why we exist and why we're here.

Moving on from hopeful Heaven to...

Types of HELLS

There are so many unique "hells" out there that many must overcome, but do not leave out the fact that anyone's hell derives from varying circumstances and magnitudes of degree. The "average hells" for most people are when a bunch of fucked up things happen in one's life; a person loses a loved one, goes through a divorce, gets fired from a job…all these scenarios can surely induce a painful state of being for anyone. (Especially if multiple negative circumstances go down in one's life during a short period of time, then Holy Hell.)

The difference between the majority who experience phases of "average hells" and my somewhat "chronic hells" is that most people live through setbacks of forlorn suffering and move on after time has allowed for healing. With me the darkness always lurks and will attack me bit by bit within sporadic cycles throughout my entire life!

If you take a seven-day week and break it down for a person with a mental disorder, the week would look like this: You have one great day, one good day, a couple average days, and three days of darkness. Sometimes it's three or four average days and "only" one or two days of darkness. Either way it sucks and can surely be a living hell.

Imagine being plagued with something like Cerebral Palsy; where your brain is functioning and you are tuned in with reality but your walking skills and speech are forever impaired. At least with Down Syndrome you're not quite in tune with reality and don't know what you're missing out on, but with CP you know what life is and could be like if you were able to function normally on a physical level. Fucking Hell.

Not including arbitrary circumstances I'd say most people live a life of 80% good, 20% bad, and the minority with the disorders and other severe issues live a life of 80% bad and 20% good. It's unfair, and not much will be done to help change these realities as majority rules and most people are fine with life as is and don't have to deal with chronic mental or physical trepidations.

If an average person lives through a few years of any negative setbacks, that's still only included in the 20% of bad circumstances category within their entire lifetime. Most people can prevail and move on from horrid circumstances because their brains are healthy. When I feel all fresh and focused I too can cope with negative setbacks much better and move on efficiently, but as stated earlier this is only a small percentage of time.

Then you've got the next type of hells that derive from a person's upbringing. So many people grow up in poverty, are abused by parents, forced to live in a foster home, etc. All the negative elements they deal with for too many years "creates" their hell from a young age. Many of these unfortunate beings turn to drugs and end up on the streets and never get out of this hell for life. However, if they have a stable mindset without any biological issues then they have the option to move on and put their hells behind them.

Look at the world of hip-hop. Many of these successful artists came from broken homes and torturous upbringings, but they moved on, achieved, and created a better life for themselves. This certainly validates the phrase "life is what you make of it", at least without any mental issues factored in of course. Sure, they had a talent that deserved to be discovered anyway, they worked hard and all but I'll bet that almost none of them had a biological mental issue or they never would have made it off the streets and into mainstream stardom, or even into a basic life with any respectable job to keep them afloat.

So again the worst type of hell anyone has to live with is that which is derived from a physical or mental handicap. To be born with a defect of any type that's going to ruin your image, mojo, and keep you out of the wonted "happy loop" the rest of their life is a "permanent hell".

When you see a person in a wheelchair you can't help but think that it sucks to be them. To be unable to walk is unfathomable for a majority of humans to perceive. To not be able to function well mentally or physically in life is just too jaundiced and I sympathize for anyone who has CP, ended up in a wheelchair, is blind, or permanently fucked in any way, shape, or form.

Mental hells are very twisted. Imagine having feelings of guilt when you're happy during a streak of good luck. Even if it's only a few days of euphoria it's a good but uncanny feeling. I feel a bit remorseful when I'm genuinely happy because it's so rare and feels so great that life suddenly seems *too good*. Inexplicable.

When I feel fresh, focused, and everything is in unison with my brain, body, and spirit, I love life! No wonder so many people are "basically happy" and live by all these optimistic quotes, phrases, analogies, and positive enhancement philosophies. When you feel generally good and you're functioning well almost every day of your life, *everything* is easier to accept and cope with. Hence the Life is Good clothing line success. (And brilliant offset of the Life is Crap alternative. \m/)

With a persistently clear, happy, functioning brain I would be unstoppable. I'm constantly busting ass and trying to make a name for myself in an already unforgiving industry, but to have a mental disorder added into the mix makes it an ongoing "hell of a life" to live. Most people just have it easier with minimal efforts required to get over any hurdles in front of them, yet most people accomplish so little in life. Sissies.

NINE levels of life (Which level are you?)

1- AWESOME
2- Great
3- Good
4- Pretty Good
5- OK
6- Pretty Bad
7- Bad
8- Shitty
9- HELL

There's also 5 distinct levels of livelihood I've come up with that possess variances when comparing one person's situation to the next:

Level 5 - The perfect life. You have pretty much everything you need working for you. Mentally and physically fit, good job/career, stability, ongoing social networks/activities, friends, a significant other…undisputed enjoyment for most things going on in life with minimal setbacks or any bullshit ever derailing your euphoric paradise.

Level 4 - This represents a good chunk of humans. You have everything a Level 5 person has but maybe it's not quite "perfect". You possess most of the components for a nice, happy living but there's a thing or two missing; no significant other, job that pays bills but not really a "dream job", most things you want you have but can't obtain all. However, you're genuinely happy and well off most of the time.

Level 3 - Most humans are living within this level. Basic happiness, average job, significant other, a few hobbies, occasional vacations...all without too many factors hindering your livelihood. But there's just enough stress in life to induce a bit of heartache from time to time and you dwell in some frustrations of not doing what you love or the inability to obtain any "dreams". Overall you're good with most of life's progress for yourself and rest of the world but still never fully satisfied.

Level 2 - Things begin to get dark and scary at this level. A person can still achieve and survive independently but there's some negative elements that won't allow for genuine happiness or feelings of peace, calmness, etc. These people scrape by with a job they don't care about, do okay at best in the dating scene, indulge in some basic interests/hobbies, etc. Yet things are more distressful due to various circumstances; chronic mental or physical issues, no family or loved ones, an outcast...there's more negative factors and setbacks to deal with than most people living in the higher levels.

Level 1 - Welcome to Hell. Living in this level is when you're at the end of the rope. Either you have too many issues or whatever demons haunting you and can't cope with reality, have no family or friends, or something traumatic happened that affects you much too harshly. Suicidal thoughts or ideations become common at this level. Life becomes optional at best.

This is my quick rundown of the 5 levels of living standards all humans live their lives at. Life should be genuinely fair, but only some people are blessed and live an awesome life, most are at a level of "good enough" and prevail with hard work, attitude, perseverance, and others will forever live a life somewhere in the trenches below Level 3.

I myself have lived a life somewhere between a lower-standard level 2-3, while sometimes dropping down into the dungeon of level 1. I might have spent some time or certain moments in Level 4 throughout my life but overall I've been stuck fluctuating between levels 3 and down to an ugly 1, far too often.

It's amazing to anyone who meets me and my family to fathom how I could ever get below a Level 3, but it's my truthful reality that I'm unable to obtain a stable lifestyle and find genuine happiness, let alone advance permanently into a Level 4 which I more than deserve after all this time on planet Earth. Level 5? Sure, bring it!

My Alter-ego Personas

1) **ROLF**- gentle, caring, passive romantic…way too sensitive, empathic, sympathetic
2) **GUNNAR**- social animal, aggressive manic adventurer…neurotic tortured mindset
3) **CYGNUS**- all the traits of both Rolf & Gunnar, but with even more ideas, ambitions
4) **SCARPIE**- who knows, just a being that knows people through digital communication

My Animal Personas

1) **HONEY BADGER** - the aggressive pursuer of adventure and achievement
2) **NEW ORCA**- attacker of elements in life with a New York attitude
3) **HYENA**- wanting to eat up all the bullshit within my surroundings
4) **MANATEE**- just chilling in shallow water allowing life to take its course

OSOGOF…god DAMMIT!

Oh Shit. Oh God. Oh Fuck. This is the phrase coined by me and my friend Jason, relating to our misfortunate dilemmas in life. We use the acronym OSOGOF constantly during phone conversations, texts, and emails. Jason also started a routine of yelling "god DAMMIT" when stories of our regrets in life are shared. He even went as far as having a hat he wore and would slam it to the ground when yelling, "god DAMMIT". This was considered his "God Dammit Hat". (And that's enough on this subject.)

Forced to Live

Jason and I have concluded we don't want to die but we really can't live like we have for all these years too much longer. We are basically "forced to live", with the notion that we have just enough to live for and it's too creepy to take the suicide route and murder ourselves. We're too neurotic to decide how to kill ourselves anyway and there's the guilt of leaving others behind to deal with our creepy death leftovers. Okay, live on(?)

It's very hard to continue living this nightmare of a life. The Earth is beautiful, most people are nice and mean well, things work out good enough for most people, but the small percentage of us are fucked.

I value so many things in life and really am a great person and fun to be around. I continue to persevere as a unique individual with so much to offer but anyone else experiencing what I have for as many years as I have would completely understand the uncanny attitude of being "forced to live".

ADD/BI-POLAR

In order to capitalize on all the horrendous issues brought up and analyzed within this book so far, this chapter is the king of the mountain for verification of my privileged yet extremely distressed lifestyle.

Dealing with jobs, girls, and people in general has caused enough grief in my life over the years, but this diagnosed "ADD" is the fundamental root of many concerns.

ADDepression is the leading cause for so much anguish and heartache within my life's plight. My mental disarray is a major reason why the finer things in life are so hard for me to obtain.

There's no excuses? BULLSHIT. These three letters that make for the acronym of a certain disorder can dishearten one's life to hapless extremes. We all know what it stands for, but many don't really see the clear picture on the dramatic effects of this biologically inherited annoyance that me and other poor bastards must live with. Worse yet is the fact that ADD has become such a mainstream phenomenon within our society that it now gets over-diagnosed and many people remain skeptical on the justification of what ADD really is, or if it even exists.

There's an epidemic happening that I refer to as "Cultural ADD", when considering the lack of commitment or any attention span that seems to be nonexistent in today's society. So how the fuck do I cope with my already diagnosed ADD when I now also must factor in this newly generated Cultural ADD? That's like trying to drive drunk backwards while playing Scrabble.

People are in the moment, nothing beyond. They appear promising after that smile, handshake, and head nodding when in conversation but rarely does anything come of it. Many people don't respond to texts asking one simple question and will maybe get back to you a few days later with that standard, "Sorry bro I've been way busy lately" bullshit of a response. Then there's this other new phenomenon where people are dropping like flies out of each other's lives for no valid reasoning at all! It's called "ghosting".

Yes, it's that bad nowadays where a term has been created to define this fucked up behavior in people. I noticed one dating site has a banner up top that states, "We don't tolerate ghosting here." (Good luck with that.)

Those of us that truly suffer from ADD get falsely labeled as lazy, incompetent, and undisciplined in being able to achieve most tasks and successes that the majority of the population can with minimal effort. Whether or not you believe in certain disorders, diagnosis, and the nifty acronyms that come with it all, I fit most all the criteria of what ADD and depression signifies.

Consult with the experts if you need further reassurance, you "don't confuse me with the facts" non-empathetic naive fuckwads.

After years growing up with constant struggles in my life, I never knew that I would ever be labeled with an actual disorder. It boils down to the fact that we are all born with certain chromosomes and biological attributes that are mixed together from the moment our father's sperm and mother's egg connect. It's called an identity; our biological DNA and there's nothing we can change about that. Our personality is derived throughout our upbringing, surroundings, and such but overall our mental and physical attributes reflect who we are and how we are from conception before birth.

Amazingly, with the help of modern technology, anyone suffering from diminishing self- worth can now alter their physical appearance. You can hit any number of surgical clinics that will gladly rebuild your frame. But as for mental issues it can be a lifelong process trying to manage every day and keep basic things in order, and all the doctors and other experts can do is give you pills and fill your mind and soul with hopefulness.

Let's compare a functioning mindset with a screwy one:

It can be hard to detect a screwy-minded individual in some cases since it's not a physical ailment, but rather a nasty bug that dwells within. This is the hardest thing to live with as you're trying to explain to someone about your dilemma and the usual response is, "Well at least you're not homeless, blind, or stuck in a wheelchair." Well ADD and other disorders are like living in a "mental wheelchair" and there's not nearly the empathy or sympathy you would get as if you were physically disabled.

A fucked-up mindset is debilitating when you have to utilize so much extra effort just to function efficiently enough to try and keep up with the demanding tasks in society.

Obviously the person who is physically challenged will not be able to indulge in many activities like the rest of us, but in contrary the mentally challenged person will not be able to maintain adequate focus, organization, stability, or sufficient amount of robustness to keep it together enough to live a normally satisfying life either.

Look at Robin Williams, this is a perfect example of how vindictive a mental condition is. He "covered up" his pain through comedy and acting all those years yet still couldn't take it in the end. As with Kurt Cobain, Robin also succumbed to the combo of depression and another ailment to help seal the deal. Even with strong support from family, doctors, other entertainers, and having adequate money, he wanted out. Robin's wife supported his decision to commit suicide because she was around him enough to witness his immense struggles onto the end.

So let it be clear that although most suicides are selfish and surely preventable there's a small percentage that are completely justified, or even necessary. Medications, therapy, and help from loved ones is beneficial, but in some extreme situations the inevitable failure to strive in life with internal peace just can't be achieved.

To a normal person this seems asinine to want to end your own life over anything, but trust me when I say life with any mental ailment and/or just the right amount of circumstantial stresses one endures in a lifetime can be so daunting that the nightmare must end. Look at it like a divorce; as when a marriage is not working out for whatever reason(s) you file for divorce and move on. So when life becomes too painful and intolerable for some they must "divorce life".

I can't feel sorry for many of these wealthy entertainers that cry on television and check themselves into five-star rehab centers. But again their pain is so intense within their own mind and soul that you have to give them the benefit of the doubt, to an extent. It's completely unfair that any person with a substantial enough source of income can utilize the best accommodations to get through their dark times, while the vast majority of the disabled have to dwell and ride out the hells within their limited amount of support and adequate recourses.

Love and support plays the best role in any tough situation someone is dealing with, but having adequate money resources can sure "buy your way" into the most sufficient means of coping with the pains of reality, as well as better one's chances at full recovery with all the accommodations and extra pampering one will receive with proper funding.

I always say that if I had a sufficient amount of coinage most of my problems would go away. This sounds arrogant and most people would argue against this assumption, but it is so true! If I came from a solid financial foundation I could at least afford to "pamper most of my sorrows away". Like morphine is to physical pain, money would help ease my mental pain no question. Not to mention being able to fund all my pre-conceived "big dream" concepts and endless endeavors that *would* finally exist. I could actually fucking LIVE!

Remember I'm an adventurous motherfucker who needs constant stimulation and interesting experiences to keep me sane. With big money I could accomplish enough to stay busy without limitations and always have something on the plate to "distract" my internal pains. Seriously, I'm happiest when free from restrain and indulging in constant adventure, even if that adventure is watching The Lord of the Rings trilogy one day, then the next day golf, then a road trip, and so on. I GO!

People will still argue that I'd get bored after a while engaging in all play and no work. NOPE, I'd actually work harder! I would of course play much harder too but also fund so many endeavors, invest in many business schemes, give to charities, and so much else to keep me occupied until death. (And like an 8-5 job isn't boring as fuck or ever gets old?)

People say the more money you have the more problems

that come with it, yet this perception is derived from experiences of many rich people who live out of control and get themselves into binds, and this gives money and excess a negative label. Having good income or any type of financial stability is a *huge* factor to rid anyone of certain demons that dwell in their life, and not depending solely on love and support. While the fortunately disabled are able to take off to Cabo San Lucas for a few weeks and relieve their sorrows at a spa resort, the rest of us have to get back to work and deal with the pain while we try to conquer all the other challenges in life along the way.

I read one story where a guy was planning on killing himself, so before he committed the act he spent the remaining chunk of his money for a weeklong stay in Mexico. He figured he might as well go out with a bang and indulge in some debauchery before ending his life.

During this one week he drank, bought tons of drugs, and had nightly sexual escapades, to only *then* realize he thought life was a blast and wanted to keep living! So really this guy "bought his way out of suicide"! I think he spent around $2500 for the week, which isn't a huge quantity but it was in Mexico where you can get a lot for that amount of money. I couldn't even afford to save myself by this weeklong debauchery method unless I sold everything I own! Fucking hell-balls.

Just like these famous icons that go into a funk and hide out alone in a hotel room for days on end. They're isolated and depressed yet have the money and connections to get whatever they want at any time during their seclusion from society. I'll take this hotel room with drugs and friends/hookers visits option of getting through dark phases anytime over the usual methods the rest of us must cope with; year after year after year…

Neil Peart, drummer/lyricist for Rush, was able to take off on his motorcycle for fourteen months, totaling 55,000 miles on a spiritual journey allowing him to properly "regroup" and feel alive again after his devastating losses. Granted he went through a lot by losing his only daughter and then wife within one year's time, but his musical success brought in a very healthy income over the years and "allowed" him to do what he wanted for as long as needed to escape reality and help rid of his despondency. The rest of us get a small amount of grieving time with limited help before we're forced right back into the grind of daily life that's already hard enough to deal with when feeling good! Most of us can't just take off for an undetermined amount of time unless we have the right connections or amount of funding to help pay for the cleansing journey. Oh well? No, oh HELL.

Although current studies with ADD have concluded that it is mostly a biological impediment, the symptoms will develop at different stages with each individual. Just as many factors contribute to the development of our personality throughout time, there are certain components that enhance a mental disorder to the point where it finally becomes officially recognized and diagnosed. If one person takes a certain medication that helps, another person reacts differently from the same medication. In addition, a mental disorder may not be diagnosed correctly so one might go through many months or years of frustrating failures and dead ends to eventually find a definitive component that will actually help.

I've spent a good part of the past three decades dealing with my mental madness; all the time and money spent on research, hospitals, doctors, therapists, medications, programs, etc. Yet with all this and the unconditional love and support I've received over the years, I'm still miserable too much of the time and can't find adequate balance in my fucking life! Throw me in a hotel room a few weeks with a platinum credit card. Allow me to escape and lose my mind in a different manor for once. Then we'll call it good.

Isn't the irony of my disorder that although I have a dark and messy mindset that needs some assistance, I'm also very creative, intuitive, and brilliant. Aren't I supposed to be a rock drummer, writer, filmmaker, inventor, radio/tv host, or something amazing in life by now?

Vocations I could/should obtain within my interests and capabilities, yet I have spent a lifetime never living a fully stable, happy life. I've instead spent my life working dead end jobs I can barely tolerate, then hopping around to various hospitals, doctors, appointments, and swallowing pills for some type of hopeful "cure".

No people, I need energizing, adventurous stimulation with no bullshit or barriers of any kind in order to obtain "genuine happiness". Show me the money! (Oh right, I must *earn* the proper amount of money. That should work out for me, only been trying and struggling hard to go this route for more than a few *decades* thus far.)

Tormenting Examples of ADD

Here is a perfect situation that could only happen to someone with ADD. During another one of my infamous jobless months I had done little to nothing of what I could have accomplished had I used my time wisely. It's so funny with me; I have more time on my hands than I could ask for, yet still I get little to nothing accomplished. I have ideas and plans in my head, then sometimes write out a "To Do" list, yet nothing happens. I have such high expectations and *mental* motivation but it's mixed with procrastination and hardly any *physical* motivation to achieve even the simplest of tasks.

I know what you all are thinking now, "I thought this Rolf Gunnar guy was athletic, adventurous, and into all kinds of activities so why not take a walk or do something to energize yourself and clear your mind?" This does make sense, and walks, bike rides, or any outdoor activity and exercise helps a bit, but it's still not good enough!

Instead of cranking away at tasks and getting anything important taken care of, (like finishing a chapter in this book without digressing into numerous tangents), I kick it in my room spending my time finishing mixed tapes or CDs and debating whether to go on a bike ride, play frisbee golf, watch TV, or just hang out and debate more.

Many times I will sleep in until noon, as I seem to hit the *off* button on my alarm clock more and more rather than the *snooze* button like I used to. Now I have left myself with absolutely no time to get anything accomplished that I had planned to from the previous day(s) of putting things off. I need to check and reply to numerous emails, make phone calls, get groceries, and perform other daily tasks. All this on my plate yet I haven't eaten, showered, and I'm unprepared for a music gig later in the evening.

By sleeping in to a ridiculous hour I have disallowed

myself to complete any necessary tasks and chores, and I will surely stay up late and sleep in for more days ahead which will postpone my tasks and chores even longer! My lack of organizing, focus, and unstable lifestyle has caused an ongoing mess to deal with, then the anxiety and depression kicks in and I'm totally screwed.

I also have a horrific time remembering instructions for the most simplistic of tasks. For instance, while working with my brother-in-law he explained how to change the bits on a drill. After he showed me the procedure a couple times I forgot how to do it by the next use of the tool and had to ask a third time. If an entire day goes by forget it. This again is the ultimate torture of trying to strive in the world living with a mental ailment. When you can't comprehend simple directions and apply them to the cause after clear explanations given, there's going to be issues for you working any job.

I can't remember simple tasks like how to change a drill bit yet I can think of an invention, detailed production of a song, skit, film idea, comedy routine, and so much more in the blink of an eye? Sure it's all in my head and needs to be produced into reality in order to have true value and credibility, but it's these endless, frantic thoughts whirling through my head that's so distracting and mentally exhausting. I can't keep up with my own racing mind or focus enough to bring many of my ideas to liFeUCK.

Hardly anyone can comprehend this sort of brain programming that's so muddled, yet also astonishingly innovative. Nevertheless, I'm more often the loser in the game of life because I can't remember simple instructions or keep up with tasks that most others can. Swell, again congratulations to the fortunately-functioning majority.

The conclusion from all this would be that a majority of the world has it easier than me and others with debilitating aliments. Maybe not *better* but definitely *easier*. From just a few weeks of anyone else living my life, (or god forbid a few decades like I've endured it), there's no doubt that almost every participant would concur that I am a complete frustrated mental wreck and tortured soul. They would experience the roller coaster ride of insanity plenty during these few weeks, as me and all my griping would finally be completely validated to the world of ignorant bliss.

Again, millions of humans out there have it *worse* than me, but there's many millions that have it *easier*.

I've been to so many top ranked doctors and therapists that specialize in behavioral analysis and they've said I fit into a realm of only about 5% of the entire world's population with how my brain is programmed. I'm so extreme hardly anyone else ever experiences the insanity I do. Wow. And let it be known when I do have a rare, blessed day consisting of good energy and focus, my head is clear, I feel content…I cannot believe the difference! I actually get pissed thinking, "This is how most humans feel most all the time? This feels great, life is easy, all is good in this state of mind."

Again, it's SO MUCH EASIER to achieve and strive in life when your head is clear and you have basic goals set. I can't believe how good so many have it without any mental ailments or PTSD type symptoms to factor into their lives. Most people only deal with "normal struggles" from bad experiences and various external factors, but not lifelong debilitating mental disorders and such like mine and what many others face that fucks our world much worse than theirs.

I have the perfect family, friends, love and support, so many talents, endless energy, good health, a natural zest for life, yet my mind is so distraught that I can't find inner peace or adequate happiness or constancy in life. It can be a nightmare living in my reality.

If you factor in EVERYTHING that makes for a fulfilling life, I'm surely below par, and mostly due to unfortunate, unfair circumstances and not much fault of my own. So many more talents than anyone I know, so much more vigorous energy, a caring, concerning, empathetic heart, gentle soul…so many positive characteristics and more that make up this wonderful being that I am, yet it's all being overrun and crushed by mental issues and a variety of other external factors that are out of my control.

I get how most anyone can't comprehend that I could have it so bad; I'm a physically fit white male who appears much younger and healthier than most my age, I possess a strong, vibrant, convincing persona, I made it through college, worked efficiently through many jobs in my life, experienced more than most…but the reality is I live a life of many more downs than ups. It really is a subtle form of torture for me to endure.

I have sacrificed so many of my prime years living on this planet due to my ADDepression. (And struggling as a genuine artist.) Again you can barely function but you know you have to because you'll have no money or established foundation to keep you afloat without having work and income. Working any job with even minimal demands is a bitch when you have any mental ailment. And from what I've read and heard I have a unique form of "agitated depression", which means I get out and stay busy even while extremely depressed. Whereas most others can't get out of bed or do shit when they're depressed.

It's *another* component against my credibility that I never "appear" depressed or distraught due to my healthy physique and ability to function or falsify my happiness so well. And because I'm somehow incapable of showing sincere emotions either I will never receive proper understanding, empathy, or sympathy in this lifetime.

This is why I can only empathize or sympathize so much for others and their struggles with addiction, or one's who get cancer or succumb to other maladies in their older years. At least most people in this category can say they lived a good life in their prime and they're just going to die a bit early. I'd rather die of cancer or something in my 50s and look back at the enjoyment and success I endured during my prime years; when you are younger and full of life is when everything counts! I'd honestly rather spend five years stuck in prison, wrongfully incarcerated against my will, if I knew once I was out that I paid my dues and was guaranteed a good life until natural death.

This is hypothetical and sounds asinine but it puts all this perspective. It's better to get any bad phase of life's severe misfortunes or complications over with in a solid chunk of time *then* relax for the duration. Five years being locked away in isolation with all freedoms taken away is still much better than being stuck in constant struggle and mental anguish for an entire lifetime!

And this is where all you cute jokesters add in, "Oh sure you'd love the shower scene in prison during that time, pretty boy." Well you gotta stay clean! I'm not going to go five fucking years without a shower, assholes! (Is there a twisted dirty pun going on here?)

Anyway just get my point already, let's move on…

I wish I was a little better off to at least function more adequately, remain stable, and feel a bit happier. Sometimes I wish I was just a bit *worse* off to get proper help and benefits from the system and accept my fate of doing nothing else but sitting around, getting high, and watching TV. At least this way I could be thankful I don't have to drain my energy and soul battling so many struggles out there in the world with the way it's all set up!

Too many things are just complicated enough so my brain can't comprehend proficiently and I get stuck working mindless jobs in order to avoid lame-ass dress codes and stressful demands that come with most "college degree worthy" jobs. Henceforth the depression symptoms escalate because I'm forced into working these dull, boring, lower paying jobs that don't require much responsibility and I feel trapped. Each workday drags by while my brain is in constant overdrive analyzing so many things; mostly dreaming about a better life that could/should be achievable, yet it's all these screwy factors and circumstances driving me towards actual insanity!

At least people with substance abuse issues, or anyone who has been incarcerated for whatever reason, they do their time and move on. If they fuck up again or relapse, screw em. Someone with a mental ailment never fully moves on, the situation never completely ends. It's "mental incarceration" without parole for me and others out there.

Who said life's unfair?

A brain plagued with a disorder doesn't function clearly or consistently, period. Neurotransmitters don't fire properly and endorphin levels are low. Depression hits me sporadically and lasts for unpredictable amounts of time during each phase throughout every year I live. Sometimes it's brought on by circumstances, other times it's completely random. Fun shit, wish it would FUCK OFF.

ADD is a beautiful disaster; so many prodigious intentions, boundless ambitions, always compassionate, creative, innovative, fun...yet overall fucked by the constant neurosis and depressive phases that layer over the beauty within.

END OF THE ROPE (with the knot coming untied...)

Way back in grade school I was sent to my first counselor for odd behavior symptoms, but some goodness came of this. I produced and performed my first play in front of the entire third grade class utilizing my stuffed animals. They took an adventure to find a hidden treasure filled with gold pieces; made from cardboard circles I cut out and spray painted gold. Little did I know that finding this treasure was the metaphor that this was the beginning of the chosen path for me as a creative producer and performer! (...years later, any fucking day now.)

In junior high I was still heavily active in sports and keeping around a 3.2 GPA, but I also discovered a new fondness for screwing around and being constantly negative towards life. I joined a new crowd that viewed things in a different manner than my "jock friends". I learned the fundamentals of spray painting graffiti, and throwing rocks at windows, cars, or anything that was breakable. I was also taught the basis of loogie hocking and flinging snot onto the lights in the classrooms and hallways. This was especially amusing as the gob of snot dripping from the fluorescent light hardened into a stalactite formation. Little did I know that this was the beginning of my life as an artist(?)

With my new lifestyle, hobbies, and troublemaking friends, I racked up hours of detention for some after school entertainment. I was still an "innocent delinquent" as I like to call it because I was loved and respected by my teachers, peers, steers and queers. The teachers saw my quiet, innocent side, but my other satanic twin would come out during passing periods, lunch, or after school hours.

On top of my indiscriminate behavior patterns, I started to notice a drastic change in my moods and attitude. As I stated earlier, this is where my "ADDepression" really started to take notice. I had a very negative attitude and dark outlook on life, mixed with periods of depression and non-talking "mute" phases. I began to refer to life as one giant curse of bad luck.

Interesting to note since turning 40 I adapted a philosophy to try harder in life and possess a very good work ethic and outlook that things are going to finally get better. But within these first few years of my 40s things have become darker and more intolerable than any other bad phase I've endured in my life! It's unreal how I've stepped up my game, brought in a whole new attitude and philosophy for life, I'm utilizing so much energy networking, attending all sorts of events, seminars, posting countless ads all over the internet to make something happen, and I'm running into barrier after barrier, letdown after letdown, and becoming less and less hopeful. I can't win! Even my faithful phone buddy Jason says he's never met someone so determined and indomitable as me, yet I'm making very little to no progression at all?!?!?

Many people who used to think I was such a great guy to be around have grown up, moved on, and completely disappeared out of my life. Now I can't hardly make valid connections or maintain relationships with the small percentage of connections I have made recently. It's so mind-boggling that I started to keep a list of people and/or scenarios that have fucked me in some way for no rightful reason at all. It's a pretty long list for just a few years enduring this phenomenon. I'm devastated and can't help but think I'm really cursed in life. Did I do something wrong in previous life so I'm being punished in this life? Would I have it too good *if all my talents, personality, and looks made definitive advancement into the world of arts and entertainment? Fuck me, let something prevail!*

The hardest part about making any sense of all this I write about is I used to have a dark, negative attitude and this "created" an abhorrent lifestyle. In more recent years I'm all about positive vibes and a "let's do this" attitude and work ethic, yet so many people and things have let me down in one way or another making external factors the main reasoning behind my current abhorrent lifestyle. It seems like something in life doesn't want me to ever be happy or succeed no matter what attitude or strategy I incorporate!

I lose sleep during so many nights as my neurotic brain analyzes everything happening day to day in my life and I can't make sense of how hardly anything is working out for me. Even with the change of attitude, determined incessant work ethic, and still maintaining my charming personality and incorporating my zestful energy into this world, I'm living in a never-ending pinball game! I'm this silver ball being constantly bumped around all over the place while remaining trapped in this one machine? Let me outta here!

My relentless drive towards success can't take many more letdowns or disobliging outcomes with all good things factored in from my efforts. These odds are impossible; to endure so many negative setbacks for so many years after so many attempts and efforts striving for the better. Life isn't supposed to have these bad of odds for anyone, let alone me who not only deserves some sort of break in life by now but I'm trying like mad to earn or "create" the fucking break!

I honestly sometimes feel I'm literally cursed. Seriously, anything I'm really good at or wanting to work out for me and progress for the better in my life, never pans out. I have moments of gratification or maybe occasional lucky spurts of greatness but they dissipate or abruptly end for no sensible reason. It's unreal. What did I do so wrong in another life? What evil karma ghosts linger around me? My mom's miscarriage's spirit fucking with me because he didn't get to live a life?

Whatever the fuck is going on, ENOUGH, STOP!!!

During my years living in Louisville, CO I've spent many late afternoons and evenings parked in this huge, vacant parking lot located across the way from many establishments that surround it. Since owning my '97 Limited 4Runner, '07 Acura RDX turbo, and latest 2011

KIA Sorento, I've parked them all in this same spot amidst the vacant lot; with thoughts racing away while entertaining my confused, darkened mindset by watching patrons pump gas at Conoco and the delivery vehicles pull in and out of the Domino's across the way. Honestly, countless nights spent alone in all of my three awesome vehicles, trapped in a state of internal panic about my life's situation and what the fuck to do with myself. Anyone care to join? Awesome sunsets are usually included.

Who knows, but my luck is so bad it brings up ulterior thoughts and endless pondering as to how this great human with so much to offer and never fucks with anyone else's mojo can be constantly let down, flaked on, fucked over, and still be getting nowhere close to my true potential. Shit, even putting half the effort into ventures like I have over the years should've produced better results in my life by now. Seriously, come on!

With all the positive qualities and traits I possess, maybe it would be *too good* if I finally broke ground and succeeded big. *Fuck this Rolf Gunnar guy, let's keep screwing with him by throwing out more negative curveballs or "teasings of hope" into his path of attainable desires. He'd thrive too well in life and be living on top of the world if he succeeded big. We can't have that!*

At one point I tested this hypothesis of my cursed bad luck during a month's time; grabbing a shirt out of my drawer and just throwing it on. I kid you not, about 70-80% of the time the shirt ended up backwards on my body. Or if I have an occasional cigar or cigarette about 70-80% of the time the smoke blows back into me on whatever side of the vehicle I'm sitting on, and not out into the fresh air that should be polluted from where I'm holding the stupid thing.

Stupid examples yes but really my whole life has been like this; 70-80 % negative outcomes against me rather than basic, impartial 50% odds like most others receive in the world. I can't seem to "earn" 50/50 odds with anything or obtain rudimentary success or happiness in any way, shape, or form. No matter how I go about things there's always more unwarranted setbacks rather than advantageous outcomes. I was literally dealt a pretty fucked-up card in life; the Joker card I presume. But there's hope! (I fucking hope.)

Anyway, I must have put my family and friends through more shit than I can ever imagine with my stubborn, non-communicating, distraught mannerisms I carried with me during my middle to late teenage years. According to me school sucked, jobs sucked, my hometown sucked, and life as a whole, sucked. It got to the point where I was unsatisfied with everything I was involved with; except of course skiing, music, and drinking. I became so locked into the belief that my life was headed towards a dead end that I decided to try and end it.

I still remember my first suicide attempt very distinctly…

Episode #1

I was fifteen at the time, and one evening I had a plan to kill myself. I took a belt and hung it from a section of one of the basement ceiling crossbeams. I remember standing there looking at the belt and how scared and intimidated I was. I climbed up on a chair and wrapped my neck in the belt loop, then bent my knees and allowed my body to dangle.

It just happened that one of my sisters came down to the basement moments later to check on laundry. This startled me and I yanked my head out from the belt and jumped down from the chair.

Soon after, while still in a distressed state of mind, I wandered up to my sister's room and started writing on paper what had just happened. I couldn't speak in the state of shock I was in. She would answer me back in writing as well and so on.

The next morning I was lying in my bed when suddenly my entire family was in my room at the foot of my bed. For almost half an hour I was questioned by my upset, confused, caring family, and I just lie there motionless. Apparently my other sister had a horrible nightmare about me dying this following evening. Things suddenly weren't looking too shiny and bright in the Hauge household now.

From this I agreed to go to a professional counselor to get some help. The first meeting I attended with my entire family and good friend Len at the psychologist's office. I recall how hard it was to talk about everything that was happening with me in front of my family and a strange man with a PhD. The hour meeting ended with me signing a written agreement promising myself, family, and friends that, "I will never try to hurt myself in any way ever again".

Episode #2

It was the summer of 1991, I was now 20 years old, and once again things were looking bleak in my life. On July

4th my “Cap Gang” friends and I decided to carry on the pointless tradition from the previous summer and have at another Case Day.

Me and my friend Brian were working as part of the Cart Crew for Hiwan Golf Club once again, and this year we were on duty July 4th. After our morning shift bringing all the carts up to the club house, then raking the sand traps and whatever else, we clocked out and proceeded to someone’s house to being consumption of many beers to kick off this Case Day.

As part of the cart crew we’re required to go back to work in the early evening to bring all the carts back down to the cart barn for charging overnight. We already had quite a buzz rolling from drinking all afternoon and at one point I lost control and an entire line of carts tumbled over this grassy incline on the way down. It took Brian and I some time to fix this issue and we were getting antsy to clock out and get back with our friends to finish Case Day.

We were almost finished with our duties until I proceeded to jump into a work cart and backed through a sliding glass door! From this incident the manager of the golf course had to come down and assess the damage. It was a frantic and stressful scene to say the least, but let’s move on.

By now I was all distressed from these incidents at work and couldn’t snap out of my bitterness and feelings of guilt from my actions. We had our bikes stuffed into the trunk of Brian’s car from earlier and planned to ride down to Evergreen Lake and partake in the annual fireworks with the rest of our high school class and Case Day companions.

We were unloading our bikes from his car trunk and my

bike got stuck and stressed Brian out. So me being me I finally had enough. I freaked out and like a little boy said, “Forget it. Screw the fireworks, I’m not going.” This made Brian even more flustered and he took off on his bike down to the fireworks show without me.

I’m left standing there alone in his driveway and decided to ride back to my house. Since my family were all at the fireworks as well I arrived home to an empty house. I had consumed 18 or so beers by this time, (not quite as many as the previous year’s 21), and from what I recall as best as possible I reached into the kitchen drawer and pulled out a good sized butcher knife and began daring myself to cut into my left wrist. I remember crying hysterically at this point and being so frustrated with life but couldn’t make the cut. (Like I’m trying out for some sports team?)

The next thing I remember was my parents waking me up on the kitchen floor with the word “FUCK” written on my forearm with a black magic marker. (Just so you kids know, there is nothing “magic” about those pens at all. They write and that’s it.) Oddly enough I was still gripping the knife in my hand and had apparently punctured a Coke can with it and it had sprayed all over the kitchen. All I heard was my mom saying, “Are you alright Rolf?” And with that I just stumbled down into my room and passed out.

The next morning I made up some story, blamed the alcohol, and that was all that became of that night. Still the point of all this is when someone possesses a dysfunctional brain and is dealing with any stressful circumstances and mixing in any type of drug into the mix it can have devastating results. In this particular case I added a depressive drug into my already frustrated, depressive state of being. Ironically I was so drunk and discombobulated I passed out before something more might have happened. The alcohol “saved me”?

Episode #3

It was the summer of 1993 during college and I was doing okay mowing the campus lawns for income and spoiling myself within an array of entertaining activities. On one particularly hot summer day I was invited to go tubing down the Poudre Canyon River with a group of people. I’ve never tried anything like this before so off we went with our tubes, Tevas, and all. It was me, a few fellow frat brothers, and two Chi Omega girls included in the tubing pack.

The tubing itself was a blast! The beginning entailed jumping off a ten-foot high bridge into the river rapids. I hit my tailbone on a couple rocks during the journey but overall everything went great. During a certain stretch we passed under a bridge and one of the sorority girls gashed her chin on a concrete support beam. She was driven to the hospital for stitches and the rest of us headed back to the Sigma Chi house to get prepared for a party to commence that evening.

As the party began to grow I noticed both the tubing sorority girls showed up, with the injured one bandaged up and on crutches from the accident. I had obtained a big crush on her from earlier in the day and figured this was the perfect time to utilize my weak-ass flirting techniques and make a move on her. And that is a perfect way to describe how I approached the situation, WEAK. I kept trying to get conversations going with her, but with all the attention she was getting from her injury and gorgeous looks I was failing.

Something lit the “frustration fuse” in my head as I couldn’t get her into my zone. With all the alcohol tweaking with my chemically unbalanced brain and another failed attempt at dialing in a girl I had hopes for, I exploded. I remember feeling the rage burning in my head as I walked towards my car while hearing Len and Brian yelling at me from the house party to not to go. I shut the car door and ripped down the street away from the Sigma Chi house.

I cruised all the way down to the neighboring town of Loveland, driving very fast through major streets between the towns. My seatbelt was unbuckled and I was reaching around 80 mph at sometimes while cranking music and yelling out loud to myself how I don’t give a shit and hope I get into a fatal wreck. I was in the most insane, dramatic, “fuck it” zone as anyone could be in. I didn’t care what was to happen as long as I only hurt myself and no other people were involved. I guess I was hoping “fate” would pick out the time and place for me to crash and die during this wonderfully senseless excursion.

After my blackout from the drive, I awoke to the knocking of a policeman’s hand on my car window. I had somehow managed to drive way off into the rural part of Loveland and was parked crooked on the side of a road. The amazing thing was the officer just wanted me to move my car off the road after I explained I got extremely tired from driving and pulled over to pass out a while. It must have smelt like booze and you would think any officer would investigate a situation as weird as this, but he just told me to pull my car away from the road a bit more and he left me be.

I drove back to Ft. Collins in complete shock and disbelief from what I had just done and gotten away with. I was still intoxicated enough that it took me over an hour to find my way back to Ft. Collins. (The usual time is about twenty or thirty minutes.)

So there's the three most planned out physical attempts for an end to the pain I've endured. It's amazing how a darkened mindset and any amount of negative external factors surrounding one's life can bring one to seriously wanting to be done.

Speaking of darkness, now I would like to list my ideas of other ways I would go about opting out if my life gets to the painfully frustrating levels it has been to before:

Interesting Ways to Go

A morbid way I thought of departing Earth, while leaving a dramatically enhanced closing statement, would be to cut open my wrist and write FREEDOM on the wall with my blood, then slowly fade away in peace.

Or better yet there's this big, flat-faced rock that sits within the first hundred yards of incline on the Chautauqua hiking trail in Boulder. I would lean up against it, put a shotgun barrel in my mouth and splatter my brains all over the rock. (When I do hike by this rock I always refer to it as, "Head Blast Rock".)

However, me being overly creative and possessing such a

"next level work ethic" with anything in life, I would also hang a sign around my neck that reads: "Welcome to Head Blast Rock. Original brain- splatter art by Rolf Gunnar Hauge, raw and unedited". I might even include a game that bystanders could play called "Pick-a-Chunk", where I invite anyone to grab any of the pieces of my brain off the rock and imagine which portion of my brain they end up with; my depression, creativity, intuitiveness, compassion, athletic skills, drum skills, sex drive...any of the many components my brain represents, one other will end up with. So pick away!

The most sinister and asinine way I recently thought of how to go out would for surely make headline news. Drive out to the Black Canyon near Gunnison, CO and dive right in. Maybe also shove a stick of dynamite up my ass, light the fuse, then put a bullet in my head just as I was leaping off the edge to my most certain death. I could even use gasoline to ignite myself in flames for more visual effects.

Although I can't imagine anything ever going up my ass, I would have to consider the dynamite stick idea just to make that much more of a dramatic statement, and accomplish something that's mostly likely never been done before in this wonderfully, executed fashion.

I could also wear a helmet cam to capture the POV footage during the fall, but the bullet or flames might fuck that up, so the most I can promise is a camera on a tripod documenting the event up until the actual plunge.

Oh here's another good one. Visit Yosemite, dress up in one of those bat-like wingsuits, jump off a cliff, and fly head first right into the flat-face of Half Dome. What a rush of excitement! (And quite a splat left from a human body plunging into a rock face at 200+ MPH.)

Fuck it, if you're life sucks enough and you're determined to end it why not comply in style? Make history while leaving a mark! (And then some.)

I know all this sounds completely twisted and morbid but that's what a brain like mine comes up with. It's especially hard for anyone to grasp how I could be this dark and dramatic with my wonderful family life, good friends, healthy looks, hundreds of photos and videos showcasing all my adventurous excursions I've partaken in over the years, but again that's the paradoxical extremity of a mental disorder and results of my boundless energy and "agitated depression".

The majority don't ride the rollercoaster of insanity, but rather sit peacefully on a Ferris wheel that rotates gracefully in control and only stops a bit here and there for a break from the ride. Boring yes, but also content, rational, and unwavering.

ADD's Positive Attributes

Even after all this bitching, moaning, and all the darkness associated with my ADDepression there are many other attributes that are positive and gratifying to live with. I can sometimes view my disorder as a "gift", that's unfortunately being mostly overshadowed by all the negative factors associated with it.

The powerful elements connected with my disability has given me the extraordinary largesse of creativity and certain depth of intuitive intelligence that most others don't possess. We ADDers are social, adventurous, creative, impulsive, spontaneous, and best of all, fun! We are open-minded, easily amused, always up for new challenges, and view most things in life with an impartial, gray area perspective. We just have a hard time making sense throughout so much of what life throws at us, and it's a never-ending chore keeping our manic brains in order, that's all.

People with ADD might be hard to understand, a bit annoying at times, and wander off on tangents, but we are really neato people. Robin Williams, David Letterman, Quinten Tarantino, Flea, and just about any other artist or entertainer in history possesses some type of "gifted curse" and have personalities that fit the criteria of ADD/Bi-Polar perfectly.

It would be a tragedy if Robin Williams and so many others that possess a unique "gift" were never discovered and able to thrive within the world they belonged in. A tragedy if any of these iconic heroes had to suffer through painstaking, dull, hourly jobs and live on hope for a miracle breakthrough like the rest of us.

Most everyone else comes home from "another day at the office" and relaxes to their favorite sitcom or an hour of positive, gratifying news stories. These 8-5 individuals need our dysfunctional, entertaining personas on their digital screens to keep the world sensible. It's a fine balance of the left brain logical masses and right brain weirdo minorities that keeps everything in order.

I really do love and appreciate who I am in life, but like all that you've read it's a challenge to utilize the positive attributes and strive forward when the dark demons are usually in control. I can't believe how creative and talented I truly am sometimes, yet how tormented I am in life overall. It sucks to know that I might live my entire life well below par while knowing what my true potential is.

I realize for most any profession in the world it's mostly attitude, focus, and perseverance to achieve success, but for the small percentage of us artistic types with unique brains that get labeled with a "disorder" it's mostly all about who we know, luck, timing, or having a substantial source of money to "buy" the proper help we need for best odds on the road towards our success. Hard work, determination, and attitude are valid idealisms as well but unlike any other profession out there the entertainment sector is mostly luck, timing, or connecting with someone who has the key to the treasure chest. And if we never get that "break" then our true talents and calling in life goes forever unnoticed and we die with everyone thinking it was our own fault and mental issues in general that were the main culprits for our failure. NOPE.

Centennial Peaks:

3 Days/Nights in the Mental Ward

After so many years battling my mental disorder(s) I was forced to spend a little time in a mental hospital. I wasn't forced like being brought in with a straight jacket and all but rather forced by too many years adding up to a near breakdown and suicidal ideations.

I entered the hospital on a Tuesday afternoon. It was a

voluntary visit to be assessed with my beloved, supportive mom at my side. After the hour-long evaluation the lady recommended I stay at the hospital for a few days to be evaluated in more detail. Well I rejected this notion as it was just a few hours before my KGLR radio show commenced. I tried to compromise with the nurse to allow me to come back and check in on Wednesday morning, but she wouldn't have it. She insisted that after all the demoralizing stories I shared with her about my history that I needed help immediately. Fine, I fucking gave in and was brought into the program. (Luckily I was not required to wear scrubs so I could at least feel civilized in my street clothes. I had to take the laces out of my tennis shoes but that was fine as I hate tying shoes anyway.)

I was set up with a good roommate, a guy about my age who was homeless for eight months and checked in after he blacked out from alcohol and attempted suicide. It was like a less dramatic version of *One Flew Over the Cookoo's Nest*; full of interesting characters that were all messed up in one way or another. The only thing most of the patients looked forward to were the smoke breaks that took place every two hours throughout the day. Otherwise we would all just sit around, read, pace up and down the hall and wait for the daily therapy sessions to commence. The food was good but we never had much time for television, which killed me since I could not focus enough to read or do anything else with all that was on my mind.

I don't want to describe anymore about this experience. It happened, I survived, and that was that. At least now I can say that although I've been a patient in a mental hospital I've never spent a night in jail, so I have that credibility in my life.

My Present Situation

After all the meds, counseling, a nice stay in a mental hospital, and years of dealing with my life's dilemmas, I have concluded that you must do what you love in life or nothing will cure the problem. All the meds do is calm my manic-depressive brain, but I'm still frustrated and miserable most of the time. I still can't find adequate balance with jobs, girls, and all the basics that make for a healthy lifestyle. Most of the meds I've tried only numb my brain enough to allow for a more day to day acceptance of situations, but they take away my energy and amusing personality that is really *me*. Ironically I have to turn to illegal drugs to bring out my true self and experience the nice buzz in life that I miss out on when I'm sober and legally medicated.

As for counseling, although therapists are great to talk to and make me feel good in the moment, I'm mostly giving them a load of money just to hear me analyze things about myself and crappy situations I can't dig out of. I'm paying to talk to someone who gets it and can add in their advice, give practical solutions, yet I still believe my "solution" is to be what I was meant to be in life; a creative, adventurous, artistic freak! I can't afford these hourly "rent-a-friends" too much longer.

Most people can only do so much for me when who I really need help from is an agent, manager, or investor of sorts. Having a disorder as nerve-racking as mine, where your moods and agendas constantly change day by day, as well as possessing a powerful brain that's full of manic thoughts, creative ideas, and big dreams, makes all the time and money I spend with meds and counseling almost pointless. I need to save all my money and pay for proper help to get me to where I belong in life!

Too bad I can barely work enough to scrape by, hence the irony of having around 50 product invention ideas and at least a few of these could be manufactured, sold, and create a foundation of money for me to work with, and coincidently pay for all my other artistic endeavors. BUTT I need the fucking money source up front to fund the process to get these ideas rolling that could eventually make bigger money in the long run! (Awesome fuck-storm of a process.)

I attend many group discussions and informational seminars to better my situation in life. I have taken the initiative to speak up during some group discussions and raise many interesting concerns to analyze. I've been told numerous times by my peers, group leaders, even strangers I meet, that I would make a great talk show host or comedian, which in turn makes me more flustered and depressed because I know this to be the truth and I just can't make it happen!

The common advice I get is to keep taking meds, indulge in daily exercise, try meditation and/or yoga, and continue with counseling and any support groups possible, but all these things take time, money, determination, and focus. I need more time, money, determination, and focus to put into my life's interests and endeavors, and not only for basic help or hope anymore. Just get me some legit leads and valid connections into the world of my interests and I will conquer the rest on my own and never be overwhelmingly depressed or stressed ever again!

Money really is my savior, not support. Like I stated

earlier, with sufficient monetary stability I could invest in some of my endeavors and never have to drain my energy on pointless, bill-paying jobs or mental counseling ever again. I could move onward in life and be happy and proud with myself, thriving in life with what I'm good at. (What a concept.)

If I had no mental issues or interests within the entertainment industry then hard work and perseverance might be enough to establish some success and happiness in life, but that's not the case for me.

Lovely to have to reiterate and re-emphasize so many things that tweak my wellbeing, but it's just out of complete frustration and giving indiscriminate validations for my reality that be. Sorry you have to read about it all, but I have to LIVE IT.

Money is *not* the root of all evils. *Not* having money is the root of all evils." (RGH)

Conclusion

No matter what your ailments or setbacks are in life, all we can do is live for the moments that we encounter every day and make the best of each opportunity. Once we die it will not matter what problems we had; whether we conquered all our desires, were rich and famous, or poor and worthless. We can only hope that this one life we live is not as significant as we perceive, where some are spoiled and others fucked.

Most people are born with a nice stable mindset with good odds for success and very little setbacks, others are born with some biological, mental, or physical issues and live life in permanent disarray. Most people live a basic, happy life under most any circumstances, while others live like a Beta fish swimming around alone and stuck in a small uneventful bowl.

I feel like I'm a product of some type of "undiagnosed insanity". Yes they label me ADD/Bi-Polar and my symptoms fit these criteria for sure, but the layers of other elements included within haunt me to drastic extremes, yet also give me unique abilities that could enable me to thrive well beyond the normal standards and accomplishments within society.

It'll be very tragic if none of my positive qualities and artistic abilities that come with my ADDepression never get to shine through in my lifetime. As population increases, technology advances to frightening levels, trends come and go as quickly as the turnover rate in the service industry, and everything becoming more expensive, competitive, and over-saturated, good luck to me.

Life is a lot like a circus tent; with some of us acting as the performers, some are the animals, and most are the spectators that enjoy what is and let things roll.

MUSIC

MUSICIAN: The aesthetically gifted curse

“Isn’t it strange that a gift can be an enemy? Isn’t it weird that a privilege can feel like a chore? Maybe it’s me but this line isn’t going anywhere. Maybe if we looked hard enough we could find a backdoor. Find yourself a backdoor.”
Incubus, “Privilege”

Or like Geddy Lee’s one solo album title that sums up being a musician perfectly in three words: *My Favorite Headache*

So, am I really “privileged” to be a musician? Or do I need to find a backdoor; another more empirical vocation to pursue in life.

How ironic and unfortunate to know that being a talented musician, and artistic in general, is really one of my biggest tribulations in life. Yes I feel fortunate to be able to play a musical instrument and my natural abilities made it pretty easy to jump onto a drum kit and within the first year be playing efficiently to Ozzy, Metallica, Iron Maiden, and even Rush. I have only taken a handful of lessons, otherwise I’m all self-taught.

Lessons can be beneficial but I believe if any endeavor in life comes naturally then you just roll with it; be original, unique, and take your craft to new and interesting levels. My “lessons” consisted of listening to the radio and many cassette tapes I owned, while beating on pillows and Tupperware that made up my first “drum sets” in the early days.

When I finally obtained a real set of drums I played along to my favorite bands from the blasting headphones of my beloved Walkman. U2s “Gloria” was the first song I ever learned. I do believe that Larry Mullen Jr. is underrated as a drummer, as is Sean Kinney and a handful of other professionals out there that are rarely mentioned for their unique, creative contributions on a drum kit.

My musical skills were adapted from a combination of the variety of music I grew up listening to and my natural abilities utilizing four limb coordination that have allowed me to become a well-established drummer. I might not be the greatest on the block but I do come up with some interesting grooves and beat patterns. So why is being a musician more of a hindrance than joy in my life?

First off, like I've griped about throughout so much of the *Spin Cycle,* most any artistic brain is not balanced or wired properly, so we don't fit in with the mainstream world of rules and regulations. Our battles in life will always be amplified and basic happiness and success is harder to achieve when you're programmed different and artistically driven rather than "logically" driven. Most of the world will never understand or grasp this truthful reasoning as they see artistic people as being delusional and having no work ethic, wanting our cake and eat it. NOPE, idiots.

Funny that true talent and perseverance are secondary to the three previously mentioned components for obtaining artistic success. And when any of the very small percentage of artistic talents do "make it" and begin to get some widespread recognition for their skills and efforts, they are now over-praised and sometimes referred to as a "genius" or "god".

Within an industry that's so unbalanced and ruthless if we somehow get a lucky break and are "discovered" then suddenly we're "gifted" or a "god" to you? When during our roughest times of heartache and struggle we're labeled “delusional dreamers”? Okay thanks, now go ass-fuck a disgruntled porcupine would you please!

Most of us artists are spending lots of time and money to perfect and implement our craft into the world that entertains you normal folks, but somehow we are only “great” and “deserve” our success if we make it on TV. (Or the self-absorbed, douchey Internet). It’s such a skewed idealism; to have any unique ability or talent that most others on Earth don’t possess, yet mostly these special abilities and talents usually make for a frustrating lifestyle. Only about 5-10% of any artistic brilliance gets that lucky break and are then rewarded to then be paid, praised, and laid.

Being a musician makes it difficult to work any type of full-time job as well, where you are required to wake up and perform for eight hours a day, five days a week. This can be mentally and physically exhausting for a musician that is gigging out at nights on a regular basis. You spend a long, crazy evening of so much that goes into one performance. Loading/unloading our gear, setting up/tearing down the gear, and of course driving to and from the venue to then get home in the extreme late hours of darkness with only a small amount of hours left before that dreaded alarm signals off for us to wake and function properly for another day of work and whatnot.

As anyone knows it’s very tough to be productive at anything on less than six hours sleep, especially if you are even more exhausted from pounding on drums or whatever the night before. Oh well, at least we’re dubious troopers to say the least.

The current times in music have declined for the worse as

well. All you hear about are stories how local bands used to pack the clubs, were given free food and drinks and could embark on small tours with little effort. Cover bands were making a living playing at local clubs and touring as well. Now local bands of any sort are playing to half empty venues at best and don't get shit for compensation; hardly any money, maybe a couple free shit beers or well drinks, and rarely ever any free food from the venue we're playing at. The venue owners now expect us to bring a certain amount of people to each show or we won't be booked at that venue again. Fan-fucking-tastic.

Musicians face another big hurdle with merchandise. During the thriving days, (pre-21st Century), a band would set up a merch booth and make some profit selling t-shirts, stickers, and CDs. Now it's impossible to sell any t-shirts, and the stickers and CDs are just given away. Fans used to pay $10 for a CD, then this price dropped to $5, and now musicians just toss a bunch out to the crowd for free. And worst of all is hardly any of these lucky recipients of the CD will even listen to it. The disk usually ends up on the floor of one's car, gets lost, thrown away...bands must now have free links to their songs on a website or any number of music related internet resources with any hope to generate a more loyal fan base. Fuck the art and authentic perks that came with albums, cassettes, and CDs, now just download a shitty sounding, over-compressed digital track instead!

The 2010s have digressed to a whole other level of complete humiliation for artists also in the realm where now all we can expect from fans is a "Like" on our band page. Even if a band reaches that "incredible milestone" of 500+ "Likes" it's very likely almost all of those "Likers" will never come to a show or go beyond skimming through a shitty sounding, over-compressed digital track or two that's uploaded into the social media world of shit. Artists end up wasting more and more time dealing with online networking and bullshit rather than just being a great artist and entertaining the (lack of) masses out there! This era sucks tainted balls.

It's so sad and cheesy to hear the singer of a band have to preach the obvious these days; "Follow us on social media, blah blah." No shit, that's what everyone does, and only *does after an inspirational performance from a band at local level. These "fans" only follow a band on social media and never actually "follow a band" anymore!*

Back in the day it was as easy as hand delivering a shitty sounding 4 or 8-track demo tape to a venue then posting up flyers around town. That's all it took to get booked and have a crowd of interested people show up. Now it's 4 or 8 times the efforts to get booked or expect any fuck to show for a gig that's been advertised all over the Internet, email/text threads, and whatever other nonsense we have to constantly utilize and fiddle with. What a fucking time-consuming crock of a joke of shit, that mostly all amounts to shit.

Being a drummer is the biggest hassle of all. Drums are the most important instrument in a band and the most gratifying to play, yet there are so many parts and things involved in a drum kit and it's so tedious to get it all loaded, unloaded, and set up on various sized stages. Since most venues don't provide a drum riser we are stuck looking at the singer's ass the entire show. This would be fine if the singer were a hot diva but for the most part is sucks.

When you have a load of drums to deal with it's just that

much more work to factor in. If I wasn't a musician or "had to play" a rather large drum set and be into the genres of music I'm into, then life could roll on so much smoother for me. Having a smaller drum set and being happy playing simple pop songs would ease a big chunk of my stresses as a musician. But I can't do that. I must remain true to my progressive rock/metal roots and play a big set of drums because of my love for multiple acoustic sounds. I'm good with a Ringo set-up but my ambitions are so much more musical than the average "beat bitch" drummer, so I have the painstaking task of dealing with many drums, cymbals, and various percussion included in my arsenal. I want to entertain the crowd with something more than just bass/snare/hi-hat/ride shit.

When I play certain gigs utilizing my full set of drums and percussion it takes eight or nine trips to and from my vehicle to get it all to the stage. Then you factor in the time to set it all up, especially if it's a frantic situation where you are scheduled to play your set at a certain time in between other bands and all their clutter of gear is in the way. To then break it all down and spend eight or nine more trips from stage to vehicle re-loading it all. THEN driving home and unloading all the same gear and having to set it up for rehearsals before the next gig!

It's funny that most people think being a performing musician is one big, fun, endless party, when really it's mostly an expensive, time consuming, strenuous pain in the ass!

"If it's all this strenuous and so grueling of a process for you then quit bitching and just quit!"

Ha yeah that's the solution. It's called doing something we love and are so passionate about we will always continue to go through this strenuous, grueling process until we're too old to sit upright on a drum throne. Determination; even during the most sad and ridiculous era in music history, I'll continue to press on.

In contrast, there's always great things happening in music and entertainment. More people pushing more boundaries and more festivals showcasing very eclectic styles of music that never existed before. Indie labels taking charge to push out the corporate monopolizing pricks, and cheaper means of recording and promoting material is available. These are great things, yet fans are still fickle and drawn towards certain genres and will only support a select number of bands they stick with.

I'm a true music fan that will see Phish perform one night, Slayer the next, then Paul Oakenfold, Bjork, Agent Orange, Yanni, Tool, and so on. I welcome *any* style of music into my world because I'm a fan of all music and an admirer of sounds in general.

It's too bad that most people's selective attention is so hazy and even though many people brag that they listen to everything and might attend many festivals that showcase a variety of great artists, they still are very selective and place boundaries on certain genres of music they won't give any chance with. And of course due to the Internet, smart phones, social media, and all this new-aged over-saturated, distracting nonsense, hardly anyone actually supports local acts like they used to. It's mostly all DJs and cover/tribute bands that get all the praise nowadaze. The positives in the modern music industry become negative just because everything is spread too fucking thin. Too many bands, too many genres, too many venues, too much social media...fans don't know what to do, where to go, or who to support. Unless you break ground and make it into the festival circuit, good fucking luck with your passions, talents, and efforts going anywhere beyond the mostly empty, dive bar scene.

To all you original musicians out there, at least enjoy those two refreshingly, rewarding cheap beers or well drinks, as that's all your worth in these times.

Perfect example how disconnected everyone is in society today and how little they care about what everyone did *care about for decades prior to the self-absorbed, digitally smothered 2010s Shit Show:*

Tonight both my currently active bands are playing a show together. As life is all about "who you know" and music is "everyone's favorite thing in the world", you'd think/hope tonight would be one big party! I've posted ads on social media, sent out personal texts, emails, etc. Now we'll see if any of these dozens of people I know and invited will actually attend...

Hey, I know there's LOT'S going on out there and everyone's digital device is beeping with all sorts of notification updates with dozens of other happenings every day/night of the year, but the fact of the matter is its LIVE MUSIC and ME on drums in both bands, mofos. I guarantee you any decade prior at least a third or maybe half of all the friends and co-workers I've invited would show up, no question. They'd be pumped to finally see me perform and wouldn't have any lame-gay-cheesy-stupid smart phone beeping with other options of what's going on that cockblocks what they should be supporting!

The final topic of painstaking tasks as a musician is really looking back to the first step within this process; getting a band together and actually keeping it together. It all starts with the posting of ads on craigslist and various social media sites, then playing message tag between you and the few interested parties that respond to your ad. I have posted ad after ad and had minimal luck getting anywhere past message tag anymore. Musicians are a mess, so getting a band together is certainly not easy in any way, shape, or form. Let alone getting any band that does come to fruition to advance past a few rehearsals or a few lame dive bar gigs anymore. (And you wonder why so many performers nowadays have become DJs, shitty-bitter sound guys, join cover bands, or just continue to play solo acoustic nonsense at coffee shops and bars in every small town across America; the much easier way to fly!)

One proud thing I give myself credibility on is nailing every single audition I have encountered over the years. For most all these auditions I was unprepared and listened to the music on the way to the rehearsal, learning the material by ear on the fly and just make my way through the session. What can I say, I'm good enough on my instrument and have a good ear for music, so I can wing it and still get hired for almost any gig. It's not that hard, yet the industry, times, and fickle fans are fucking impossible!

Many people are naturals at certain things in life, and for me it was certainly sports, music, and anything creative, intuitive, and innovative/entrepreneurial. I was born to play drums and percussion and make a living as an artist in general, but all the griping and factors brought forth from the previous paragraphs on this topic are the brutal truths; that nothing might ever come of it all outside of fun moments, a few crazy stories, some pocket change, and maybe an occasional slice of hair pie.

I'm here to make greatness in the arts and entertainment world by taking things to new and interesting levels, yet I can't establish enough interest or generate a worthy "buzz" out there, year after year after year...I don't get much credit for pushing new boundaries on my instrument or incorporating my outlandish musical ideas because I'm never playing in projects that allow for that type of innovative, percussive freedom, nor do I play out nearly enough to audiences that appreciate unique, astute musicianship.

Put it this way; the times, trends, and "scene" in music have become so shitty that bands like Pink Floyd *or* Rush *wouldn't stand a chance making it to the level they did if they were up-and-comers within today's putrid market. Not due to anything of their negligence, but only due to the times, trends, and shit standards that be. Those bands more than deserved their success no matter what factors are/were included, but in today's foul, shitstorm of an industry, they'd be fucked like the rest of us.*

Just like in the sports industry where coaches and players are revolving from team to team and never remaining true to their original unit (huh-huh) anymore. Record labels also have no patience or tolerance for keeping any band signed that doesn't have an immediate Top-10 hit. Back in the day the contracts were written so bands had more time to nurture and more chances to prove themselves and grow with the record label. Not anymore! And with the younger generation fans having no fucking attention span or appreciate raw talent or can absorb any musical composition that's longer than 3:33 in length, the industry as a whole is a complete shitstorm of putrid crap.

Hence the Incubus lyrics I included to start off this chapter; relating to being born into the world as a genuine artistic being and having to pay the price for this "privilege". With all hopes for a lucky break to show the world you're another of these "gifted gods" and not a "delusional chump". Fucking really?

Check out Joe Rogan's podcast interview with Shirley Manson of Garbage, *where they discuss this wrongful epidemic that be in a nice 15-minute segment. Even Adam Jones of* Tool *stated how we're becoming a minimalist society and hardly anyone cares about the depth of the music or art that's put into the package deal of album covers, promotional posters, merch, and such.*

The Eras of Influence: Radio, Mixed Tapes, and Beyond...

Turntable Times

Although my parents were never music connoisseurs, I must give them props for being the launching pad for my initial musical discoveries. They owned one of those classic home stereos that consisted of a turntable and radio only. (Sorry no 8-track on this one.) My parents also had a pretty good size collection of records stored in the cabinet below the main receiver, and I had the privilege of thumbing through many albums and playing the ones that grabbed my eye.

The Beatles were the first group that interested me most and I spent a good portion of my pre-teen years continuously playing what became my four essential Beatles albums: *Magical Mystery Tour, Sgt. Peppers, Abbey Road,* and especially *Rubber Soul*. I would play the entire record and soak up all the artwork and lyrics included with the album during each listening.

The Beach Boys, Jan and Dean, and the Ventures were among the three most enticing surf rock bands that appeased my interest. I was taken in by the fast, twangy, reverbed guitars and busy, flamboyant drumming. Many of the instrumentals like "Wipe Out" gave me the first taste of how great the drummer's role could be in a band. And from this influence arose the formation of my first makeshift drum kit set-ups; consisting of pots, pans, and Tupperware.

The Boom Box Era

Ever since I was a young child I was fascinated by radio and how the DJs presented the music; being especially fond of Pete McKay's "nostalgic rock" show on KBPI. I remember hearing "Won't Get Fooled Again" by The Who and being very enthralled by this lengthy composition full of so many musical parts, especially the cool synthesizer sounds during the intro and mid-section. I was heavily influenced by the radio and eventually created and recorded many productions of me pretending to be a DJ.

Around the age of eight I purchased my first ever cassette tape; The Cars debut album. This was the launch of what would become a rather large collection of tapes I would acquire for years to come. *The Cars, Who's Next, Asia,* and *90125* became my most listened to albums for a few years until I began to discover many more interesting artists by the mid-80s.

I began listening to a bunch of the new wave 80s bands like Human League, Naked Eyes, Pet Shop Boys, Tear for Fears, Duran Duran, OMD, as well as some heavier rock from the likes of Van Halen and especially the Scorpions. I was then exposed to the modern "college rock" of the mid-80s. Bands like The Cure, REM, U2, Men at Work, and Talking Heads caught my attention with high regards.

U2 became a very special band for me to listen to and I was heavily into all their albums up through *Joshua Tree*. To this day it's hard to say which of their albums is truly my favorite. I took a liking to *War* for a while, even *Boy*, then *Unforgettable Fire* and *Joshua Tree*. Over time I've realized how underrated *October* is as well, but if I had to pick one U2 album as my favorite it would probably be *Unforgettable Fire*.

Under a Blood Red Sky is a classic video and I still own it on VHS. I have worn that concert tape out after years of viewing it, and what makes it so special to me is I remember the day that footage was shot. It was my last day of grade school and I rode down to Denver with my mom to run errands and vividly recall looking over at Red Rocks and all the fog that had rolled in to give such a beautifully eerie appeal. I was a bit too young to hit the concert scene at the time but I wish that epic U2 concert would've been my first live music experience. Talk about going down in history!

Men at Work ended up being my first live concert experience. It was during Fall of 1983 and my mom took me and Craig. It was scheduled to be at Red Rocks earlier that summer but was moved to the CU Event Center due to rain problems or something. I remember the ticket costing $12.50 and the t-shirts being around the same price. The highlight of the show was Craig and I filling up a small jar of cigarette butts thinking they were joints.

Classic Rock

There's no question that classic rock is the most important era that ever prevailed in rock and roll history. From The Beatles to The Stones, Hendrix, Zeppelin and the dozens of other bands that originated in the 1960s musical movement, I have to commend this era of importance.

There's so much that has been analyzed and spoken of classic rock that there's no need for me to reiterate anymore. I always say that the greatest, most important and influential decade of music ever was the mid-60s through the mid-70s, no question.

The 80s

This decade of music featured more keyboards, sequencers, and drum machines within the songs. Clothing and hair styles were a bit over the top; combining bright colors, big puffy teased up hair, and thick makeup. All of this excessiveness catered to men and women equally, to where it was sometimes hard to distinguish which gender was performing on stage.

Unlike the raw guitar, bass, and drums foundation of the 60s and 70s eras, the music during the 80s made way to fresh electronic sounds. Many of the bands that gained fame in the 70s jumped on this 80s trending bandwagon by cutting off their long, greasy hair and writing more simplistic, pop-friendly rock songs that disappointed many diehard fans who were used to the raw, organic sounds of their earlier material.

Any way you look at it the 80s have become a very prominent decade of music for fans of all ages that appreciate the happy, singalong structures of so many great pop songs that were released in these times. Many people still like to host 80s theme parties with their friends and usually pick an 80s song when willing to embarrass themselves on a karaoke mic. And like a lot of the 70s classic rock it's also the 80s music that is still the most featured selections on corporate radio and in the cover band circuit all over the world; year after year after year...it's all a bit overcooked, but rightfully so I suppose.

Hard Rockers

Proceeding onward with the evolution of my musical influences I will discuss the importance of heavier rock. I was introduced to Van Halen in the early 80s and owned their second album which I played pretty regularly for a couple years until *1984* was released. I also took a huge liking to *5150* but then lost my interest in the band soon after.

It was really the Scorpions that grew on me as my favorite

heavier band. I heard the album *Blackout* and soon after *Love at First Sting* which was an epic for the times. Len and I used to jam out to these albums in my room with our air guitars, or utilizing tennis rackets as guitars.

MTV's Headbangers Ball was also at its peak during the mid/late-80s. This show introduced me to other hard rock music I might not have discovered otherwise. I was watching these other bands like Anthrax, Iron Maiden, and Suicidal Tendencies. As the decade came to a close the show was moved to later and later slots as hip-hop took over.

I will admit that I did get into some of the hair metal of the late 80s and would watch the MTV Top Ten Countdown every day after school. Many of the bands that were featured in the daily top ten were hair metal bands. Bands like Poison, Cinderella, and of course Bon Jovi were hogging the top slots for months. Bon Jovi won me over with *Slippery When Wet* and soon after it was bands like Queensryche and Guns N Roses. "Welcome to the Jungle", "Sweet Child of Mine", "Jet City Woman", "Silent Lucidity", "Rock You Like a Hurricane", and "Still Loving You" were all the videos that gave me the perfect glimpse of this new raw energy of anger rock and the beauty of ballad metal.

Rap

As with punk rock I never got into rap too deeply. I refuse to use the term "hip-hop" as back in my earlier days it was simply all just "rap". (Which sounds tougher anyway.)

Beastie Boys and RUN D.M.C. were at the top of the heap for a while. Both these rap bands spawned at the same time during the mid-80s and were both connected with famed producer Rick Ruben. "Fight for Your Right" was an instant hit and I bought *Licensed to Ill* which became yet another album where every song appealed to me. It wouldn't be until years later that I learned that Kerry King from Slayer played guitar on the tracks "Rhyming and Stealing" and "No Sleep Til Brooklyn". Why? Slayer was also involved with Rick Ruben, duh.

Bryan and I made our own video production of "Fight for Your Right" in drama class during 9th grade, and Len played the nerd. We had a pie fight and everything. It is priceless footage to say the least.

It was classics like Sugarhill Gang and especially Grand Master Flash that Len's older brother got us into a few years before where I first discovered rap. Len and I would ride down to Denver with his brother and he would always play "White Lines" and other catchy tracks by Grandmaster Flash.

I purchased the Furious Five's *Greatest Messages* and proceeded to learn pretty much every line of every song on the album. I remember the song "New York, New York" being my favorite by offering such catchy, punchy rhymes. There were other classics like "The Message", "Scorpio", and "Freedom".

Gangsta Rap

From the old-school rap of the East Coast came a whole

new attitude and style with "gangster rap" on the West Coast. Deriving right out of south-central Los Angeles in the late 80s and early 90s, this form of rap contained some controversial messages about issues in their world.

The first "shock rap" to become exposed to the public was Luke Skywalker and Too Live Crew. These guys were rapping some hardcore antics, but like hair metal most of it was about partying and pussy. It was soon after that the real intense "gangsta" stuff was making an appearance on radio and MTV.

Just like the alternative rock boom, and coincidentally during the same era, the true gangster rappers of the West Coast began to dominate the rap scene by the early 90s. Public Enemy, NWA, Snoop Dogg, were a few of the biggies from the era. Public Enemy were the instigators and rose to rap fame first, especially with the help of Anthrax that took them on tour and created the first official "rap-metal" project ever! Hats off to Rage Against the Machine for perfecting this concept within one tight unit.

I remember seeing Public Enemy perform at the Boulder Theater in 2008 and Chuck D. yelling out to the crowd, "Today's hip-hop is shit-hop!" (Oh truth hurts don't it.)

Alternative Rock

By 1987 Jane's Addiction was beginning to make a huge impact on the scene, after riding the coat tails of the Red Hot Chili Peppers. (Although the Pixies have been credited as being the first unofficial "alternative band" for that movement and era.) I also remember seeing the "Cult of

Personality" video on MTV and was fascinated! To see these four black guys, who make up Living Colour, all dressed funky and playing such interestingly, intense music was a radical change from the boozing, girl-chasing, white boy glam metal. The guitar solo was so crazy and the ending sequence just after the JFK quote blew me away. I bought their debut album *Vivid* and just like *Appetite for Destruction* every song was so exciting to listen to and once again I had something new and inspirational happening in my musical world.

From here arose an explosion of alternative bands that would sink into my domain of interest. As the dawn of the 1990s came about there was a huge movement developing that became "grunge" music. Nirvana and Pearl Jam had just hit the airwaves and once again I was hooked. *Nevermind* and *Ten* were the next two albums played many times in my car stereo. Soon after was Rage Against the Machine, Alice in Chains, Smashing Pumpkins, Soundgarden, Fishbone, Tool, and Primus.

Primus is a funky trio and one of the most unique bands I had ever heard. To this day they remain in my top five "island bands". How was I not supposed to like a band that starts off their debut album with the intro to "YYZ" by Rush?

311 is a very unique, eclectic rock band as well. I discovered them while working a landscaping job in college. It was the summer of 1993 and I was listening to the radio with my headphones on while planting flowers. I remember hearing "Do You Right" and was taken in by the distinctive sound of this tune. When the song ended I thought the DJ said the band was 911 or something so when I tried to find the album at the music store the clerk

had no idea what I was talking about. Turns out I was one of the first people on the planet to hear about this new funk-rap-metal band from Nebraska. They were so unknown that when they made an appearance in Ft. Collins, CO I had to convince the skeptical club manager that he made a good decision booking them.

It ended up being one of those classic shows where the fresh energetic band is playing to a smaller, packed club in a hip college town. Nathan and I ended up front row squished against the small stage, cool shit!

Lollapalooza Era

Then the real deal came about; Lollapalooza. This festival was founded by Jane's Addiction front man, Perry Ferrell, and remains to be (arguably) the greatest running musical festival ever. I missed the first two years but ended up catching the third tour in 1993.

This all-day music and arts festival would turn out to be one of the better concert experiences of my life. I was still in college at CSU and we had a huge posse of friends ready to go on this hot July day. A couple groups of us drove from Ft. Collins in two separate cars, only to have someone in Len's group forget their ticket half way to the event and Len had to turn around and backtrack to Ft. Collins at 90 mph to grab the ticket and make it back to Denver in time. (Will Call sure saves us from this hassle nowadays!)

We gathered at a mutual friend's house in Denver. She happened to be making a huge batch of mushroom tea, which would not only give us the perfect trippy buzz for a big portion of the festival but also keep us from getting the munchies or craving beers in the 95 degree heat. We ended up surviving on Mountain Dew all day instead, a great choice over beer for the body and wallet within scorching heat.

Coincidentally the lineup of bands featured at this particular show consisted of many of my favorite bands at the time. Rage opened the show on the main stage, but we missed them due to lagging in the pre-party department. There was Front 242, Arrested Development, Fishbone, Alice in Chains, and headliner Primus. I also remember passing by the second stage at one point where Tool was performing.

As anyone knows who went to any of these Lollapalooza festivals it was always filled with so many artistic freaky things to check out and play with as you walked around. The best area we discovered to hang at was during the peak of our trip. There was a tent with misters flowing and you could sit in chairs while wearing these weird goggles. You looked up into the sky and many shapes came about, like that of a kaleidoscope. I remember a few of us sitting there for at least 20 minutes getting off on this craze.

One other funny event that took place was in line on the way in. Len had a pint of vodka shoved down his combat boot he was wearing. The bottle slipped down under his foot and broke open, drenching his entire foot with vodka as he limped his way into the venue.

Homage to the Diva Bands

Testosterone was not the only thing writing and performing great alternative music of the 90s but female rockers were beginning to make a statement as well. It wasn't until some years after the whole alternative/grunge movement that I realized how awesome the female performers were. The early 90s spawned so many amazing bands with talented musicians and a bunch of these musicians happened to have vaginas.

Most all my favorite chick bands came from the Lollapalooza generation of music. The Breeders, Veruca Salt, Tori Amos, Liz Phair, Juliana Hatfield, Luscious Jackson, Sneaker Pimps, Belly, Bjork, and Lush were just some of the many great female bands to derive out of that era. There was also the radical poetic rock of Ani DiFranco that began to spark a new realm of interest, or Drain STH who have a heavy metal vibe rolling.

All these female artists never really got the respect they deserved as they were up against so many male-based bands that were hogging all the attention. (Sort of how Megadeth is to Metallica.) These diva bands had such an impact on me since their debut into the music scene that I began to make mixed tapes and CDs based around all my favorite female fronted bands.

Even today I continue to discover other outstanding female fronted bands; Lorde, Metric, Lili Allen, School of Seven Bells, The Naked and Famous, and especially Phantogram. God bless all you divas!

The alternative music era was such an epic time for the music industry. All these rappers and alternative acts sharing stages together and many people were gathering at these shows and absorbing it all in. I can't say enough about this era and how much of an amazing impact this all had on me, others, and the history of rock and roll as a whole.

Fusion, Jam, Metal

The next big phase for me musically was modern jazz, jam music, and heavier metal.

I heard Len playing a Phish album on the porch when I came home from class one day and was intrigued by the variety of styles that existed on this one album. I bought the album *Picture of Nectar* and immediately dove into this jam band world. It all made perfect sense as jam band music incorporates a lot of jazz and fusion influences. The mixture of all this interestingly complex music with an open-mind for improvisation really boosted my musical world into another realm. Phish is kind of like Allman Brothers, Frank Zappa, and Yes combined in one musical unit, but because they are labeled as a "jam band" a lot of "anti-jam band" musicians will never give them a chance.

During the early part of the 2000s I was getting bored with all the constant noodling of the jazzy jammy band era and needed some angst back into my life. I got back into Rage, Alice in Chains, Smashing Pumpkins, Megadeth, and especially Tool. They had just released *Lateralis* and I remember driving around Boulder with a friend cranking this album while smoking bowls. I had seen them live at Red Rocks during the *Anema* tour and was now fully ready for the next tour to commence.

By the mid part of the 2000s I was inspired by heavier

bands like Slipknot, Pantera, and Slayer. I craved the intensity, speed, and complex arrangements that all these thrash metal bands possessed. There's nothing like playing any of these heavier bands full blast on the car stereo when in need of a kick in my day! (Just be careful not to get a speeding ticket while rocking out to *speed* metal.)

Modern Music of the 2000s

I have discovered and listened to pretty much all the styles of music available on Earth. By the turn of the century I was listening to bands like Incubus, Deftones, The Strokes, Queens of the Stone Age, and Ultraspank. I also rediscovered previous favorites like Weezer and Radiohead.

In the past few years I have also discovered some really interesting music when I stay up really late and watch "Insomniac Theater" on VH1 Classic. Cool bands like MGMT, Owl City and some other weird shit has won me over.

Creatively Complex Compilations:

The mixed tape era

Right out of the days of me pretending to be a DJ and putting on mock concerts with my stuffed animals I was now utilizing a lot of my free time producing mixed cassette tapes of my favorite music. I realize that almost everyone did this same thing growing up but I took it all to a whole new level.

I would spend hours on each mix; picking the bands I wanted to include and the order of the songs to permit the best flow possible. I would generate themes within so many musical categories and take it as far as using colored pens and draw artwork within the tape cases. I would even re-create the exact logos of the band's whose music I was mixing by freehand. I made mixes for everyone.

Girlfriend mixes are the hardest to produce as girls tend to pay closer attention to vocal and lyrical aspects of the music more than guys. With me this is even harder as I don't pay much attention to lyrics at all. (I'm slowly making an effort to change this way of perceiving the music, but I can't help being the oddball who notices every little detail of the musical side rather than vocal elements.)

Most of the mixes I've made throughout my lifetime are still located in my tape cases. They are sacred to me as they not only define who my favorite bands and songs are but they also represent certain eras where my tastes went through changes, or maybe just a particular mood I was in during a certain creation. From photo albums, videos, artwork, and music mixes, it's all worth saving as it represents a major component of my life.

Rock-a-Sonic

These were a series of mixes I recorded off the radio on my Panasonic boom box, hence the title "Rock-a-Sonic". I would listen to the radio for hours with my finger on the record button waiting for any song that I deemed worthy of recording onto the tape. Then I would go back through the tape and mute out as much of the DJ talking as possible between each song. These tapes are currently missing in action but I think I ended up recording about five or six volumes of Rock-a-Sonic tapes during the 1980s.

Decade's Best

By the end of the 1980s I came up with the idea to pay homage to all my favorite bands that I was listening to during an entire decade. "Decade's Best" became the title and the mother of all mixes that would reflect the ultimate bands I was into during the 80s. I got my friend Brian to partake in this project and we spent two full days in his parent's living room producing these mixes. The challenge obviously was making sure to pick the right bands and narrowing down all their songs to just one that would act as the best portrayal of them on a single cassette tape. Overall we both produced a fine mix.

Here's a list of some fine mixes I've made over the years:

Random Rush (vol. 1, 2, 3) songs spanning through all of Rush's discography but focusing on the more obscure selections

Trip at the Jane (1989) a mix made specifically for ski trips to Mary Jane; the title derived from the Suicidal Tendencies song, "Trip at the Brain".

Vacation '91 made for the west coast road trip with Len

Metal Mix (1991) favorite metal tunes of the time

Dogmatic Alteration of Life (1992) after meeting a girl during college

The Cheesy 80s (1993) made specifically for an 80s party during college

Drive (1994) made for a family road trip to Vegas

Road Trip '96 made for trip to Seattle with Len

Random Compilation from Hell (1996) heavier tunes on one side, softer on the other, featuring mixed genres

Talented Tunes (1996) songs representing more "musicality" in nature

Aggressive Progressive (1998) heavier progressive rock

Good Firkin' Musica (1999) first side alternative rock, second side instrumentals

Couch Days...Revisited (1999) in relation to once again having to reside on a friend's couch, so I mixed away (2 cassettes total)

Bi-Polar Schizo Mixo (2003)- last official mix I ever made on cassette tape, good production with many extras added in between certain songs

RUSH

Validation behind the greatest band ever.

If Led Zeppelin are the gods of rock, Black Sabbath are the gods of metal, and Pink Floyd are the gods of art rock, then Rush could be considered the gods of all gods.

Any rock band that can maintain the same three members in their lineup for forty years running is an amazing feat in itself. These three Canadians have held a very special place in my heart throughout most my life now. They so deserve the praise they receive from the industry and other musicians, fans, and critics. I would consider Rush one of the top three most important components in my life.

Let me begin by sharing the story of my discovery and growing fascination with Rush:

It was sometime during the early 80s after a friend and I traded some albums and I ended up with *2112.* I was enthralled by the album artwork and a bit humored from the photo on back of all three band members standing together wearing white robes of sorts. Being that I was a bit naive in my early teens I perceived the red star logo as representing evil and when the "Temples of Syrinx" would kick in I was overwhelmed by the singer's screeching vocals and thought he was saying, "We are the priests, and the Devils of Syrinx".

So with the red star logo and misinterpreting the lyrics I never listened to much of the rest of the album. Although I really did enjoy the opening instrumental, "Overture", with its trippy, futuristic synthesized intro and would listen to this opening suite of *2112* over and over, as well as including it on a few mix tapes as well.

A few years past since my attempt at *2112* and by the fall of 1986 I had a growing interest in wanting to play the drums. Then one day while sitting in Speech & Drama class a friend handed me a cassette and told me to check out the drum solo on it. The cassette was Rush's *Exit…Stage Left*.

I got off the school bus, ran inside and popped in *Exit* immediately. I skimmed through the tape so I could hear the drum solo first, which is found in the middle of the instrumental, "YYZ". I was blown away! I had never heard such an amazing, musical display of power, stamina, instrumentation, and unique solo composition in my life.

From this I rewound the tape to the beginning and proceeded to listen to the entire album. I dubbed a copy for myself and this became my influential listening tool for months to come, or actually YEARS to come as *Exit…Stage Left* is my very favorite album to this day!

This album not only opened my ears to how far a rock band could take their instrumentation and idealisms in a musical setting, but *Exit* introduced me to what would now become my favorite band forever and expand my musical awareness into other uncharted territories I might not have discovered without Rush.

From the miraculous inspiration I got listening to

Exit…Stage Left, I proceeded to buy every other album released by Rush since their inauguration in 1974. *Hold Your Fire* was released a year later in the fall of 1987. I fell in love with this album immediately. From the cover artwork to the musical concepts and great production I was once again intrigued by these three guys that could have so much energy, talent, creativity, and innovative aspiration. I feel that *Hold Your Fire* is their most beautifully mixed album of their entire catalog. Only *Power Windows* or *Snakes and Arrows* can compare in possessing a perfectly mastered production.

Many old-school fans of Rush gave up on the band after the *Signals* album. You hear this story more than any other within the confines of Rush chat. The reasons are that of many; they were writing shorter, poppier songs, bringing more keys and synths into the musical equation, and they parted ways with their longtime producer, and "fourth member", Terry Brown. These three factors alone scared off a good chunk of hardcore Rush listeners but I have never bugged out! I am always excited and impressed with anything they release.

The 1980s showcased Rush experimenting with new wave, reggae and all sorts of synthesized/sequenced sounds. Shorter songs were prevalent but they still possessed the originality, creativity, and superior musicianship that Rush will always own.

I believe Geddy and Neil came up with their most innovative bass and drum patterns during the 80s. Their music wasn't as epic or complex as their mid/late 70s era but the patterns they used in these shorter songs were way outside the box compared to any other rhythm sections within the rock world of the 1980s. It's too bad so many

Rush fans by- passed much of this 80s era. (Trent Reznor would back me up on this statement.)

Sometimes a curious newcomer will ask me which album to get first for themselves. Are you kidding me? Let me burn you a mix, or mixes, as there's a lot of ground to cover even if you do narrow it down to only 10% of their catalog. The best thing to do is start off with a viewing of their documentary, RUSH: Beyond the Lighted Stage. This will give a detailed analysis of who Rush is and great insight to their entire musical career.

As for Neil Peart alone, I bet I'm one of the few die hard Rush fans that notices the subtle intricacies he assimilates into his playing. For instance, when Neil utilizes the hi-hat with his foot on the & after each snare backbeat during the chorus sections in the song "Chemistry". It is so faint in the mix I'm sure most Neil Peart fanatics have never noticed this detail in the recording. He does the same thing with the hi-hat during the song "High Water", but the foot accent on "Chemistry" is much harder to detect. (Headphones a must to hear this minuscule yet flavorful detail Neil added to these songs.)

On another note if you listen closely you can hear John Bonham click his sticks together during "Black Dog" after Robert Plant finishes each verse and the band needs a cue to punch back in with the music. Or if you're really in tune you will notice that Matt Cameron of Soundgarden hits the crash cymbal *and* open hi-hat at the same time to end "Black Hole Sun". Again I bet most Soundgarden fans, even drummers, have ever noticed this obscure, effective detail that Matt utilizes, but you can hear the open hi-hat sustain after that final crash of the song. (He also was the drummer who played on Geddy Lee's one and only solo album, just FYI.)

From YYZ to Xanadu, The Trees, Jacob's Ladder, Witch Hunt, Digital Man, Red Lenses, Mystic Rhythms, and so many other songs in Rush's catalogue, Neil Peart showcased innovative skills and techniques that were unheard of or ever played by any other drummer in the rock scene before his reign. Referred to as The Professor, (which is ironic being that he's a high school dropout), this nickname makes perfect sense as most any drummer will confess they listened to Neil for ideas on what the drums could do outside of basic rock beats. He's the lead "instructor" of new and interesting ideas for all who came after him. More music fans have air drummed to Neil's playing than any other by far!

No other rock drummer up until the time of The Professor ever incorporated jazz influenced triplets on the ride cymbal, as all other rockers played straight quarter or eighth notes in songs. Neil makes the choruses in songs more interesting by adding china cymbal accents within many basic ride patterns; emphasizing the "&s" on the china to give the chorus an upbeat "punch", which adds more flavor to the groove. Neil introduced crossover accenting patterns between the hi-hat and snare which was a new, exciting detail on drums to witness. When Geddy punctuates a bass note that's locked in with each hi-hat "choke" it's just too cool. (see, "Subdivisions")

Neil is the master at composed drum solos that incorporate his entire arsenal of drums and various percussion that surrounds him; all while his drum riser rotates 180 degrees so he can showcase both the acoustic and electronic aspects within one solo. Neil tastefully blends odd time technical proficiency, African influenced beats and sounds, new wave disco grooves, reggae, and a tasteful amount of percussive instrumentation (i.e. melodic cowbells) into his arrangements which make his playing so innovative, exciting, and unique. Even many non-drumming musicians within the industry refer to Neil as their favorite musician.

Then you must consider the multi-tasking motherload of musical demands Geddy Lee endures while on stage. He's playing complex bass lines while singing and adding in keyboard parts at the same time, sometimes playing patterns with his feet! Alex Lifeson gets overlooked a bit by this immense and busy rhythm section but when you focus on the guitar you hear some very unconventional soloing, phrasing, and a multitude of innovative layers and sounds coming from any of the arsenal of guitars and pedals he uses.

Once you add up all the amazing elements that make up Rush, and the fact that these three guys have stuck together and made incredible music throughout four decades of history, it's unbeatable. There's bands that are heavier, faster, more technical, and definitely more popular and profitable, but considering what constitutes for musical awesomeness within the rock and roll world there will *never* be another band that will cover as much territory in as many interesting ways as Rush.

I'm 100% sure of this in the way the music industry is heading, and besides Aerosmith and the Rolling Stones there's no other bands out there that have survived as long. And the icing on the cake being Rush is only a 3-piece outfit and they integrated so much more into rock and roll than any of the other epic bands out there. They were the first ever progressive rock band to incorporate metal influences, they are musically proficient and technical but not overwhelmingly so like many other progressive rock bands…Rush did it all, and did it all so well. Just right for the spirit of rock and roll and all that symbolizes great music.

And there's more! Another very important element within music Rush taps into and most other rock bands never do, are instrumentals. As a fan of instrumentation and sounds in general I always welcome the surprise instrumental track some bands will include on their album. Rush gave us seven brilliant instrumentals within their vast discography over the years. Each piece is so musical and tells a story without need for vocals. The vocals and message of a song almost always seem to win over the average music fan more than the arrangement and quality of the music within a song. After all, it's *music* not poetry.

Maynard James Keenan of Tool said in an interview that when recording an album they drop the vocals down in the mix and don't include lyrics with any album they release so fans are more focused on the music. And this statement is coming from one of the greatest singers in music history!

Yet most fans will still focus on the voice and meaning behind the song more than the fucking music! Unbelievable. Music rules, words drool. (Ha, whatever.)

Finally, let's bring up another detail with the music of Rush that is so exclusive. They took things in a very interesting direction on certain tracks where they add in a very unconventional mid-section "bridge jam" of sorts. The songs that come to mind include, "Circumstances", "Freewill", "Mission", "Red Sector A", "Animate", and "Afterimage". Each of these songs contains a mid-section that goes completely against the grain of any other ordinarily structured rock song. Check out these song's mid-sections and be prepared to change your undies.

Twenty studio albums and ten live albums all that include a variety of styles and influences they experimented with during the trends of each decade. Then factoring in the innovative musical ability of each member, the three hour long concerts which include the eagerly anticipated nine-minute drum solo with a rotating drum riser, the lyrics, the album artwork, their humor and genuineness, other great bands they've influenced…are you kidding?

RUSH RULES ALL.

As 2112 *bought Rush their freedom, so do I hope for* Life in the Spin Cycle *to buy me mine.*

Rush Laser Show (Produced by yours truly, at Fiske Planetarium--CU Boulder.)

2112: Overture

Twilight Zone

Force Ten

Peaceable Kingdom
Main Monkey Business
Headlong Flight

Jacob's Ladder

Mystic Rhythms

Countdown

Cygnus X-1

Rush Tribute (The more obscure selection of songs to showcase)

R30 medley

Big Money

Kid Gloves
Ceiling Unlimited
No One at the Bridge
Different Strings
Territories
Chain Lightning
New World Man
Time and Motion
Ghost of a Chance
Body Electric
Lessons
Before and After
Twilight Zone
Baachus Plateau
Best I Can
Armor and Sword
Double Agent
Earthshine
Natural Science
In the End

By the way, it took me almost two full YEARS to finally get Fiske Planetarium to put together a Laser Rush production. After attending many Fiske presentations and laser shows over the years I couldn't believe they didn't have a Laser Rush program for fuck's sake. I mean besides Pink Floyd, Tool, NIN, and small handful of others, no other band in history fits the idealism of space or has a repertoire of music that fits trippy lasers as worthy as the music of Rush! I expended so much time and energy pushing for Laser Rush during this two-year phase, until they finally budged and made it happen. DUH.

I was very happy to be given full control on what the setlist would be, however the only letdowns were we couldn't get "Overture" *edited out of the* 2112 *suite to act as the show's epic opener, and when I took a hot date to the second screening the fuckers cut out the show's climactic, concluding song,* "Cygnus X-1" *and instead ended it with* "Countdown".

That's Anti-Christ for Christ's sake! Do they care? NOPE. I do.

No biggie, we made it happen, but two fucking YEARS of pushing this concept? Pushing something that's so obligatory and befitting for any space-themed auditorium to include in their list of laser shows; showcasing Rush's amazing "sci-fi, laser-friendly" music. Hello?

Too many things of greatness that are so benefiting for society and easy to make happen take way too fucking long to materialize, or never happen at all. We (I) made it happen but it never should have been such an arduous task.

Rush to Conclusion

As everyone has their Top 5 lists that represent their

favorite artists, movies, hobbies and all, just to pick my Top 5 Rush albums is a frightening task. It's painstaking enough trying to narrow down my Top 5 favorite bands of all time, let alone having to select 5 of 20 spectacular albums by one band that represent my "favorites". But I love games of torture, let's give it a shot. (In chronological order please. I'm not going to literally torture myself condensing down 40 years of greatness into only 5 worthy representations of "favorites", THEN shuffling all these favorites into an exact order trying to showcase "least best" to "the best". Fuck that sideways and a half.)

Caress of Steel, 2112, A Farewell to Kings, Hemispheres, Permanent Waves, Moving Pictures, Signals, Grace Under Pressure, Hold Your Fire, Snakes and Arrows, Clockwork Angels.

Top 10 right? I mean 11. Oh wait, 5? Fuck, sorry, here we try again…

Hemispheres, Permanent Waves, Signals, Hold Your Fire, Clockwork Angels.

As for live albums, I'll just narrow it down to 3 "must haves" for any authentic Rush fan or newcomer to be.

All the World's a Stage, Exit...Stage Left, Different Stages (which includes a bonus 3rd CD of a live performance in London, during Rush's *A Farewell to Kings* tour, 1977.)

And finally, here's what I consider the three most epic eras in music history:

1) Classic/Prog Rock Era -- mid 60's through mid 70's

2) Punk/New Wave Era (and most prominent Rush Era) -- mid 70's through mid 80's
3) Alternative/Grunge Era -- mid 80's through mid 90's

BANDS O' MINE
(Original and Cover projects)

Although almost every project I have ever had the luxury of playing drums in has been an interesting lesson in life, most were very short-lived and lacking on the "worthy gigging stories" element. I have yet to take my musical visions and abilities beyond the inconspicuous experiences I've had so far during my life as a musician. Besides the dozen or so bands I've been in for days, weeks, months, or a few years at best, I have joined in on many open mic jams, free jams, fill-in work for many interesting gigs, and a few recording sessions over the years. It's all been very good, just not entirely gratifying.

Trilogy/Gunnar (1989-90)

After so many years of playing competitive sports I changed paths after my sophomore year in high school and formed my first band, Trilogy.

During my last year of junior high I met Dave O. When Dave first moved to Evergreen the entire school was scared of him and thought he was a NARK; as he had long dark hair, a mustache, and intense eyes. But thanks to him pushing me further into the world of heavy metal, my drum skills really skyrocketed during my first year of playing. He had me listening to Ozzy, Metallica, Iron Maiden, and of course we both dug Rush.

Dave and I auditioned my friend Bryan as vocalist. We had him sit in my room with the door shut and sing "Closer to the Heart" into my boom box as we jammed the music outside the room. He didn't get the gig, but what a classic way to try someone out for a band; having them sit alone in a room and sing into a fricking boom box while the band is outside the room jamming the music.

We settled on another mutual friend, Steve, for the singing duties instead. With him and a bassist on board we were now a 4-piece band, yet still went by the name Trilogy. This name was a great fit for us as it sounded intelligent and "proggy" but with four members in the band it just didn't make sense. It was too late to do anything about it during the time as our bassist, Jim (originally of Symposium) had already made up the flyers for our first official gig under the name Trilogy. Oh well, rock and roll!

Our first official gig was a classic. It was held at the local teen center in downtown Evergreen. On show night I think we had about a dozen people there, which included some friends from school, a couple friends from Denver, and my mom! Being the sweetheart my mom is she actually paid the cover charge to get into the show to support her son's first rock gig ever.

Another surprise guest was a girl I met on a teen chat line a few years before but had never met her in person. We only made $15 total from this gig but we had a blast playing for the first time in front of a crowd. I even performed a drum solo! (A spectacle that I would not carry out again until twenty years later in my band Free Radt.)

Unfortunately there is no documentation from this first Trilogy show. The name Trilogy was soon replaced with Gunnar, my middle name, which all three other members voted on against my will, as I thought it sounded like a hair metal band.

Our next gig as Gunnar was a big all day "Battle of the Bands" festival which took place on the EHS football field during a very hot summer day. There were about a dozen bands performing and I recall driving the Loogie down onto the field to unload my massive drum kit with nerves beyond comprehension. It was a great feeling setting up all our gear in preparation for a big show when others we knew in attendance were working as security or sitting in the hot sun as the observers.

We performed four originals that day and didn't make the cut into the top five acts, so no prizes were earned. It was really disappointing as our originals were much more creative and difficult in arrangement than most of the other bands repertoire. One of the bands that beat us out of the 5th place slot played one original and three covers for fuck's sake!

What kind of bullshit is that to have these professional judges vote us out by a band that played three covers? Jim couldn't handle this and quit the band immediately following the show, as the rest of us headed out to a party that night and drank our sorrows away.

It turned out the party was a bash for all the bands that participated in the battle, so it was very rewarding to be a musician that was part of this incredible day. Dave and I couldn't stop bitching about this band that beat us out playing those cover tunes, but I did have one starlit moment when someone knocked on the front door in a broken pattern and I said, "Was that a paradiddle?" Amidst our bitterness that comment received many laughs from the crowded room of musicians.

My friend Nathan (aka "Beef") then set us up with his football buddy Randy (aka "Tank"). He became our new bassist, and soon after we replaced Steve with a restaurant coworker of ours named Silver. Tank fit in perfect as he was into the same music as Dave and I and just as goofy. I remember each time Dave had to tune his guitar, which was quite often, Tank and I would go into what I call the "space-reggae" section of "Natural Science" by Rush. Dave would turn his amp up at full volume and tear our ears up with those fucking harmonics as he tuned.

Me, Dave, and Silver all worked at El Rancho Restaurant together so we could listen to our recorded jam sessions on the kitchen radio. "The Spirit of Radio" was such an accomplishment for us to learn and I remember playing it for the kitchen employees and one of the cooks commented that he thought it really was Rush. Wow, thanks!

The Commons Gigs

The Commons was a large, open area in our school located between the cafeteria and performance theater. the site of the school snack bar. On certain occasions bands were allowed to perform in The Commons so Gunnar jumped on this opportunity right away.

We played The Commons a few times during our two-year

career and each time it was the same ritual. I would drive the Loogie to my house before lunch with Len riding shotgun and acting as my drum roadie. We would load my gear and head back to the school cranking Rush to get me pumped up. Each performance usually consisted of an hour set of music so it was a great opportunity to showcase all our tunes in one sitting.

I can't remember any of our originals during this time but I do recall performing "It's So Easy", "Crazy Train", "Fade to Black", "Heartbreaker", "The Ocean", "Working Man", "Bastille Day", and "The Spirit of Radio".

For the record I feel that "Heartbreaker" is Led Zeppelin's worst song ever. The guitar riff and overall arrangement is bland and the lyrics are lame. The drum groove is magical but otherwise this song drives me bonkers!

During our first Commons performance two unforgettable moments took place. As Steve was still our singer during this first show, we played "It's So Easy" by Guns and Roses and he very perceptibly yelled out the "Why don't you just...FUCK OFF!" portion of the song. It was just like the Doors on the Ed Sullivan Show where there was an agreement to change this particular line in "Light My Fire", but like Jim Morrison Steve just sang it out the way it was. We were a bit shocked but how rock and roll of him.

Another amusing moment was during the vocal bridge section in "The Ocean" when Dave was trying to harmonize the "la-la" parts with Steve, and someone yelled out "Boo!" This prompted Dave to hold up his middle finger at the heckler as he continued his "la-las". Needless to say there must have been no teachers observing this show as we were able to play two more shows in The

Commons soon after.

I really wish I had documentation of these Commons performances, but we did make it into the yearbook. There's a picture of Dave and Steve rocking out in front of my roto toms with the caption: "Trilogy performing in The Commons". Okay we were Gunnar by this time but what the fuck ever, we made the yearbook!

First Demo

Upon graduating from high school Gunnar was history and summer break commenced once again. Dave and I still wanted to be in a band together and found a new bassist, then tried out a couple vocalists. The first vocalist to audition was this guy Mike, who years earlier wanted to kick my ass after I broke his Vaunt sunglasses with a basketball pass to the face. He was from a rough background and it was a trip having him there in my parent's basement with us. We were jamming out ideas and the music was now more edgy as Dave was transitioning into more of a hardcore punk guitar player.

The vocalist we settled on was a mutual acquaintance and amateur ramp skateboarder, Aaron. With him and another Aaron on bass we composed four heavy-edged songs and wanted to record a demo tape. (Aaron disappeared just before the recording session so we had a studio employee lay down the bass tracks for us.)

It was a smooth, gratifying experience and we made a pretty good four-song demo after two evenings of recording sessions. Gratifying enough that the three of us loaded a big fat bowl and drove around Evergreen in Dave's army green station wagon that we referred to as the Iguana. Little did I know Aaron had laced this pot with PCP. I was sitting in the back seat and as we were driving through downtown each person that we passed would turn and look at me and their shadow would start running after the car! I didn't say a word to the other guys but I was tripping out.

We ended up at the infamous Dedise Park and finished the rest of the bowl; just as all the trees came alive and the large bolders of rock took form of dragon heads. What a way to celebrate completing my first ever recording session.

Scattered Atoms/Normal Kids (1990-91)

Soon after this amazing experience and the post-recording "trip", I headed off to college. During winter break I was back in my parent's basement jamming with Dave once again. Aaron the bassist was back and since I only had three weeks to jam during my break we rehearsed as much as possible to get ready for a show at singer Aaron's party.

During a practice session we took a smoke break outside and began the process of trying to come up with a band name. Dave had the idea of Splattered Atoms but Aaron and I agreed that Scattered Atoms sounded better, so that was the name we used.

I loaded up my gear on a cold, snowy night and drove over to Aaron's house party. I was wearing my brand new Sorel boots I got for Christmas just days earlier and when I took them off to play our set some fuck-stick decided to take them. It was a tragedy for me as Santa had just brought them to me and I only got to use them this once before they disappeared. Oh well at least I got to play some hardcore music at a crowded party; a time where moshing was becoming the new craze and I was in panic about my gear the entire show.

By the time I finished my freshman year in Durango, I moved back home for the summer and found out Dave and Scattered Atoms were now performing as Normal Kids. Their most classic song I can remember was titled "Marijuana/Mountain Dew".

Normal Kids lasted for quite a long time and they still have an active website to this day. My name is even mentioned in the band credits as "the original drummer" so I have a bit of satisfaction that I was remembered as a "founding member".

Diatribe (1993-1995)

Diatribe represented the perfect blend of musical influences, instrumentation, structure, humor, and practically every element that makes for a great rock band. I had become good enough on drums by this time and really wanted to form a band again. I posted an ad at a local pawn shop during the summer of 1993. It was quick and to the point, listing my influences of that time: Rush, Living Colour, Jane's Addiction, and Primus.

A guitarist named Jeff gave me a call. I invited him over to my house to chat and it turned out Jeff walked into my front door right when I was having a heated argument with my dad on the phone. Jeff is a small, skinny guy with this skate punk gone hippie vibe. I apologized and said it was revolving around some birthday drama. Jeff asked when my birthday was and it turns out we are both the exact same age; born on July 23, 1971. (Leo cuspers, look out!)

Jeff and I started to jam in the shed located behind my house in Ft. Collins. I was now playing my basic 5-piece black Ludwig drums, with the three roto toms, and new additions of my first double-pedal and china cymbal.

After a couple sessions of messing around with some ideas and playing a few covers by Nirvana, Metallica, and Rush we had composed our first original, "The Bong Song". It was a shorter song comprising of an interesting structure; mixing reggae during the verses and punk rock in the choruses. From here we realized it was time to move forward and find our bottom end guy and inevitably a singer to front our project.

I will never forget meeting Matt for the first time when he showed up for one of our shed rehearsals. He had long, straight black hair, sported a black leather coat and round wire rimmed glasses. He looked kind of like a cross between Mick Mars and the Proclaimers guys. Matt never really liked it when I would sing, "And I would walk 500 miles…" on occasion just out of stupid amusement. But most importantly he could play bass! His style was a whole new ambiance of ultra-low-end thunder meets innovative noise making. Matt was a techno guru computer geek and loved to fiddle with gadgets. He constructed a bass rig that consisted of many sound effects that helped take our music into another world.

We were pumping out ideas rapidly and every song had such originality and innovative qualities. I was psyched that things were rolling along well, and all we needed was the addition of vocals. We had since been forced out of our shed from a noise complaint and moved into a dance studio that Jeff discovered above a bakery. We had access in the evening hours to play as long as we stashed our gear clearly out of the way for the daytime dance classes.

After only a few quick auditions I found a singer who went by the name Turtle. He was a member of the fraternity across the street from Sigma Chi where I was affiliated at the time. Turtle was short like Jeff but was a dark-skinned preppy guy that dressed more like me in flannels and jeans. He had this amazing low range voice that mirrored Eddie Vedder. Turtle happened to be from Portland and was really into the Pacific Northwest grunge scene of the times. It was only too perfect that we learned a few covers by Pearl Jam and Chili Peppers that really spiced up our earlier performances with the help of his voice. Turtle pushed us to play "Daughter" by Pearl Jam before it was ever heard on the airwaves, and the girls loved it.

Going by the name Divining Rod, we rehearsed a few times a week in the dance studio and soon had our first gig booked. It was at Buddy's Run, a small house annex located next to Turtle's fraternity house. This was perfect because we were guaranteed a crowd and free booze! Booze isn't the only element of being a true rocker, as just before show time I found Jeff out in the garage with a grin on his face eating the last of remaining mushrooms he had in a zip lock baggie.

The show was everything it should have been; crowded with pumped up spectators and a multitude of drinks in their hands. We played two short sets of our originals and a few covers. My proudest moment was opening the second set with Primus's "Too Many Puppies". That gave me the spotlight playing the opening 8th notes on the bell of my ride cymbal. Neato.

After our inaugural party show, the flood gates opened as we had a house full of heavy rocking frat guys that loved us and Jeff was starting to book us around town at various dive bars. Since Jeff was an art major, that gave him more free time than us business majors and he would create the most interesting flyers for our shows. In our first write-up with a local entertainment newspaper he described our sound as "Motorhead with a twist of Barbara Streisand." (That was dead on! Nice Jeff.)

The name Divining Rod was scrapped and replaced with Diatribe, a suggestion by Turtle's mom. Turtle's dad was fairly wealthy working as an executive in the Hostess corporation. He owned the factory located just north of downtown Denver off I-25 that I had been driving by since I was a child. But either way Diatribe was the coolest name for a band of our stature, and it stuck.

For the remainder of the school year we played numerous gigs at house parties, fraternity parties, and local establishments. We even landed a couple shows out on the campus plaza in front of the Lory Student Center during the lunch hour. Talk about great exposure as hordes of students would flock around to watch as they were coming from classrooms and ready for lunch. My biggest worry during these performances was the sun and heat! The sun was baking us as it reflected off the concrete and I didn't want to drop a stick or lag in my stamina.

But we made history as our second performance became the last time this sort of event was allowed on the plaza ever again. A couple professors bitched about the noise being heard in the buildings where some classes were still in session, and that was the end of live rock performances on the plaza. FUCK YEAH DIATRIBE!

The music we wrote kept progressing into multiple realms of styles but we began to realize that although Turtle had a great voice and acted as the perfect front man, he really wasn't musically inclined and didn't have natural rhythm. He was constantly getting the phrasing of the lyrics wrong and had a hard time finding the "1". Of course it was left up to me to break the news to Turtle, which occurred soon after we had recorded our first demo in the summer of 1994 at a home studio just down the street from my parent's house in Evergreen.

Mastertouch Studios was the perfect place for us amateurs to record our very first demo tape. Obviously the location was ideal as we could run over to my parent's house for snacks, pooping, and such, plus the owner Robb was really easygoing and had just enough insight on the recording process to get the job accomplished.

We ended up with three good tracks that Robb saved on ADAT: "Too Low", "Numb", and "Wisconsin". These three tracks represented Diatribe's unique blend of funky-grungy alternative rock to a tee. To this day people still think "Too Low" is a Pearl Jam demo track. However I assure you it's Diatribe, I promise.

By the fall of 1994 we were gigging regularly as a 3-piece with Jeff stepping up as the new singer. His vocals were more in the range of Layne Staley and Kurt Cobain instead of the Eddie Vedder vibe we had with Turtle during the previous year. (At least we kept the vocal element in the spirits of Seattle.)

Our music began shifting away from grunge to the funkier sounds of Chili Peppers and Primus, and with Jeff taking the role as our singer, his guitar playing began to get lazy and he was overusing his wah-wah pedal. It was cool at first but after a little while I was getting annoyed with each song containing this funky wah-wah sound. I never let it get to me too much as I was just happy creating strong and busy rhythmic grooves with Matt.

Although Jeff's guitar playing was becoming less "rock" he was still a great artist and musician in general. He had more of his art school buddies pushing gigs for our band and getting many peeps to attend shows as well.

All was rolling along fine and the three of us recorded our second demo tape at Mastertouch Studios once again in the summer of 1995. We got four songs down this time around; "Running Down", "Groovy Sunday", "Better Way", and "Paul da Painter". (An instrumental tribute to our number one fan, who also happened to be Turtle's best friend.)

However, unlike the successful ride we had with our first demo, we didn't really capitalize too much after recording our second one. We began to play shows during the fall semester as usual but again Jeff wanted to make a change to our sound, this time adding a trumpet player to the mix. I really didn't care about this addition as the sounds of brass became a hindrance to our guitar/bass/drums rock foundation. (And to this day I've kept my word to never be in a band with any brass ever again.)

We were now practicing in a dark, gloomy room underneath a vintage clothing store that Matt coined as the

"Brown Reckluse Lounge". I was not too enthusiastic about Diatribe by this point and with the "help" of a girlfriend's input, I quit.

Years later I regretted this decision as we still had momentum to take this amazing music we created further. But really the decision was about me losing interest, and letting a girl convince me that it wouldn't do anything for me in the long run.

Diatribe carried on for another year or so under the name Sector 7G. (The quadrant where The Simpsons takes place. Nice one Matt.)

I would like to add the biggest show I ever performed in my career thus far was with Diatribe. We performed at a huge warehouse party put on by a few fraternities in Greeley, CO. It was Halloween night and we played in front of about a thousand people packed in this mighty warehouse. I played my drums wearing a cow costume.

Ounce for Ounce (1996-97)

Ounce for Ounce (Oz 4 Oz) was a foursome I joined right out of college. It was my first time playing in a project that featured a female on vocals and exhibited a much more pop rock approach than I was used to. *The benefits of drumming to more simplistic styles of music was ability to expand my creative approach to the drums evermore. I had just upgraded to a brand new Yamaha Stage Custom drum kit, in Cranberry Red finish!*

We played all originals and like most bands I've been in we

never progressed any further than performing at a few smaller venues around Denver. I think we played Cricket on the Hill a half dozen times alone.

Saucy Jack (2002-2003)

Funny enough this was the same project (Oz 4 Oz) but under a new name and a keyboardist added into the mix. The female singer was now playing the bass as well.

I was re-introduced to my old band through a friend that worked with the new keyboardist and it all came together. Saucy Jack was playing a few of the older Oz 4 Oz tunes and a handful of newer originals.

The highlight of this short-lived Saucy Jack project was recording a demo album at this mountaintop studio in Idaho Springs, CO. The experience was enhanced as the incentive was an extra $50 charge to sleep over at the studio and use the hot tub.

Speaking of $50, there was one occasion after a performance where the band and select friend's all gathered back at the rehearsal pad for late hours fun. After a few hits off this Ghandolf like pipe I went into "stoned out blabber mode". Seriously, good weed for me is like euphoric coke; I feel trippy and goofy yet also very lively and talkative, even adventurous, and sexual. ANYWAY…

I'm holding the Ghandolf pipe in my right hand, beer in the left, and I'm bantering away some analytical, comical nonsense. One of the select friends in attendance made the comment, "Dude I would honestly pay $50 right now to see a performance like this with you in this exact state of being. Seriously, exactly like this!"

Yes my calling being called out once again, by another new face I had just met. Hence why the 60s and even more so, the 70s, was the American Dream. Everyone was open minded, experimental, engaged, and fucking HIGH. It was all partying and fucking yet still maintaining jobs, careers, families…holy shit what amazing times! (Just a bit un-sanitized and full of stinky, hairy crotches meshing together, but who's stressing that element over all the other awesome ingredients that made for the perfect recipe of those times.)

Fall Out (1997-98)

Fall Out was my first experience in a cover project. I saw an ad posted at a music store and they listed a few bands I liked and decided to give it a shot.

The guys in Fall Out were all cool dudes. Spence, guitarist, was a tough talking muscle head and funny as heck. The bass player, Kelly, was probably the most talented and had a great singing voice. Chris was the lead guitarist and always annoyed Spence with his habit to "tweak" on his guitar in between songs. "If you don't quit your tweaking..." was the usual statement relayed from Spence to Chris.

We played all sorts of hard rock covers from bands like Metallica, Green Day, Smashing Pumpkins, Corrosion of Conformity, and many others. This project never made it out of the rocker suburbs of Denver; playing a number of gigs at a local blue collar dive known as T&R's. I soon left the band.

I re-joined Fall Out some months later as I wanted to keep playing music and had no other worthy options. I remember Spence saying, "If another drummer says he's taking his gear home to clean and polish it and doesn't come back..." (This was the lie I used to quit the first time and I guess the replacement drummer had said the same shit as me! Fucking drummers.)

Church Band (1998)

I joined a church band at one point; a night church that catered to underprivileged teens. We played some good rocking music, but the best part about drumming in this project was our trip to Atlanta.

The band was flown out to Atlanta to perform at some big church related event. A storm rolled into the Denver area and I missed my flight. Then I missed a second flight. By the time I made it onto a third flight I was rewarded by sitting next to a girl my age who had a bottle of Captain Morgan for us to consume. I got her number so I could have someone to hang with while in Atlanta.

I reached the hotel where the band was staying but the front desk had no idea about them being there. Since these were the times before cellular phones I could not get in touch with any of the band members.

Long story short I never ran into my band during the few days I was in Atlanta! I instead hooked up with the girl I met on the plane and went out one evening with her and some friends that were tripping on ecstasy. I had some drinks and ended up spending a good amount of money for a cab back to the hotel after that crazy night.

And that was that; flown out to Atlanta to play a church convention and instead having my own solo adventures for a few days around the city.

Sex Exit (1999)

This project was an offset of the same one I tried to be part of during my first trek to Santa Barbara, CA. My friend Josh kept in touch and we discussed the option of me moving back out there and getting a band going again. He had found another guitarist, Patrick, and the ideas were flowing between them. Josh had come up with the clever name of Sex Exit on a whim.

We rehearsed on the UC Santa Barbara campus where other bands also rehearsed. (One being Ultraspank, who had just been signed to a label and was preparing to tour with System of a Down.)

Josh booked a recording day at local Orange Peel Studio. I drove up from San Diego and spent a couple days and nights in the studio rehearsing the parts of the four songs we were to record. Josh and Patrick stopped by both nights to jam with me and we were a go for recording on Halloween day, 1999.

I had to learn the drum parts off a drum machine that Josh had programmed and it was a challenge I had never faced before. I recreated the parts almost exactly as they were from electronic programming onto my acoustic drums; a painstakingly fun process overall. But I give Josh credit, he's a great songwriter (on guitar and drum machine, haha).

The Fanatics (2000)

After meeting Joe, a bass player and awful singer, and discussing the plan to jam in his Jawbone project, we crossed paths with Don. Don was an English guitarist virtuoso and he could shred! I've never jammed with a guitarist having such skills and unique sounds deriving from one instrument. The problem with this is the more talent you possess, the more crazy and neurotic you are in general. Talent breeds insanity. Funny also that me Joe and Don were all ten years apart in age so we represented three different eras of musical generations.

Don was being sought out by Angelic Entertainment, a large Christian label in San Diego, and this news had us bouncing with joy. (Or jamming with 'tude'?) Just after I was fired from my Blind Melons bar job me and Joe rented out a rehearsal space and rehearsed through Don's original songs every day to prepare for a very important showcase gig we had with Angelic.

We played very well at the showcase but the event itself was a joke. Only a short while later Angelic backed out of all the promises they made with us. The main promise broken was a good money deal to have our music featured in movies, and our music was perfect for film. Oh that genuine, Christian American spirit shines on!

With this it wasn't long until The Fanatics disbanded. Yet another ball buster in the business of music for me.

Lipslide (2002)

Although the Lipslide project was short lived it consisted of a talented group of guys, two of which were good friends of mine.

I met Trevor in Boulder during the late 90s and made a couple attempts at throwing a band together with him, but I eventually moved to California. My connection with Douglas was even more exasperating.

I came across (huh-huh) an ad of his posted in a local music store; needing a drummer for a band that was influenced by Red Hot Chili Peppers, Jane's Addiction, and Tool. I was excited after discovering this ad and wrote down the number. The next morning at work my other drummer friend, Brendon, flaunted his enthusiasm telling me he was trying out for a killer band that evening. Yes it was the same project advertised at the music store, and I was planning to call them that evening but Brendon was onto it quick and ended up spending a number of months jamming with Douglas on bass and a guitarist.

This coincidence of timing would delay me ever jamming with Douglas until 2002. And to be finalizing edits in this book some 17+ years later, with me and Douglas still living in Boulder County? Scary cool.

Back to Lipslide…

Trevor contacted me again with interest in working on some more music. He told me he found a tall, dread-locked black guy for a bassist and I immediately figured it was

Douglas, so I was in.

The three of us began jamming in Trevor's basement, working on originals and a few covers we agreed on; "Take the Power Back" by Rage Against the Machine, "Head Up" by the Deftones, and "Set the Controls for the Heart of the Sun" by Pink Floyd. We recruited a friend of Trevor's on vocals and a DJ to add in some spice to the music.

As a five-piece we played only a small number of shows but each one rocked! We all were the same age and came from the same background of musical interests and the chemistry was magic. Despite Trevor's dictating antics we had some amazing shit coming together.

One time we performed a show at The Basement on Pearl St, which is now Nitro strip club. Another time we played a show in Vail. I drove up with me, girlfriend, Douglas and our gear packed in my Toyota Camry. The gig went fine but after everyone packed up and departed to their rooms Douglas was left behind; alone wandering around freezing cold Vail during the early morning hours. Oh well I got laid in a nice warm room.

For the record both Trevor and Doug are really good friends and great musicians. They deserve props and more written about them and all our times together. Trevor has the ability to jump into any current music trend and make something unique out of it; utilizing his prerogative to "Trevorize the trend". Just take my word for it that Trevor and Doug exist and have been major attributes in my life; as musicians and friends.

Slugworth (2005-2007)

Slugworth was my second run at being in a cover band. A name derived from Tim, my friend and lead singer of the outfit. The original band name was Five Hole, a term used in hockey as a puck is shot between the legs of the goalie.

First of all, who is Tim? He is a guy I met after I posted an ad back in 1996 wanting to form a band with anyone who dug Rush. After answering me add Tim and I chatted on the phone for a long time and set up a jam at his house. Tim had just moved to Denver from San Francisco so we had Rush and our Bay Area upbringings to chat about.

Tim showed me all his Rush memorabilia and we jammed "Red Sector A" in his bedroom. The first and only time I've ever played that song. Since this jam we kept in touch and hung out on occasion, only to finally be in a band together nine years later!

We proceeded to rehearse in the guitarist's basement for a couple months before playing out. Others in the band were Brad on guitar and programming, Greg on rhythm guitar and another muscle head, Kevin, on 6-string bass. After our first rehearsal Kevin said, "Just don't fuck up." However it turns out Kevin is really a great guy with a fucked up sense of humor like me. Love it!

Our first gig was in October 2005 and I documented part of the show with my camcorder from the side of the stage. This was a "test show" since the bar owner had to see if we had what it took to entertain the masses with four long sets of music. We nailed the gig. We had such a powerful set of music and an immaculate stage show that Tim had created, so all was well.

We were mixing in more metal and 90s alternative songs than all the other cover bands out there that usually stick to classic rock, hair metal, or mostly fucking 80s. We threw in some 311, Weezer, Sublime, Tool, Pantera, and the likes during our sets. At one point we had the "And Justice Medley" down and even "Eulogy" by Tool. The opening song we chose for many of our shows was "You Call My Name" by Ra. It had the perfect anthemic intro to kick us into gear for a long evening of great cover tunes.

Like a couple of the other bands I've been in, I left Slugworth (or was actually kicked out) and ended up re-joining months later, as the other drummers they used just weren't cutting it. Either way it was still a good two-year stint and one cover band that should have made it bigger than we did.

You Make the Call: (First of all we need to re-incorporate this idealism into Monday Night Football.) The first time being fired from Slugworth was a frustrating, twisted situation and basically unjust. I will now share the story of all the events that took place which brought about my firing from Slugworth, then allow you readers to make the call.

I was away on a quick vacation and knew about our gigs the following week; the usual Wednesday through Saturday at Eck's Saloon. Because I had to bail on the vacation group early to make it back for my shows I had to have my "date" drive us back from Lake Powell to Denver, leaving early Wednesday morning.

During the ten-hour road trip back I had to make multiple

calls to the band with updates whenever I had signal to do so. (Funny that on the way out to Lake Powell my date had to make many business phone calls during the journey that occupied much of the road trip experience. Fucking jobs.)

When I realized I was going to be late I then had to call my drummer friend, Brendon, and have him drive up to Evergreen, pack my drums, drive them back down to Eck's, and set them up.

In the meantime I was still communicating with Tim giving constant updates of my progress and situation. Tim and the guys had to call on a previous drummer to fill in on my drums until I arrived at Eck's.

After a very frantic, stressful ten hours I arrived at the venue having only missed most of one set. I played the rest of the evening and all was okay.

By the end of the weekend I was informed that I was fired from the band. Now take into account all that happened; I had to leave a fun-filled getaway with great friends that included boats, booze, bud, and do all I could to make sure Slugworth wasn't completely let down. Wednesday nights are a fucking joke anyway and this annoyed me from the start, that a pointless Wednesday night would be the cause for a shortened getaway with friends and then cause me to get fired.

Either way the show prevailed due to the efforts of many. I felt the guilt and pressure from my end and Slugworth was stressed on their end, yet we pulled it off. Still with all these elements factored into this entire debacle, was it a just decision for a firing? A threatening final warning to never put the band in that stressful situation again would've been sufficient, but the guys focused on all the negative aspects of the ordeal and not all everyone did to make sure things still worked out overall.

I got my drums delivered and set up at the venue, they got a previous drummer to fill in for the first set until I arrived, the show went on and all was well. Fired? Fuck that noise.

And worst of all is after months of anticipation and build-up I would have gotten laid by the sexy female companion who accompanied me to Lake Powell, had we stayed the very same night of this ordeal. (NO) FUCK.

Another tormenting story with Slugworth, just weeks before the Lake Powell incident, was when we decided we absolutely needed to practice on St. Patrick's Day. I had dinner plans with my dad at Conor O'Neills in Boulder, CO, and due to the line being so long to get into the venue I had to bail on my dad and get to rehearsal.

The following day I hear my dad's stories of how crowded the venue was with girls kissing everyone, including him, and the band's drummer was late for their show, so the singer announced in the microphone: "Any drummers out there?"

I missed what would've been the most memorable St. Patrick's Day of my life for a band practice, *not even a gig! We musicians sacrifice a lot to indulge in our craft, but to make a sacrifice within the sacrificial avocation is too much. Fuck a bloody duck.*

**Maybe "karma" from backing out of the big New Year's gig originally?*

And now onto describing my last attempt at joining an established, original rock project that had good potential within this cluster fuck, rat race of a music scene.

Free Radt (2009-2012)

After promising myself to never again drum in a band with a female singer, I broke my own rule by joining this outfit. I couldn't help myself as I listened to their tracks online and really loved the diversity and complexity of the arrangements. And nothing was happening with Douglas or anyone else so I had to get involved with something.

Free Radt was made up of Katz on vocals, Jeremy on guitar and violin, and Angela on Bass. Yes two females in the band this time, and the band name has an implication of freeing yourself from the rat maze of life, hence the spelling of the name as Free Radt.

Free Radt had recently won Denver's Battle of the Bands just before I joined to replace the original drummer, and we had a live radio appearance coming up so I had to learn most of their debut album quick as possible. I can't tell you how many times I would listen to each track over and over during the car ride to practices, even pulling over at a nearby park to really pay attention to certain parts and take notes before possibly embarrassing myself at practice. Like I stated it was complex, dynamic stuff.

However, it was only a short amount of time before the girls had a feud and Angela left the band. After her departure we spent months searching for a replacement bass player with no luck. One of the prospects turned out to be the brother of the guy I worked with in the mailroom up in Evergreen. But like me he's not into female singers and couldn't commit. We finally had to settle on a mutual friend, Samantha. I had known Samantha for years through other means and Jeremy knew her from working at a music store together. Samantha was more basic punk rock trained but pulled off a few gigs with us as we decided to continue the search for someone that would fit best for our style of music.

My friend Douglas ended up filling in on bass for a short while. With him we recorded some tracks and played the next Battle of the Bands at Hard Rock Cafe. No first place that time around, it was a disaster.

Katz's sister-in-law set us up with a guy she worked with at a health food market named Jeff. The interesting thing with Jeff is he used to be in a band I knew from years back that featured a local Evergreen fellow on vocals. Jeff also came from punk rock roots but went through a progressive phase and loved Yes and Rush.

We spent weeks practicing with Jeff and realized he was mega loud and had the most aggressive style we had jammed with yet. This was all great except our practices were tough as it was hard to hear distinct parts from any instrument through all the thunderous noise. At least we clicked well enough to learn a few Rush tunes that were great to play as warmup jams.

After a few gigs with Jeff he had decided to move back to Florida to be close to his ailing mother. This was fine and soon after I was burnt out on Free Radt's lack of progress after three years of exhausting efforts and left as well.

I loved this band and the music we created, and we had potential but like every project I have drummed for it never made any progress past the smaller rocker bar circuit. Even after having won the battle of the bands when I joined, and a radio show appearance, we didn't amount to squat. So rad(t).

Finger Pie (2012-2015)

"Hey Gunnar, how would you like to join a project where we don't give a shit and just play old school punk rock. Saying, 'Hey! Ho! Let's Go!'" "Sure." (I respond without hesitation.)

Way back from the days of my high school band, Gunnar, lead singer Steve called me on a whim just after I left Free Radt to offer this drum position playing some Ramones influenced punk. (Or "irreverent diner punk" as we described ourselves as. I had never played punk nor had a desire to, but after all the recent years of musical debacles I endured, I obliged.

With me on drums, Steve on lead vocals and bass, and Koobs playing guitar with some backing vocals, our 3-piece outfit lunged into the Denver dive bar scene; sharing the stages with many other local punk bands. It was very different for me, yet gratifying to be playing numerous songs with fast, driving 8th notes to loud, gritty guitar strumming, and goofy-ass lyrics on top. I was having a blast!

We recorded a 4-song demo at The Decibel Garden; a very large, exquisite studio full of many rooms, corridors, and interesting artifacts. I even convinced the band to learn and record my neat little forty-second song, "The Pink Blob Squad".

It was a good three year run we had and the only major letdown for me involved the Suicide Girls. Yes those hot, alt girls full of body art, colored hair, and piercings galore. We had written a song about them, oddly enough titled "Suicide Girls", and this one song went through almost a dozen revamps and edits before we considered it worthy to record and pitch to the colorful divas to use as their website theme music.

When the Suicide Girl's burlesque show came to town I nominated myself to attend the event and pitch our song to them. I splurged on a VIP ticket at $75 so I could get in with the right people to talk to, and just before the event began I managed to meet, explain my purpose, and get a card from the tour manager.

Only days later I received an email from one of the head managers of Suicide Girls that included a contract form so we could officially submit our song to them. But unfortunately, after all these months of preparing the song, spending a chunk of change on a show ticket, making the proper connections, and now having an official contract to work with, Steve decided not to roll with it as he's a teacher and didn't want to be associated with sexy, kinky, nude women.

How un-punk of us, and a primo opportunity that might have led to bigger shit. After years of hoping for any type of break with any band I've been involved with, a day job fucks things up for the musician's cause; the one time something does look big and promising. Ho-ly SHIT.

Oh, one more concept I tried to throw together with Finger Pie *was having us be the live band that performs at* Film on the Rocks. *I've attended so many of these events since the very first one,* Braveheart, *and they always include a local band as entertainment before the film begins. Usually a band whose music fits the theme of the movie they are showing that night.*

I spoke with one of the organizers during a film night and contacted headquarters the next day to pitch the idea for them to show Rock n' Roll High School *and have* Finger Pie *as the opening band. We play a handful of* Ramones *songs and sound a lot like them anyway, so why not?*

Nope. I bugged them a few times and listed all the reasons why, blah-blah, they don't care. They'd rather show any 80s comedy over and over each summer than any other worthy curveball feature, especially a cult classic film with a local band that fits the bill perfectly and can entertain the outlandish crowd beforehand! They'd sell the shit out of PBRs *during a theme night like this, to say the least. And I guarantee some respectful reviews and post-event hype would come of it all.*

When will my credibility and unique, praiseworthy ideas ever gain attention or any ground in this stubborn, vanilla-coated, conformist state of ours? Fucking Colorado; so great yet so lame. I'm soon going to be forced to push for an "Anti-Vanilla Movement" here.

Anyway, look for Finger Pie's non-existent album; *Slurpees, Milk Duds, and Blowjobs* at a non- existent record store near you!

Dillusiac (2011-present)

Perfect name for this project I coined as Dark, Heavy, Psychedelic Instru\m/etal. After Landon answered my ad (see *Posted Musician Ads* below) we set up a jam at my studio (#6, Dog House Music). Since this evening we've remained intact as a casual, improv project, usually jamming at Landon's pad while high on homegrown weed and organic coffee. Dark trippy improvisational madness = Dillusiac.

We've played out with a rotation of bass players, but we have also performed as a duo; either way with an advantage of its own. Jeff from the Free Radt era has been our most prominent bassist over more recent years but he's now back in Florida again.

Landon provides some impressive lighting and three video cameras to capture angles of the jams and edit it all together into one fine production. We have audio saved from almost every jam during the original Dog House sessions back in 2011-13, and many more jams performed and recorded at his pad since. TOO MANY.

We played a few shows at Owsley's in Boulder which features a covered stage that's connected to a patio right by CU campus. You would think this would bring in great exposure but nope, even though the trippy-jammy element of Dillusiac is "so Boulder" it's a new era of digitally-distracted Millennials with earbuds in staring at their phones as they stroll by outside, without a care of our live music proceeding just yards away.

The inevitable, disappointing letdown with this establishment came after the bartender/booking girl promised us a regular bi-weekly performance night at Owsley's, being paid $150 a pop. But she had a falling out with the owner and quit, leaving it in the owner's hands to save the deal, but he, like so many on the business side of the music industry, didn't give a fuck and never booked us again.

A highlight performance for Dillusiac was opening for Banyan in the summer of 2015. Banyan is "fronted" by Jane's Addiction drummer, Stephen Perkins, who co-founded the group with trumpetteer Willy Waldman in the late-90s as a "fuck singers", all instrumental, improv, funky jam project. As I've been a volunteer drum tech for Stephen over the years he agreed to have Dillusiac open for Banyan on this particular occasion.

I constructed a hybrid, monster drum kit on stage by incorporating various percussion, effects cymbals, and extra drums of mine into the house kit we both played. Dillusiac performed a solid 45-minute opening set, which thankfully was captured on video by Landon's girlfriend, Michelle, utilizing three cameras and various lighting we provided. As Banyan performed I jumped up on stage at a point in time as percussionist; incorporating my two Rototoms and one 18" floor tom.

Check out the multi-camera, edited version of our performance here:

https://youtu.be/51xwbpJaAyU

(Stephen jams with me a bit at the end of the clip. If you watch closely you seem him acknowledge how I broke both

Deccabon heads during our 45-minutes of playing \m/)

Stephen complimented my drum skills and Dillusiac's mission in general. He knows it's tough out there. But ironically *not* that tough to be a good musician, and be worthy of bigger success from many achievements attained, if they go noticed by the right eyes and ears, ever.

One time Stephen had to leave a gig early for the airport so I filled in on drums and played a long set with Banyan. Unrehearsed, drunk, stoned, and playing with a group of experienced veterans in the music scene, I passed the test.

Following the set Willy also complimented my playing and asked the band what they thought. "He did great", was the response from John Avila. (Original bass player of Oingo Boingo.)

So why the fuck am I still working pointless day jobs and not making any kind of living at what I'm naturally good at? Lack of skills, effort, karma? Fuck no, just mostly all BULLSHIT.

Dillusiac is such the perfect project for underground events and festivals across the nation. We are ideal as the side-stage performers or even parking lot tailgate entertainment at least. Just need to gig more and prove our worthiness!

We were actually booked to perform a couple times at Fiske Planetarium, but wouldn't you know it, both times the promoter booked another band last minute in our place. And this is *another* example of being fucked out of a promise for something that was earned and set to be. It's endless letdowns and bullshit like this I endure so often I truly wonder if I'm cursed, or I'm incapable of grasping the concept of what this world wants from me.

It's such an aggravating game out there, so tough to deal with all that goes into being in a band and getting anywhere with it all respectively. Dillusiac is a nice detour from all my other more structured musical projects I've been in over the years. It's a great release for me to jam freely and improvise on the drums in this glorious project of ours!

One excellent concept I came up with is **Dillus-i-Cruise**. *Rent out a cruise ship that caters to trust fund hippies, ravers, and artsy-musicians alike and have us perform! What a boatload of interestingly awesome people that would be; cruising the ocean together in musical harmony. If* Dillusiac *wasn't jamming away, Landon could integrate his solo DJ project,* Employee, *to entertain the masses. Or I could integrate my Roland SPD-SX sampling pad and perform as my one-man solo show;* The Sybian Experiment.

All of this and more is doable; just need to maintain focus, perseverance, putting together the right business team, getting the proper funding and sponsors involved, legalities squared away…HELP!

Free Jam Society (2002-present)

Similar to Dillusiac, The Free Jam Society is a revolving door style project I've been honored to be part of for well over a decade now. I remember the time I discovered this phenomenon one chilly evening just months after moving back to Colorado in 2001. I was wrapping up a phone call while strolling around Boulder and I heard music and saw lights coming from a nearby outdoor amphitheater known as the Boulder Band Shell. As I approached the scene I observed two musicians, one on keys and the other playing guitar and all sorts of gadgets. I interrupted their flow to ask what was happening and David, a full-on hippie and main organizer of this free jam, invited me to join in on drums the next time a jam was to take place.

About a week later I had my drums set up on that same stage and proceeded to jam with these two freaks, only to have the city enforcement stop by and put an abrupt end to our session. We then moved the Free Jam Society operation to the stage at Red Rocks.

Most people still can't grasp the fact that anyone has permission to jam on the stage at Red Rocks but it turns out it's free game as long as no concerts are scheduled. David had one of those old person electric carts and three wagons in tow in order to get all our equipment from the lower parking lot up to the stage. It was quite an exhausting process but we jammed long into the evening hours numerous times in order to make up for the long hauling and set up time involved.

David and I still commence jamming on the Red Rocks stage after a decade since we met, with David performing up there almost every weekend during the off season. I average about 3-4 jams at Red Rocks each year and David can top 50! No joke, as he will jam into the winter months if weather permits. What a dedicated musician and the reason I'm proud to be part of the FJS after all this time.

Apart from Red Rocks we have performed at various other

empty venues throughout the Denver metro area. David will invite me to a number of places he discovers and is able to jam at. We've performed at race events, art shows, microbreweries, and other interesting locations. Recently we performed at a Renaissance Festival, and as I write this David is performing solo at some fashion show taking place at a hookah bar right now. I must get going so I can catch it!

David has been a true blessing to have in my life. Thanks for everything Dave!

www.freejamsociety.com

I also tried out for the Blue Man Group at one point.

Music Projects I'd Like to Form and Play In:

For what it's worth, here's a list of all the projects I have always wanted to (and still might) create and perform with for my own satisfaction and homage to all the music that influenced me over the years. For any reason I should perish, let it be known that I had these ideas engraved within my brain and soul since my 30s commenced.

Anomaly (3-piece; featuring mix of prog/alt/metal/fusion)

Elastic Penguin (100% improv; electro-trippy-jam music, rotating musicians)

? (100% improv drums/percussion, set up backwards on stage; including looping sequenced patterns, blacklight, lasers, and showcasing slideshow of my photography/videography on the backdrop screen or wall)

Lollapapozers (Tribute to all bands featured during

those first 4 tours; 1991-1994)

ALL 90s (Play any great song from 90s; Pantera, Phish,

alt/grunge…showcase ALL)

Darker Side of the 90s (Feature all the heavier

alt/grunge/metal of the 90s)

Porno Addiction (Music by Jane's Addiction & Porno for Pyros)

Everlasting Gaze (Smashing Pumpkins tribute)

In Sound From Way Out (Play entire catalog of

Beastie Boys instrumentals)

Shuffling Madness/iPod Shuffle/Juke Box

Heroes (Covers, anything goes)

Pixies/Pumpkins (Both great bands, each containing

female bassist)

No Vox (Band that plays all instrumentals; originals

and/or covers)

Epics (Play longer cover songs; The Camera Eye, Three

Days, Echoes…)

Almond Bros (Allman Bros tribute; members dress like

almonds. Nope, fuck this.)

Carlin Crusaders (Music and lyrics based around

George Carlin rants/idealisms)

MC Teretz (Nathan on vox/drums, Me on drums/mouth harp)

Bleach & Blue (Nirvana/Weezer tribute)

Sloppy Seconds (Perfect name for a cover band, think

about it)

Drunken Fuckits (Offset of DDP, we get wasted and

jam nonsense)

MixTape Madness (Perform shows from various mixes

I've made)

I also have a concept rolling around in my head for a theater production of Rush's *2112*. It would consist of my friend Tim as the individual who finds the guitar and presents it to three priests of power. I would be the drummer in the band that performs the music as the play goes on. Being that it's now 2012 I was hoping to make this happen and call it the 100-year pre-anniversary of the actual year the original concept takes place, but of course nothing has come of it yet.

Divapalooza

I want to create and help promote a summer tour, or one time weekend event, of all the girl bands from the 80s/90s era. Artists will include:

Breeders
Bjork
Belly
Hole
Lush
Drain STH
Sneaker Pimps
Tori Amos
Veruca Salt
PJ Harvey
Liz Phair
Sundays
Kittie

L7

Another interesting thing about my musical preferences is that I usually favor the "sophomore" album release over the debut with many bands. Here's a list of examples from second album releases I feel are more worthy of praise than their debut releases:

Jane's Addiction- *Ritual* over *Nothing's Shocking*
Beastie Boys- *Paul's Boutique* over *License to Ill*
Living Colour- *Time's Up* over *Vivid*
Alice in Chains- *Dirt* over *Facelift*
Van Halen- II over I
Pearl Jam- *Vs.* over *Ten*
STP- *Purple* over *Core*
311- *Grassroots* over *Music*

OR we can painfully pick which of any band's two "epic albums" I prefer. If I actually had to choose one, it would be like this: (Realizing again most would choose opposite)

Rush- *Permanent Waves* over *Moving Pictures*
Metallica- *...And Justice* over *Master of Puppets*
Beatles- *Magical Mystery* over *Sgt. Peppers*

In fact, it's prominent that many things I support in life are usually the underdog or constantly take 2nd place in the polls. But I always say I prefer silver to gold anyway so I'm good with it. And here they are:

CSU over CU (Ft. Collins over Boulder)
Rocky Mountain Pass over Epic Pass
Goodfellas over Godfather

Michael Myers over Jason
Lamborghini over Ferrari
Movies over Books
Salts over Sweets
Blood over Sweat
Silver over Gold

Posted Musician Ads

InstruMetal project

Drummer looking to form instrumental electronic/industrial metal project. Stuff that would be featured in a Michael Bay film or performed at a gothic strip club with cage dancers and black lights.

NIN, Ministry, Korn drum grooves, dense heavy Tool-style bass, audaciously innovative guitar with lots of effects and looping sequences, maybe a MOOG or Taurus pedals as well. Very dark, crunchy, drop-tuning realms of the deep that will rumble any venue.

Have 24/7 rehearsal place @ Dog House Music in Lafayette

Lollapaloozers/Lollapapozers

I play drums, and since it's coming up on the 20th Anniversary of the Lollapalooza festivals from the 90s I feel it's the perfect time to pay tribute to most of the bands that performed in those epic shows. Why not play a few tunes from each of the best bands of the Lollapalooza era:

Tool, Rage, Jane's, Primus, Soundgarden, Pumpkins, Fishbone…

All you need is knowledge and love of that era and the right equipment/experience on your instrument, then it's just a bunch of homework learning multiple tunes, some rehearsal jams, then book some shows.

The hardest part is attempting to mimic and play such an eclectic mix of talented music. Hence the idea for the band name, as to not take it too seriously in respect to these artists and not being able to play as good as them anyway. This is not a "practice three times a week" commitment, just a side project for fun and chops mostly, but it's the era of tribute bands and this would be off the hook and rally all the Gen-Xers who really understand and appreciate some of the greatest music of all time!

Gunnar

KGLR (greenlightradio.com)

Snapping and whistling both SUCK. As Baachus and I try to get our rhythm flowing but the power of the Sharks Breath is killing our mojo.

After having an interest in radio since childhood and being involved with radio all through college, I am now involved with a pirate radio station that's broadcast out of Boulder, CO. So how did all this come to be?

While I was wrapping up my four-year working stint in Evergreen I surfed the internet for my next options. I saw an ad posted on the internet looking for DJs to get involved with an underground radio station based in Boulder County. I soon later moved back to the Boulder area and set up a time to meet with the guy who posted the ad; DJ Baachus.

I was invited over to his apartment to get a rundown on all that was happening. It was the classic scene of a true bachelor pad and underground station set up. There were beer cans, pizza boxes, pipes, and ganja scattered all about, as well as microphones hanging from the ceiling by duct tape.

Baachus gave me a very quick overview of how everything works, then asked me which song I'd like to play on the air while I was there. I picked Slayer's "War Ensemble", so Baachus clicked on a link and boom my request was now playing to the masses of listeners throughout the Boulder County area. (Or anywhere in the world, since it is internet radio.)

Soon after connecting with Baachus I attended my first radio crew meeting at the house of another DJ. I brought my friend Dan (aka DJ Rhythm) along, and as the five of us began discussing plans around the kitchen table I recognized another guy who I met at a party some weeks before, and we chatted about a pirate station becoming reality. Cool.

A few more months passed and my schedule finally allowed me to be a weekly host for my own three-hour show. It still broadcasts to this day, on Tuesdays from 6-9 pm. I named my show "Eclectic Mayhem" which appropriately refers to the wide array of music I play during my three hours on air.

I usually put together my playlists at a coffee shop near the KGLR studio, (aka Baachus's Basement), each Tuesday during the couple hours, or handful of minutes, I have before show time. Most of my themes revolve around progressive, alternative, and metal genres. (As an 'up yours' to Boulder County and Millennial's likings for hippie jam bands, bluegrass, hip hop, and DJs/EDM redundancy.) I also include some instrumental music and the occasional surprise of some George Carlin dialect to enhance my shows.

Nothing against any person's choice of music tastes or any genres out there that I may not prefer, just that so many people overplay the stuff that's already well over-cooked in the main course meal pot. Let's call this the "Limp Noodle Syndrome"; ANY style or genre of music that's overplayed and can't be avoided, to the point it makes you cringe! Hence, tune into my show and go on a wild ride of mixed genres and themes from my library of 6,666 songs of musical mayhemic madness!

Here's a copy of my radio show bio found on www.greenlightradio.com

Cygnus is bliss! Deriving his handle from an 11min epic Rush tune about a black hole (Cygnus X-1) he realizes no one cares, so anyway... While living his manically chaotic lifestyle he spent months contemplating his dream of hosting a 3-hour slot (huh-huh "slot") here on KGLR. Good news kids, hermaphrodites, and necrophiliacs, "Eclectic Mayhem" now exists and features an interesting mix of songs to enjoy each week.
Cygnus was a DJ in college so this radio thing is familiar

territory with him. While studying Custodial Arts he mixed various substances with poop hoping to find a cure for worldwide naïve flaky self-absorption and hypocrisy, but nothing came of it. Poop on that.

Check out his neat little show on KGLR every Tuesday 6-9pm. (And remember to wipe!)

Check out other DJ's bios as well. (Then go masturbate to Care Bear Porn.)

Let it be known that Baachus is a great guy and KGLR is made up of a fantastic crew of music-loving bitches who love to share their favorite songs to the selective ears out there in the world. Baachus is so dialed in with the community and he's sufficient enough with technology, which keeps the soul of this station thriving. He's a strong individual; an old fashioned good guy with an edge. Genuine yet a bit crazy, like me. He is also one of the most unique "power rappers" I've ever heard and we both share a passion for drums.

Very cool to still be connected with Baachus and this awesome crew of radio DJ peeps; broadcasting music, hosting events, working fundraisers, charities, and partaking in many other fine extracurricular activities of debauchery together, for an entire decade! (And counting…)

Just too bad AGAIN digital technology and self-absorbed narcissism has ruined what could have been so great with our intended mission. Competing with Spotify and so much else out there now we're the nomads of the music world anymore. For DECADES radio ruled the land, and if we had jumped onto this pirate ship some years earlier there's no doubt we would have been the rock stars of Boulder County, and beyond.

Musical Conclusion

Music is the only universal language in the entire world, and it's almost always in everyone's top 3 favorite things of their lives, just so unreal what a painstaking avocation it is to pursue, and try to keep enjoying along the endless, rocky path.

I can play drums like a motherfucker, but I can't wait tables or bartend. I can think of endless creative ideas and hear every note of ever instrument being played in any song, yet I can't remember names or minuscule details regarding simple things in life. Hum…

It's brilliant madness. Being naturally creative is such a chore! I remember the roommate of this girl I was dating, an art major, saying, "Being creative sucks." This statement summed up *so much* in three words of truth; and strangely validated by a good, wholesome, Christian girl, who also happened to be artistic and naturally creative herself. She knows, as well as the many other small percentage of humans who are also stuffed in this odd boat floating along in a river of muck, that being right-brained dominant and predominantly creative in life is fucking hard! There's no guarantees! No matter how big a resume you build, how much effort and perseverance one puts into a creative endeavor, the odds against us are tenfold compared to any other fucking skill on the planet. It's fucked! (But also very fun and gratifying, that's why us stupid-ass, stubborn, masochistic artists and musicians carry on and don't give up!)

EVERYONE has pain, heartache, and issues in life to deal with, but with artistic people there's a whole other layer of stresses that come with our craft. A craft that is praised more than anything else out there, (besides NASA), yet we get our butts kicked by the systems, trends, and so much bullshit compared to the average person who only has to deal with "normal setbacks" and basic shit in their lives.

Did I already cover this? Probably, and this book will most likely conclude with a rehash of this justified, cantankerous bitching AGAIN, but fuck off and take it society! You have it easier and don't live in such a dense jungle of fuckness like us artists, period. I've simplified, worked 8-5 and all that, it's EASY compared to artistic paths of any sort. This isn't biased ranting, it's the unbiased, unfortunate truth of how it is out there. I choose to endure it, because I'm not a sellout wussy and it's "me".

I will continue to rock my drumming skills in multiple projects until my body is thrown in a casket (or ashes flushed down the toilet of a local dive bar that features live music). I will continue to push my creative ideas and "big dreamer" concepts as well, until maybe with a lucky-ass break things will come of it.

Everyone always says how fortunate I am to play music as proficiently as I do, how clever I am, taking amazing photos, being a great writer, entertainer, adventurer...and how I'm building the ultimate resume as I chug along. Right, my resume is like 33 fucking pages long! I've beyond proven my skills and worthiness that could easily be at professional levels by now after all these years, yet

I'm just adding more pages to my prolonged resume and living like an intern bitch in this unbalanced, tweaked world of ours. Where even in a semi-perfect world I'd have a quadruple PHD in the Arts/Entertainment fields of significance by now.

Jesus Dammit, why is it *this*?

SUCCESS IS THE ULTIMATE REVENGE.

I couldn't agree more. From this bumper sticker slogan found on an anonymous vehicle, it speaks 100% truth. (Especially in the world of arts and entertainment.) Because, AGAIN, things are so askew and set up so unethically in this industry, and with most of society (and even your own friends and family) calling you a "delusional dreamer" and to "be more practical", just one stroke of luck or the right timing can get you "made". To where you're actually making a living within this crooked industry, and only *then* are your skills and years of efforts credible, and everyone who dissed you over the years suddenly gives you kudos and will never again admit, or even remember, the shit they gave you during the shit times, before lucky "discovery" or "stardom".

As just after writing this segment I get in my KIA and hear these lyrics on the radio, "These are the good times in your life, so put on a smile and it will be alright."

Really? Agree? Laugh? Cry? Vomit.

Funny enough, even after you "make it" there's still so much bullshit the artists deal with. You always hear the cream of the crop, most deserving successors in entertainment *still* complaining about what an unfair, fucked-up industry it really is.

Artists get shafted no matter what level we make it to. However, the payoff at the next level is huge! At least at the professional level there's perks that don't exist at all within the lower levels of arts and entertainment. The money, the pimped treatment, sponsors on gear and such, roadies, and occasional backstage blowjobs, rather than endless sodomy. (Or if an already famous person is still getting it in the ass from the industry, at least the industry is considerate enough to use lube and wear a condom with them.)

So please karma gods; no more ass fucking, allow me to shine! It's time for my zipper to come down and let all the real "delusional dreamers" (i.e. average chump, hypocritical skeptics) to quit fucking, and start sucking.

Hey, even the artists themselves *become* delusional just after they "make it" to a level where they're living at their craft, or embarking on a first-ever tour. (Or whatever is considered an earnest step up from performing in a tight corner of a local coffee shop or half-empty dives; consisting mostly of patrons sitting at the bar fiddling with their phones.) I'll get in discussions with other musicians about how bad it all is and sometimes there's that one musician who disagrees and says, "Hey, we did it. You can't be negative, you just have to keep pushing and work harder than the rest and it will happen."

Well this same musician I bet was bitching and moaning for many months or years prior to their "lucky break" (i.e. hard work and perseverance) because most of us *are* busting ass at the same magnitude as them, and most of us *don't* ever get a deserved break or "promotion" like they did. Fucking people…

You're one of the lucky few, I'm glad for you, enjoy. But be real concerning the big picture here, as the only musicians who never bitch are usually the solo act, acoustic guitarists basking in the streets for pleasure or playing Jimmy Buffett covers in a mountain town cafe or ski resort lodge. The rest of us have something unique and bigger to offer and bust ass to assemble, promote, and showcase our special ingredients that make up the exclusive recipe we would love to have the world to get a taste of!!!

Put it this way, almost any interest, goal, or craft is capable of success to any degree of satisfaction from basic efforts exemplified, except music! Look at gardening; whether you're a botanist or a clueless beginner with desire to construct the ultimate garden, you can obtain all the help you need and succeed. Read books, watch online tutorials, go to Home Depot and they help you pick out all the right ingredients, supplies, and give their pointers as well. You're golden, now get to it and construct that ultimate garden!

With music it's too much of a crap shoot. Our help, or "Home Depot" along the way, is an agent, industry connection, or the proper amount of money to buy the right source's interests and be in the garden of our desires! We've had the right ingredients, supplies, and such ready to go for a while, (and it all costs *loads* more than what anyone else puts into their "gardens"), just that our plot of land is fenced off so we can't construct our wonderland and have people take notice of our constructive achievements that are or should be.

Anyway, MUSIC RULES.

CAREER OPPORTUNITIES

(Sponsored by The Clash)

Business Ventures Compatible For RGH:

"Snowdog Soda" Website featuring and promoting ALL my creative endeavors; music projects, radio stuff, a bit of photography, stickers, shirts, this lame book…Home page you enter through a pink curtain (that's secretly a big vulva) and direct the cursor (a sperm) to whatever "egg" (big round category icons displayed on the homepage screen) you want to dive into (impregnate) and bring that topic to life. Maybe have a small toilet at lower right corner of homepage featuring the poop pic of the day. Click on toilet, lid opens and shows poop! (Maybe not, but the vulva, sperm, and eggs for sure.)

"Drop D" I create and run a big club featuring live music acts that play all heavy alt/grunge/metal/electronic music. (I play drums in the house band of course.) The ambience would be very dark with trippy décor. Included in this venue would be an ergonomically friendly in/out door back entrance for all musicians with musician only rear parking spaces, leather couch lounge room, couple pool tables, blacklights abundant and sexy girls serving/dancing with glowing body paint. Sell various memorabilia including shirts/stickers with the phrase: "Just say no to blues, classic rock, 80s". (*Drop D* logo included.)

"Cygnus X-1" Afterhours hangout near *Drop D*. Come to the black hole lounge!

"Common Sense Counseling" Out of home counseling business; the real deal.

"Crafty Crapola" Grassroots business selling shirts, stickers, various artifacts.

"Photo Phreak" My photos of landscape, bands, erotica, bathroom stall graffiti.

"PROmoter" Create huge music/promotional tour--been done, but not my way.

"Down Under" My own basement talk show, video podcast, or something.

"Cam-man" Hidden camera footage of my random strolls; internet reality success.

"Art Walk Girls" or **"Dog Park Girls"** Calendar featuring the hotties on site.

"FIG" (**F**reelance **I**dea **G**uy/**G**al) Companies hire FIGs to help develop/launch ideas.

"Ultimate for RGH" I purchase and reconfigure a big RV, hire a roadie/companion, then travel all over the country as a public speaker/entertainer. The companion runs the merch booth to help sell all my books, stickers, shirts, etc at each event. And while I'm drumming away there's a screen behind me showcasing a slideshow of all my photos and video clips of interesting places I've been and crazy things I've done over the years. The day of or prior I've given my "motivational speech" of sorts and give out free pass invitations for the music/visual performance that follows.

How awesome, got sponsors?

JOBS (THAT SUCK ROTTING COCK)

The Permanent Intern

You name it I've probably worked it, and most all of it has sucked. As George Carlin put it: "If it requires a uniform it's most likely a worthless endeavor."

Aside from the military this accusation is usually true, even for those cheese ball office jobs that "only" require a modest business casual dress code. I don't even feel comfortable tucking in a shirt at all let alone wearing a tie or dressing "appropriately" for some company I'm going to give my hourly time to five days a week while they rake in the profits.

First let's not confuse jobs with *work*. I don't mind hard work at all. There's nothing wrong with a good day of accomplishing tasks of any kind; even painstaking stuff like spending an entire day digging and moving piles of dirt. Its *jobs* that are evil; these institutions that suck us in day after day, week after week, and pay us less than adequate wages after giving them the production they need.

Fuck this, and why do so many of us conform to this shit cycle? I would love to visit the grave of the guy who thought of the concept of M-F, 8-5 (formerly 9-5 during the "more practical era"), dig up his bones, light them on fire, piss out the flames, then re-bury the mess.

Job after job I've always hated the anticipation of that alarm going off the next morning for another day of work. It can be awful sometimes when you wake up about an hour or two before your alarm goes off. This is the worst because it's just too little time to get anymore adequate sleep but long enough to lay there staring at the ceiling with harrowing thoughts about when the alarm will sound off. All the while your racing thoughts are contemplating that "white lie" scenario to get out of your work obligation that day.

Now let's reminisce over some shit jobs I've worked throughout the years:

The very first job I worked after graduating college was getting paid $6.50/hr to represent Great Expectations, a nationally recognized dating agency. I fell into this position through a recommendation from one of my career counselors just before I graduated. It consisted of ten-hour work days for fourteen days straight! It was the annual Western Stock Show, where I was stationed at a table for ten hours each day, trying to get attendees to sign up for a dating program. My only amusing entertainment during these grueling days was watching the Smart Mop demonstration guy at the booth next to me. (I also spotted Carl Weathers at one point).

The next phase of jobs for me was temp agency work. I lived off these "temp jobs" for almost three years after the dating agency job. Talk about degrading! All the hours of testing you're put through at each agency while dressed up business casual, just to be qualified and get your foot in the door at some company doing braindead work that's only (luckily) temporary anyway. In some cases it's "temp to hire" opportunities, where one might be hired on permanently, yea!

Within the first two days I moved out to Santa Barbara in the late 90s I landed a sweet temp gig working in an old hanger at the airport. It was me and another guy sitting in a small dusty back room counting nuts and bolts all day. This went on for two days straight, I almost cried. Can you even fathom showing up for that second day of work after suffering through eight hours of it the previous day? (Oddly enough I do have a work ethic and do my part, no matter how shitty the tasks or atmosphere is, I always do my job.)

Another unpleasant two-day temp assignment was the time I experienced what it's like to work in a sweat shop. The temperatures were well below freezing outside at the time but inside dozens of us workers sat at tables in a big room putting clothing buttons on cardboard displays for stores to use. Like the nuts & bolts job in Santa Barbara I again sat through this strenuous, degrading bullshit for two days. At the end of the shift on the second day my car wouldn't start and I was stuck at that place an additional three hours until a tow truck could get to me.

How do I make it through so many of these pointless, dead end, bullshit jobs so often throughout my life? (I'm a stubborn, impervious, masochistic, Irish-Norwegian Leo.)

Poke Man

This was one of the worst jobs I had to endure in my lifetime, and of course it only lasted days. It was a telemarketing company based out of San Diego in a cramped office fitted with tight plain white cubicles and phones. We were to cold call various companies around the country and open each call with the question, "Do you sell Pokemon?" We then had to try and convince these stores to purchase swag from us or something. Funny part about this was I had no idea what Pokemon was and just thought it sounded funny to say.

Pokemon had just become the newest craze and I hadn't heard of it or gave a shit after I did know about it. There were about five or six of us working this awful job and I didn't even last a full week. It was just a job I had to work and feel good that I was doing something while hunting for more praiseworthy options. (Sure)

And that's enough, there's plenty more demoralizing stories I could share from my times spent in the working world but I don't want to make anyone dig out the noose from the garage shelves just yet. Take my word for it that most all the dozens of jobs I've worked have most certainly sucked rotting cock.

It's just not right to be stuck in a lifestyle where you must be somewhere you don't give a hoot about for five days a week, eight hours a day. Most of the world lives this lifestyle and it's just not ethical. Life is meant to be fun and full of experiences and not revolve around so much work or a "job". I know we must work in some way or another to survive but a four-day work week at six hours a day would suffice. I guarantee we citizens could accomplish just as much in four days as we do in five.

All we'd have to do is replace lunch with a midday break and drop an hour or two off each work day. People would crank out their tasks more efficiently without wasting time taking multiple mini-breaks and a daily lunch break that puts everyone into the dreadful "food coma" anyway. Having three days off a week is imperative for us to get enough leisure time to ourselves, and that extra day acting as the "catch up on our chores and errands" day. Nominate me for President and I will make this change happen!

I will conclude that it's really a boss who can make or break the complacency in any job. You can shovel shit all day and if the redneck, toothless boss is cool to you and pays a respectable wage, that's fine. However this is usually not the case, which in turn makes almost every job on the planet suck balls in my opinion.

I can't stand the abundance of greed and lack of respect from upper management in the working world. For this I do call a "no work ethic clause" in life. If you do a good job and must beg for a worthy raise or lie to get out of work for an operation to receive a new kidney for survival, fuck that boss and fuck that job. You only live once so move on! Or just do the bare minimum, enough where the managers stress but can't fire you. I despise these Type-A, micro-managing dill weeds that get in your face with demands and conduct quota meetings even when things are rolling along just fine as is. People of authority in this country always feel the need for a change or upgrade when it's rarely needed.

To the greedy owners, upper managers, and Type-A micro managing nincompoops around the world:

GO_FUCK_YOURSELVES.

I get depressed every time I drive by construction sites or highway repair work sites where all the employees possess that sullen look on their faces with cigarettes hanging from their lips. Grunt labor jobs, office jobs, temp jobs…most all jobs are not worthy enough for an adequate, happy lifestyle. Too many jobs are unhealthy for our souls and rather are time consuming nonsense during our years spent living this one life we get on this beautiful planet.

I would like to thank Mike Judge for inspiring my hostile feelings towards corporate America with his wonderfully brilliant and realistic viewpoint on the stagnant job world he depicts so well in the film Office Space. *(Beavis and Butthead kicks ass too!)*

JOBS (THAT LICK A CLEAN BALLSACK)

There's always those "tolerable jobs" out there. The ones that have a good boss, cool coworkers, comfortable environment, flexible schedule, and any incentive to keep you at work...at least for a while. Let's dig into a few of these more tolerable jobs I've had.

Hiwan Golf Club

Working at this prestigious golf club during the summers of my senior year in high school and freshman year during college was some of the best job experiences in my life. In a quick nutshell, I was working with one of my best friends, Brian, and other guys I grew up with. I was outside on the green grass of a beautiful golf course and had the best boss on the planet. His name was Gary and he just drove around in a red pickup truck with his two golden retrievers in the back. (These dogs always smelt awful as they would jump in the ponds and chase Carp.)

I was part of the grounds crew, yep just like Bill Murray in *Caddyshack*. Fuck waiting tables on golf yuppies when you can hang out below in the cart barn area and cruise around the golf course all day working on the sand traps, changing the holes, mowing the greens and fairways, and even repairing damaged grass from elk urine. Even though it was hard to wake up every morning while it was still dark, once we parked our cars and punched in to start our daily routines, it was mostly a smooth operation.

The daily routine consisted of pulling out all the carts from the barn where they sat charging all night, linking them together in a train of about eight carts total, then hauling them up to the club house by tractor. It was quite a scene to witness this big line of carts being hauled up a steep dirt road by a tractor, but it worked.

After this task was finished a couple of us would head out to rake every sand trap on the course. One guy would ride the ATV that pulled the metal rakes behind it while the other got the crap job of riding in a golf cart and hand-raking the edges of each sand trap. From here we would tend to any other little things that needed fixing and go home.

Hiwan was also the host of the Colorado Open golf tournament, consisting of up and coming golf pros. One bonus perk during this event was stealing a bunch of booze from the beer trucks and stashing it in the woods for later. During one tournament the ultimate in amusement for me was when I was asked by Gary to hurry up and fix the green on hole #7, which was one of the nicest on the course. I drove a work cart out to the location and saw that someone had taken gasoline and wrote, "Golf if your GAY". I was in such shock that I almost forgot I was there to fix the mess, and there were golfers already teeing off to begin the tournament.

Copper Mountain Resort

I got a job as a lift operator soon after graduating from college. I convinced Len to join me and we began our short stint as lift operators; or ticket checkers as we scanned everyone's ticket or pass with an electronic scanner. Me and Len decided this would allow us to slack more than being an actual lift operator and give us opportunities to joke around with all the skiers in line. (Or "maze" as it's referred.)

We found a cool apartment in Leadville, which is a small town located about twenty miles up the mountain from Copper. This is the town to live in if you are strapped for money, as your only other option is the nearby, pricey town of Frisco or Breckenridge.

We worked at Copper about four months and closed out the season, but in that time we experienced a lot and met some really cool people; a few that are still friends to this day. This job was tolerable, as although it paid shit and was sometimes a painstaking day if weather or hangover pulled rank, it was mostly casual and fun.

One day while I was working a lift over at the beginner area of the mountain I took it upon myself to climb a lift tower and yell out, "RICOLA!" to a packed lift line. (Hey at least I didn't act out a Mentos commercial instead. Although...)

Schwinn Cycling & Fitness

Schwinn headquarters was located in Boulder, CO and I got a job there as an inside sales representative. My friend Brendon was working the same gig, as well as my old ski buddy, Chris, as an engineer and designer for the fitness equipment department.

We had so many employee deals on bikes and gear it was insane. It was this job that allowed me to purchase my first real mountain bike; a 1998 Schwinn Homegrown XT in bass boat orange finish. It retailed at $2200 at the time but I got it for $850 at cost with the employee discount.

The only downfall with this job was the workload. It was a customer service job; working directly with a few outside sales reps who drove around your specific territory to various bike shops. I am by no means a phone guy and this job entailed a lot of incoming and outgoing phone calls throughout the day. Not to mention we had to keep track of faxes and email orders coming in as well.

Brendon is so enthusiastic and such a natural at sales he ended up making bike deals with local radio DJ Uncle Nasty and even Danny Carey of Tool. He then proceeded to leave a voicemail on Maynard James Keenan's phone at one point and played me back the return message from Maynard which stated: "I heard you can get some type of bike deals or something, and that's fine but if you give my number out to anyone else I'll kill you."

TV/FILM WORK

Ironically my "career" in TV and film began while I was working a temp job at some insurance company in Denver. I worked with this big black guy whose wife happened to run a talent agency. He thought I had just the right look and charisma to be in this industry and told his wife about me.

Not a few days later she called me offering a great gig opportunity. An advertising agency needed a person who resembled the look and size of John Elway for a national television commercial. I didn't hesitate for a second and gave her a full description of my physique and she set me up for an "audition" with the two main ad execs that were staying at a nice high rise hotel in downtown Denver.

I was riveted with excitement as I knew this was the easy, high paying type of work I craved. I was paid over $800 to hang around a film studio for two days dressed like John Elway, while grabbing free snacks from the food table and occasionally getting in front of the camera as a "stand in double" to prepare the camera team for the real Elway.

Brainless, boring work but very interesting and way better than a stressful 40-hour per week job that pays much less.

After this occasion they used me for two more commercials in that same year! It was the late 90s, the time when the Broncos won back to back Superbowls, so I was needed.

One highlight I recall was when we had to act out a football play, consisting of me being Elway on a rollback hand off routine. John grabbed the ball from me and said, "Here's what I would do." Imagine one of the greatest quarterbacks of all time showing me one of his moves on an actual football field. I'm not really the star struck type at all and my friends got off on my story of this event way more than I did.

Let it be known this was not my first introduction to John Elway. I was almost run over by him in a golf cart while working at Hiwan Golf Club.

The Final Lap (Featuring the EMC)

After my experience with those John Elway commercials I landed work on some film shoots for Stu Segal Productions in San Diego. The best shoot ever was The Final Lap, which ironically would serve as my launch into the realm of extra work for the next year to follow. The Final Lap was a Disney film about a motocross champion that gets injured and his twin sister takes his place to win it all. The title of the movie was eventually changed to *Motocrossed.* Get it? *Moto*crossed.

Me and my new posse of "extra friends" spent three weeks hanging out on this shoot at a motocross track out east of

San Diego. Every morning we would drive the half hour to get there in complete darkness, check in, then grab our breakfast burrito and coffee before we had to begin "working". Daily work consisted of hanging around the set most of the time just bullshitting and getting to know who the cool slackers were that we could include into our slacker gang. We grew very close in the first few days and became known as the EMC. (Easy Money Crew).

I had already met a fellow Coloradoan named Jeff who was also milking the movie extra profession. Jeff and I met on a set for a low-budget television series called "18 Wheels of Justice". I remember him mentioning Ft. Lewis College during lunch and we hit it off immediately.

Our Motocrossed days consisted of hiding in the back of a trailer, chatting, and smoking weed; basically avoiding having to work any scene at all. When we were called to work a scene or two it was still fun anyway; as we were already high, feeling adventurous, and it got us out of the trailer for a bit each day.

My position in one big scene was acting as the 30 Second Board Operator. I was the guy who held the sign about 50 yards out from all the motocross racers on the actual track. There was a lot of them, most professional riders, and I would drop the sign as they came buzzing towards me. At one point the director got mad at me because I was running off too early as the bikers were almost hitting me, and he responded with, "I don't care!"

What made this worse was he yelled it in front of a hundred people as I'm standing there in the middle of the track, plus he was one of the family members who owned Mammoth Ski Area, the Vail of California. Fucking prick.

As for other extra work, I was involved with two local TV shows and a few other movies. I became established enough around the set to have landed some "featured extra" roles as well.

One time I worked on this low budget military film with Antonio Sabato Jr. and James Remar, the main villain from *48 Hours*. At one point he got in an argument with the director about a scene and blurted out in front of the entire set, "Hollywood is so full of shit." And during a break on the set James was telling us stories about all the fun times he had during the 80s; mostly about the sex and drugs.

On another film shoot I worked with John Stamos. I was his valet during a scene and the crew used a red, convertible sports car like the one in the Aerosmith video for "Rag Doll". I made a comment about that and we discussed music for a bit while waiting for the cameraman to set up for the scene. Pretty cool.

Sony

Of all the slacking jobs I've worked over the years I think this one takes first prize. I was hired through a temp agency to work as a video game tester for Playstation 2. My friend and fellow EMC co-founder, Jeff, joined me on this job.

We would literally sit in these huge reclining chairs all day and play video games. This sounds like heaven for most gamer geeks but it made for a dragging day. We would become so comatose after hours of play that if one of us dozed off and the manager came by we were awaken by the code word: PICKLES. I don't know how we came up with *pickles* but it was the key word to bring us back to reality if needed.

Jeff and I were part of the testing team for NHL Hockey. Since this game was in its initial phase we got a kick out of how many glitches were abundant. The player's faces looked like zombies, they shot pucks on automatic rapid fire, and funniest of all they would skate onto the ice like they were still in sitting position. We called these players "witches" and they would skate all over the place remaining in the sitting position, even venturing into the stands and through the crowd. Glitches, fuck yeah.

Mailroom

One of the better 8-5 jobs I've ever had was working in the mailroom for a massage insurance company, ABMP, based in my hometown of Evergreen, CO. I spent four whole years in this world with steady pay, flexibility, casual atmosphere, and great perks that included many picnics, bowling day, and that sort of fun.

My companion and I would crank music all day (usually punk or metal) and keep busy enough to have the day cruise by with very little qualms. The only issues I had with this job was being a bit low on the pay scale, with minimal raises each 6-12 months. Also my manager in particular had me bouncing around between the hectic mailroom and the publication department which really stressed me out. Thankfully the business kept growing fast enough that I became a permanent mailroom scrub.

Why did I ever leave this job? Well the big factors were being back in my original hometown of Evergreen with limited social life and my lame boss. Otherwise I could have milked this job a few more years or so, but never as a "career".

Valet

While I was working the mailroom job I picked up a part-time evening valet job in Denver. This was a great experience, as with valet work you're constantly moving and driving a variety of nice cars. It was also good to be working, once again, with my friend Jeff, so that made the atmosphere fun and interesting.

During the downtime we would play wall ball in the ally or feed bugs to the spiders that lived in the bush where our valet stand was. After our shift we would hit one of Denver's top ten dive bars, Lancer Lounge, for drinks and rounds of pool.

Dog House Music

Teaching music is a great job for most starving musicians. Me and a few others were hired on as music instructors for a teen rock camp program at Dog House Music. It is full time during the summer and part time in the winter months. Each instructor working the camp has a specialty instrument that they play and can teach the campers more about that particular instrument, as well as help a group of kids write some original music in the jam studios.

We started off the day with an hour lesson on whatever instrument each kid wanted to play and then put together a band with kids that have similar tastes in music. From here we work with our assigned band and help them write and produce music all week long. This could be quite a chore for the week if you had someone in the band not cooperating or that had no clue how to play an instrument, but usually things went okay. Then each Friday the campers put on a live show of their created music at a local venue and the instructors are then rewarded with paycheck and beers to close out the week.

Again this job sounds ideal for any musician that needs a good amount of pocket change while embarking on their own rock fantasy, but for me it was a challenge. Each morning while driving to Dog House I would have anxiety over what might happen that day; knowing there was six hours of work to go from the time I arrive and having to maintain enough focus and energy to deal with teenagers.

From my description of the job duties it sounds ludicrous for me to have any anxiety relating to a job like this, especially for only six hours a day. But for me it was a bit too extreme; being stuck in a cramped studio all day with hyper kids playing loud music and the time usually dragging by as you give basic lessons and work on the same three songs all week.

It's a wonder why my brain doesn't allow me to enjoy even the most pleasurable work situations, but I can say that my mailroom job was much more tolerable than this Dog House experience. Weird but true.

PROMOTIONAL WORK

I've been milking promotional work for years now. It all began when I was involved with a couple talent agencies that were not hooking me up with acting or modeling work so they suggested I could work some promotional events; as another one of them khaki pants wearing BAs (Brand AmbASSadors) out there. Okay…

Promotional work is perfect for college students, starving artists, or anyone looking for easy, good paying, flexible work opportunities. Usually every event is a fun experience and most all the companies, products, and managers we work under are respectable and easy to deal with. I've met, worked with, and stayed in touch with many awesomely charismatic people over the years as a result working in the promotional industry. *Many* stories could be shared with my experiences in promotional work and all the interesting characters I've worked with over the years.

In fact, I came up with a concept for a film based on the promotional world; based around all the interesting stuff that goes on throughout a standard day within the promo world. So much happens while standing amidst that footprint area dealing with customers and coworkers alike, or when out in guerilla sampling warfare things can get pretty interesting. It's unreal, and definitely "film worthy".

I shared this movie concept with other BAs and they love the idea. One BA, who works in film, also had a similar plan and we tried to get something rolling, but like anything artistically ambitious it's a fucking process to bring these concepts to life. Yet it would be so awesomely epic to have a film like this exist!

Maybe a documentary? Nah, a movie, and the name of this film would be Khaki Pants.

The promotional industry has the same cursed blessing as the service industry; you get out of the game for a bit then you're right back in, as most other jobs on the planet are crap compared to what these revolving door "tolerable industries" offer.

The problem these days is too many people are finding out about this line of work and many opportunities are taken within minutes after any email, text blast, or social media posting is uploaded containing information on available work. Ever since smart phones became the norm it's turned into a rapid-fire response type of competitive market. The smart phone addicted Millennials steal the job opportunities because they have their notification alerts set, ringer volume up, and faces glancing down at their phones most of the day anyway, so they will respond to any job alerts within seconds.

This just in! I found a job as a sign holder. Yep after a month of no promotional work to keep me busy I've had to resort to sign holding for income; being one of those schmucks you see holding and spinning signs while dancing around on street corners throughout cities and suburbs nationwide. They are usually teenagers or early twenty-somethings but now they have a middle-aged man taking the position. It's just another cheesy job I can add to my pathetic resume. (Someday I hope to laugh about all this, but for now I'm demoralized.)

Windows Phone

Back in the "golden days" of promotions a group of us

were flown out to Chicago for a three-day training to promote the new Windows phone. (The very first smart phone on the market at the time.) The hours of training in the conference center was extremely hostile for my fragile, non-tech savvy, ADD mindset, but our group from Denver was so much fun and the hotel room gatherings at night were quite interesting as well.

Back in Denver we were split into three teams; each representing a kiosk at a certain mall. I was teamed up with a couple familiar faces and a cool guy who was thankfully a tech savvy Millennial and was already tuned into the smart phone culture. This allowed for us Gen-X technological 'tards' to focus on the hustling and bring customers in as Mr. Millennial explained what all these little squares were on the screen of the phone.

Cherry Creek Mall was my first location, standing many hours in front of our kiosk while trying to grab people's attention in a crowded, frantic Holiday mall scene. I usually avoid these type of work settings as I can't handle the pushy "sales vibe" within the promotional industry, but I sucked it up.

The final weekend of long hours standing in front of a kiosk took place at Colorado Mills Mall. This mall is interesting as it's shaped like a giant racetrack with the food court in the middle. Our kiosk was set up near one of the main entrances in the middle of the race track, and better yet we were next to another kiosk that was selling remote controlled helicopters. Our entertainment consisted of watching these two guys fly various models of helicopters all around our area, occasionally selling one of the many models on display.

Middle of the afternoon on the final day I'm standing in front of the fucking kiosk, near brain dead, still watching helicopters, and everyone else was on break. I glanced over after hearing a guy's voice say, "I'll meet you back at this store, I'm gonna check out the Game Stop." And as he walks in my direction I realize he has a very familiar face.

"You look like Trey Parker", I casually call out. He stops in his stride, let's out a sigh and hesitantly responds, "I am Trey Parker."

"I went to Evergreen High", I immediately followed with. And just after hearing this he suddenly expressed the "oh cool" face and turned towards me.

From here we only chatted about a minute, where I brought up some mutual connections I crossed paths with while living in SoCal and he was slowly remembering a couple of them as one was in his class. No I never mentioned shit about SouthPark, but…

After our brief chat I watched as he slowly made his way to the Game Stop, leaving me with a strange grin on my face; an expression derived out of so many thoughts and emotions crossing my mind of what all just happened within the past 60 seconds. What this grin represented was mostly the product of the reality of how much he's accomplished and the impact he's made on the world, and here I am from the same town, similar upbringing, college degree, creative and musical myself, yet standing in front of a kiosk making chump wages.

Many thoughts raced through my mind like, "I should've given him my card, why not, I already had the Evergreen card dealt to give him an actual card." and "Fuck I should've mentioned at least one quick idea or something to let him know I'm a creative maniac, instead of reminiscing about high school and SoCal connections." and finally "That's it, there he goes out of my life, probably forever, snooze ya lose."

Like all famous people Trey gets approached and praised constantly so I didn't go there. It was the Holidays and he was with his parents, but we have the Evergreen connection and if he only knew what I was really about instead of just Evergreen and being stuck working this pointless job in a fucking mall.

FUCK! FUCK! FUCK! (In Dante voice from *Clerks*)

Noosa

Yes, Colorado's finest yoghurt! Thanks to our team of BAs that helped promote this product and advance it from #7 to #1 within a year's time during our work contract. This promotional job was near Heaven. It was a few days per week, 4-10 hour shifts, and casual. Mostly we just roamed around the outskirts of big events, dragging a cooler full of yoghurt samples and people would flock over for a taste. Noosa sold itself, which made my job even easier not having to talk about the history, contents, etc. Sometimes we were set up at a booth during certain events with two huge troughs full of samples, but usually roaming around somewhere on our own.

This job lasted over a year and during a shift in my home turf of Louisville, CO we met one of the head managers of the company. He loved our team and promised we'd have work to keep us busy the remainder of the year. It was early October so I thought this was great as I could milk this

Noosa gig a few more months and rake in more easy money. I budgeted a ballpark figure of how much more money I would probably make and was psyched that I would be stable enough and rolling well into the new year. Well…

Out of nowhere our team was informed the program was coming to a sudden halt, or rather it quickly changed to "another manager took over and was hiring her own team of BAs". I contacted the marketing headquarters and demanded a few of us original BAs get to stay on with the new team, out of respect for all we've done up to that point and the promise by Mr. Manager. But the marketing company's response was, "It is what it is, we're moving on" type bullshit.

Out of frustration I then contacted Noosa headquarters to explain the situation, to which they replied they couldn't do anything about it as the marketing company is in charge of the promotional aspect of Noosa.

This brought me to spending an afternoon trying to find the marketing company headquarters in Boulder, CO so I could confront them and negotiate in person; to which the first two addresses I found online were wrong! Third time's a charm though, I found the offices and by this time they were closed for the day.

I re-emailed the marketing offices to explain all I've been through and how ridiculous this whole scenario had become. Didn't matter, no response, to which then I left a final more hostile email rant in one of their inboxes to officially "burn the bridge".

Unbelievable, and how disrespectful the working world can

be when you're further down on the totem pole and do so much for a company, and completely asinine how this outcome came to be after all the original team did for Noosa! Nothing against Noosa themselves, it's the cold hearted, incompetent marketing company cunts that screwed us. And for me this was HUGE because any type of decent work is hard for me to find and I had budgeted a good amount of income I was to earn for nearly three more months of work!

Unreal, and throughout the whole year following this ordeal I've paid the price for it all tremendously. I missed out on hundreds of dollars I would've made, putting me way behind on expenses, leaving some financially supportive goals unaccomplished, and having to expend so much energy hustling more promotional work that I wasn't expecting to have to do for the remainder of that year.

Fuck all this job shit. My next job will be dealing with a huge pile of scratch off lottery tickets until I uncover the winning numbers and never work again. That's what we all say and want right? (And for good reasoning; F--- J---!)

God damn people, fucking jobs, and…

CHICKS

The Good, The Bad, and the Not So Ugly

Let it be known I will be referring to the female race as women, girls, ladies, and chicks intermittently throughout this chapter. For no other reason other than that's the way it is.

Dog Food is Cheaper Than Sushi

This interesting phrase comes from a movie I recently watched, *National Lampoon's Adam & Eve.* A guy used this saying to metaphorically scrutinize all the bullshit involved with dating. Stating that you're better off just owning a dog.

Men are from Mars, Women are from Venus. NO FUCKING SHIT. I know you should think positive and put valiant effort into most endeavors in life for success, but with women this is not the case. The harder you try to get a girl it will only curse you with the inevitable failure to close any deal. The whole thing is a game and always will be. Both sides of the gender coin love to fuck with one another to the point where there will never be a laudable understanding of each side's odd behaviors, differentiating values, biased beliefs, and screwy idealisms.

The way I describe it is: Too many guys are inconsiderate, sexist, lying dickwads and too many girls tend to be fickle, irrational, unconcerned, psychotic freakoids. (Notice I say *too many* and not *most,* because most guys and girls are good-natured overall, but unfortunately too many of each gender fucking suck.)

First off, I'm plagued with that nice guy curse. Besides the fact I tend to clam up and sort of "geek out" in front of women I'm attracted to, I believe one of the main reasons for many of my failures dialing in the female persuasion has to do with being one of those old fashioned, passive nice guys. I've always been too passive and nice, and these are the wrong ingredients needed for succeeding in the dating world during these foolhardy times we currently live in.

Women of the modern dating world are much more creeped out by amiability and enthusiasm than they ever were back in the day. They tend to prefer the chill, unemotional, "bad boy" types rather than nice genuine guys they always claim they want.

I also believe women have a natural sixth sense and can detect when someone is not comfortable or stable within their own skin and surroundings in general. Women have this intuitive ability enabling them to detect a guy's aura and they know if that guy is the real deal or not. (Interesting though, even with this special keenness women possess they still so often end up in relationships with assholes or losers. Nice job ladies.)

How about humor? Women always say they love a guy with a sense of humor. This is true only to a very minor extent. It's good to be cheerful and funny but the more you analyze and joke around the stranger you come across and most any woman pulls back.

Comedians joke about this all the time how they get the least amount of pussy out of anyone else involved in the entertainment industry. They're too funny *and* overly-intelligent and these amazing traits come across as too creepy and scare off women rather than attract them.

All the cool, attractive women seem to end up with lazy, no-good bastards or older rich guys. Women say stuff like, "Are you kidding? We would love to meet a nice

gentleman for once, someone who's intelligent and real".
Right, of course. (And is anyone "real" out there anymore?)

This is a false proclamation that is used to cover the actual truth; that many women can't admit they prefer money or status in a guy over looks and personality. I've only heard a handful of women acknowledge they tend to date the assholes and more well off guys. I've also heard some of the more intelligent women I know analyze and acknowledge how most of the chicks in the world have an inner psycho-like persona which can make its presence at any time. (Cool fuck it, keeps life exciting!)

I've known and dated many women over the years who have brothers and/or sisters or kids of certain/mixed genders and asked them how they feel about the opposite sexes. It's amazing how many of these women have admitted straight up without hesitation how bat-shit crazy women can be. (And much of this is a result from previous centuries of world-wide male dominance and so many arrogant-bastard men out there prowling the streets.)

I will confess that throughout all my years working so many jobs, when women step up into these managerial roles they tend to "psycho up" a bit too much. I don't understand this at all; as when I'm working with them on the same level it's all good, but as soon as they are promoted to a higher ranking they turn into these hyper, illogical, micro-managing nutcases. It's like, "You were fun and cool to be around since we've worked together on the same level, now you're suddenly a hypomanic, micro-managing anomaly. Why? How?" Most guys never resort to this asinine behavior.

Sucks to have a certain amount of pre-job anxiety knowing

you're working under an overly-anal manager during certain programs. Driving up to the job site with the thoughts of, "What tiny batch of spilt milk is she going to flip out over today?"

Just chill and do your job ladies, and be who you were since we've worked many events together and all's been fine in the past. A promotional boost in life doesn't call for a boost in exorbitant comportments!

In the past few years I've experienced the absolute worst outcomes with a variety of girls I've met and hit it off with. There's ups and downs with anything in life but my downs with the female persuasion have become more of a gut wrenching, soul damaging experience lately. All these mind games that girls play without even realizing how hurtful they are is absolutely astonishing. Guys know when they're acting like dupes and just lie to cover up their stupid behaviors. Girls are so unorthodox they don't even know when they are being unfair, cold, or imprudent sometimes. Fucking wow.

Guys seem to cheat and break hearts more often, but when girls engage in any kind of hurtful behavior they do it in such an arcane, malevolent way. They sport a happy grin thinking all is well no matter what has occurred and the guy is left hanging with this feeling of discontent and wondering what the fuck has just happened to this entity who was so sweet and genuine for months prior, and cant' even see or admit to their most recent changed behavior pattern(s).

I realize this isn't always the case and being a guy writing this will surely bring up some retaliation from the other side but I state the absolute, unbiased truth here from plenty of experience and research conducted from both sexes. I know many screwy behaviors and mind games come from both sides of the coin but again women take things to extreme levels with their weird, taciturn, nonchalant tendencies.

Does the gay community have it easier? You have Mars on Mars and Venus on Venus, so at least overlapping the same planet and the brain chemistry is similar. With us heterosexuals this ongoing gender dilemma is a mindboggling cataclysm from Hell.

During the 80s, 90s, and even to an extent the 00s, so many of these cold, bizarre dating behaviors didn't exist much at all in our culture. Considering my nice guy shyness curse I did pretty well with women and dating during these eras, but since the latter part of the 00s and introduction of smart phones, social media, online dating, and all else lame and unfortunate in these dreadful 2010s, society is losing their fucking minds. People are becoming much more sanctimonious and only worth a shit in the moment before they back out of a deal and are gone out of your life like a fart in the wind.

Phase 2

This brings me to the next perturbing phase of outcomes that occurs after you make it over the hurdles of the early stages in modern day head game playing bullshit. You meet a girl, get her number, set up a date, have a great time and assume we will try for another round soon to come. Nope, even after a good time is spent with someone and the evening is great, that someone will move on and leave you hanging. It's usually without any valid reasoning, or maybe some little miniscule thing they don't want to admit to?

After the milestone of reaching *Phase 2* and the opportunity to live in a moment of mutual bliss with the few women I've connected with from these online sites, they usually disappear after an initial meet up and I never hear from them again. Why do today's odds usually lean towards a "nothing more after this" scenario? Jesus, what the shit fuck hell is happening with society these days? When did simple, fun, casual dating and cool, sincere human bonding become so outlandish and taboo?

Because my age now begins with the number 4 this drops my chances of dialing in any of the younger women by drastic percentages. If my age was still 39 at least girls see the 3 and it immediately signals their brain that I'm a thirty-something and not in my 40s. It's so annoying to have this reality working against me because if these girls would just check out my photos and read my bio they could see that I'm physically healthier, more interesting, and more adventurous than most guys within their lower age range discrepancy.

Look at the photos, read my profile! 40 going on 30 bitches. With a heart of gold, and unfortunately balls of blue. Thank YOU.

Oh to have big money or fame. My age could begin with a 5 or even 6 and I could pull many of these younger picky chicks no problem. This has been evident truth since the beginning of humankind; powerful men and hot women can get whatever they want no matter what the age or any other bullshit factors included.

I have also come to realize women get bombarded with

messages from guys on these dating sites, so really *that's* the main factor for not getting any response after I message so many. *Sorry about that ladies, all you've read up until this point can be forgotten.*

I recently had a nice, casual date with a girl who moved to Colorado from Texas. The model statement she made during our conversation was when she said, "I love it here so much, but god people are flaky!" Yep I concur, must be the mile-high climate or something as Coloradans are certainly flaky motherfuckers. (Or maybe it's more of a Midwest thing, since so many of them have migrated to Colorado in recent years and they're bringing with them that slow, stoner-paced farm town culture?)

But this Texan hottie validated my ongoing complaints in one sentence after only living here a few months. It's so bad, yet Coloradans are more active and "genuine" than most of the rest of what inhabits other states in our union out there? Yikes.)

Most people are so predictable and so much of our culture conforms in formulaic behavioral patterns that it eventually becomes a redundant standard, or even stereotype. It's not always about being negative or judgmental, it's stating a fact, and being that the word *stereotype* is perceived as a judgement rather than stating the "generalized truth" it's not a well- accepted idiom in our culture. Yet pretty much every stereotype in existence is truthful and right on the money for what it's targeting. Truth hurts, admit it, carry on. (Or god forbid, BE ORIGINAL.)

I mean come on, what's wrong with the black or Jewish stereotypes? Black you got natural athletic/musical abilities, great vertical, and a big dick. Jewish, you wonder where that stingy with money label comes from? Sure, when the Jewish race pretty much owns and runs New York, Hollywood, Las Vegas, and any number of smaller *money- making empires out there.*

Gee, awful stereotypes. But yeah, the average-sized dick white guys of the world have caused stereotypes to "be all bad" and not just simple truth!

**Must also give my Jewish friend credit when he's performed comedy and once stated how he prefers to buy the day-old bagels on display by the register, since they're cheaper.*

It's like the word *drug,* which usually gets a negative label associated with it, when really drugs have been a good thing for humanity over centuries of time! Legal or illegal many drugs have done great for the world, but the "average person" can't handle some drugs or moderate their erratic behaviors. So drugs bad! Because so many humans don't know how to control their impulsivity, or they have addictive tendencies, they acquire bad habits, abuse drugs and whatnot, and *this* causes the systems to crack down and set rules, regulations, and many drugs become illegal or very hard to obtain for those that really fucking need them!

MODERATION, WILL POWER, COMMON SENSE, you god damned reckless retards of the world. You're fucking it up for the rest of us that need drugs and do much better on drugs in order to escape this messy reality you assholes have produced and keep shitting into this world with your idiotic comportments. (Wow, never knew this word existed. High-five Thesaurus!)

Most people focus on the small percentage of rock stars

that die in overdoses, rather than looking at the stats of how many more rock stars have survived with drugs and made amazing music; ironically with the help of those drugs. Steve Jobs admitted to taking LSD while coming up with the concept for Apple. Trey Parker and Matt Stone were tripping balls when creating the entire first season of SouthPark.

Are you kidding? If you're not another conformist chump and rather an imaginative weirdo roaming the planet with innovative tendencies and cycling vexations spinning within; pondering and assessing all the 'what the fucks' of the world. Fuck it, do drugs!

Now if Nancy Reagan had said, "Just say no to some *drugs"...*

Shit, back to CHICKS…

A classic example of a text exchange with a typical modern day chica:

I met this girl while working at the Aspen X Games recently. We were both personable and hit it off well enough after a few minutes of talking so I got her number. She insisted that I meet her for drinks later that day as she was attending the events alone!

Hours later we exchanged a few texts and were set to meet up after each of us re-grouped, but for some reason my final texts to her were ignored and we never did meet up.

This was so frustrating and maddening for me to where I had to come back with a final text the next morning, then another follow-up text the next day to see what happened. (A bit psycho yes, but for a cause. Fuck this ghosting, game playing bullshit. LET'S MEET AS PLANNED!)

Here are those exact text exchanges after nothing came of our proposed meet up in Aspen. And remember that everything was all good up until the ignored texts. (Although I'm sure I was most definitely cock-blocked since it was the Aspen X Games and just enough time had passed since we met in person earlier, still I fucking hate all these scenarios of excitement and anticipation that fall dead before the next step of action is able to occur!)

Me: (Feb 2, 5:28pm) So what's up how did the rest of your X Games experience end up today? When and where do you want to meet up?

Aspen girl: (no response, usually would've made another text attempt but didn't)

Me: (Feb. 4, 2:10pm) Sweet good deal

Aspen girl: (Feb. 4, 2:36pm) Can u stop texting me? Thanks

Me: (Feb. 4, 3:40pm) No problem, a simple response is a miracle from people anymore. Our society is so fickle and moment to moment you just validated this unfortunate truth even further, so thank YOU!

With women there's a small window of opportunity to make something happen or you've lost all hope. Just today a girl I know contacted me out of the blue to hang out but I was working, so I responded that we should try for next week and I got no response back. I'll bet anything that nothing happens with this girl because I couldn't take advantage of a prime, spontaneous, small window moment. This blows because I'm flattered to be thought of on these rare occasions, but after one of these sporadic offers is made and you can't jump on it, that's it, there's no second chance. Fucking WHY?

This particular girl can't even respond to my counteroffer? Do I try to reach out to her again? Sure, but then you become the desperate "stalker type" in their mind, when really you just want a simple connection to work out when time allows for both parties, who both dig each other anyway! God DAMMIT.

I can't fathom myself how many opportunities with girls I let drift out of my reality. Countless times throughout my life I will see a girl, check her out to factor in all the "is it worth it to make a move" elements, then too many seconds have passed and it's over. Even if she catches my eyes and reciprocates with a smile I'll quickly look away with embarrassment. WHY RGH?

Just today, while working another fine promotional event, I was walking some product from the van back to our booth and noticed one of the attractive guests walking out of the event just yards away from me. As I kept my eyes upon her she glanced over once, then again with a smile, as to say: "Hey there coconut boy."

I stopped walking and watched her get into her Audi to only then realize I could've offered her some coconut water to take home with her. FUCK. You don't get a better "in" than that. Offer the free shit, then the gate is open for a cheesy pickup line that has potential for a connection.

In the minutes that past I analyzed the 4 most probable outcomes, had I made a move:

1) I offer the coconut water, she accepts or refuses, then I throw out the, "You're leaving already? Up to anything later?" line. She declines by stating she just wants to get home. (Standard outcome.)
2) I offer the coconut water, she accepts or refuses, I throw out the pickup line, she accepts. We exchange numbers, I meet her after my shift. (Old school outcome.)
3) I get her number, we exchange texts, she's too tired to hang out, we agree to try again another time. Maybe more texts are exchanged but nothing ever happens. (New School outcome.)
4) I get her number, I text her and get no response. A bit perturbed I try again a few days later; to which she doesn't respond again. I've been ghosted! (Newest School outcome.)

It's such an injurious, draining game trying to dial in chicks and people in general during these days. Having extreme confidence and/or game playing skills, or especially being a well-known figure or a basic rich guy, is the only way to easily dial in girls or gain anyone's interest without the bullshit games the rest of us must deal with. Otherwise the dating and networking game of complete self-absorbed, cold-hearted, flaky nonsense is prevalent. (And there's extra innings piling up with no game's end in sight.)

GAME ON! (and on, and on, and on…)

It's come to the point where I now realize why many guys resort to hookers. At least with this tactic you're guaranteed a fuck, rather than being fucked with. (Ouch, sorry, not me.

But really, FUCK ME!)

Okay then, why don't some guys resort to "Sugar-mamas"? Well that's surely an option, but there's still catches to this tactic. As again women are more complicated, and although a Sugar-mama might take care of you she'll expect a lot in return. "How come you're not helping around the house? Why aren't you working a better job? Do you have to go play poker every Thursday?"

Whereas a "Sugar-daddy" is simple; he just wants the younger trophy girl as a charm for sex and fun adventures. A daddy don't care what that girl does for a living or if she makes any money, as he's already rich, yet women of power still expect stuff out of a guy who's with them and will nag away until he complies with her "mentally self-produced contract" list of expectations.

Women have it so easy with looks alone, whereas guys are definitely easier to deal with. Hence why Sugar-daddies are far more common out there than Sugar-mamas.

If a hot chick has one idea or talent that's about a third of the value of any one of my many ideas and talents, she'll win. Her looks alone will put her in the special "spotlight of importance" category well over me or anyone else without these certain looks and appeal that can sell easier to the public domain.

T.O.T. (**T**its **O**ver **T**alent)

Another subject of concern with women is concerts. How many times are we males thrown into the gauntlet of debatable fire when a killer band is in town and we have to decide between going with our dude friends or the girlfriend as our show companion(s). A lot depends on the band at hand, but usually if it's a musical act that's a bit wild and outside the comfort zone of what most women prefer, you have to be objective and inform her this one's a "guy's thing". Because if you pick the girl and take her into a world you know she doesn't relate to or appreciate, it can ruin the entire evening for both of you.

Fishbone was playing a show at the nationally acclaimed Little Bear in Evergreen, CO one evening some years ago. I had my girlfriend with me and was all psyched to introduce her to this amazing band who happened to be performing at this bosomly authentic, hometown venue I grew up near.

All was fine, my girlfriend was into it, then about half way through the show a mini-mosh pit broke out on the dance floor. As we were stationed on the front row of the mosh circle looking inward it was our duty to bounce patrons back into the pit who came crashing into us. Well my girlfriend was having a blast with this; shoving drunk patrons all over the place, until she got knocked into a table and banged her arm up pretty good. She was okay, just a bruise, but a very sensitive, fragile girl in general.

Upon the show's end word got out that the band didn't have any weed to smoke, so I offered to bring my stash onto the bus and smoke them up. They were good with this, (especially when realizing we had a mutual friend in the music scene who also happened to be from my hometown), but the "injured" girlfriend wouldn't have it and demanded we go back to my parent's house where we were staying that evening.

I tried to tell her the importance of this opportunity that

came to be but she was still shaken up from the accident during the show earlier. I gave in and drove us home; with irritating thoughts of frustration spinning in my head of what we had just passed up.

I did the right thing? Seriously, what was the *right thing* in this case? Yes you take care of loved ones first and foremost in any scenario or circumstance, but she wasn't that hurt and rather just shaken up from the whole ordeal.

No, I pulled the "nice guy *wrong* thing" to do in this scenario. The right thing would have been, "Throw some ice on that arm and suck it up a bit longer as we get high and have conversation with the members of Fishbone and a few of my Evergreen friends who are present as well. Weed will help numb your pain and this is a rare, essential, historical opportunity here."

This is a case where both parties in the mix have to look at the whole picture of what's happening and come to a practical conclusion that satisfies both as equal as possible. Had my girlfriend been injured to a bigger degree then no question we leave the venue and get her home, but in this instance it wasn't that bad and she could have allowed the final moments of the evening to commence as planned and I guarantee she would've been satisfied and had great stories to tell her family, friends, and other boyfriends to come! (Huh-Huh, I said…)

OKAY, WHATEVER, ENOUGH! GAHENGA.

One last thing before we enter the next chapter here ladies; didn't Lorena Bobbitt show you how to handle asshole men some years ago? Pussy Hat marches and such are weak, cookie-cutter strategies in order to try and make progress for change, instead reach for the blade and do some real cutting for definitive change! (And yet even with this tactic whitey male *still* came out on top once again. John gets his penis chopped, then sewed back together and makes money in porn, television appearances, published writings...as entropy pervs wanted to see his newly attached retard-cock in action and hear more about his "life after slice". Lorena just disappears as John reaps the rewards from this incident. Fucking men win again.)

I will always love and respect women to the fullest. Ask any of the many I've known over the years and they'll validate I'm a rare breed, sincere, unpretentious guy. It's just that so many females on the planet seem to need a big dose of sanity injected into them. Dr. Gunnar will collaborate with scientists and come up with a "formula of saneness" and personally inject it into every female on the planet, just to be safe.

I'll need about 3.5 billion needles and syringes so we don't spread any disease of course. Then I'll have to open an online fundraiser account to pay for all that's required in this grueling but necessary process. (I'm sure tax payers would love to jump all over this. Sure, starting with Republican males of course.)

So now even more *work for me and my already over-worked, stressed out, ambitious requisite to fix so many glitches in this world! I must incorporate more of my (thankfully endless) energy out there to be part of a bigger cause; rather than be smart, self-absorbed, let things go, and carry on like most others in the world that be.*

I'm American! United We Aren't, Divided We Sit. What a

crock of...

Don't worry ladies, I'll also have 3.5 billion needles and syringes full of cyanide ready for the guys! Just don't say anything, they'll think they're being injected with "I'm a Golden God" serum.

In conclusion, we all know it's mostly the mighty-whitey male who has done more damage to this world than any other race, or the other gender, in human history. So FUCK YOU VERY MUCH to my own kind! All the previous generations of white cock that fucked all others and everything in their path, is now forcing us newer generation white males, (who don't hold any discrepancies towards other races or genders nearly as much), to walk on eggshells and deal with these cold-hearted, fickle-freaky mindsets of modern day women; moslty as a result of you older generation while male bastards!

Operation Bobbitt \m/

420, brah!

It's all about the **P.O.T.** (**P**roduct **O**f the **T**imes)

These times we live in now are so crazy, shallow, unforgiving, and everyone's struggling more than ever to maintain a basic, stable, fulfilling life. People are constantly bombarded and distracted by an array of external elements, which then results in a society that has become more distressed, unreliable, and possesses no attention span or patience for much of anything anymore.

Everyone's stupid bitch smartphones are constantly 'beeping' with notifications so people can't stay set or true to a simple plan made or commit worth a shit. Henceforth, this obviously affects the dating scene tremendously as well.

I *always* take the most rudimentary things a step further in life; adding some spice to normal, boring redundancy. (That wording sucked, but let's give an example.) For instance, I printed out a shitload of business cards that have the appearance of a mixed tape; with "***Tunes from Uranus***" written in cursive-ish font on the front side and a small photo of me and my contact information on the back. Almost everyone who sees this card loves it, and I figure it will help me stand out more and they'll remember me with better odds they'll follow through after our meeting. NOPE. I've handed out around 100 of these business cards over a 3-year span and maybe 2-3 people tops have ever gotten back to me. And even with these 2-3 who actually remembered, cared, and took time to get back in touch, we all know by now the odds of any of them taking our connection to the next level, (meeting up again in person to further discuss our plans of intent), is most likely 0%.

Here's another example of how **P.O.T.** fucked-up something good. (That back in the day would've surely grown into something, no question.) I set up my own Meetup group over a year ago called Reaching for the Stars! The intent was to get outside the box, innovative, entrepreneurial-like individuals together and make big things happen together. Simple concept, what Meetups are all about, and with a clever-catchy title that over time generated well over 200 members!

Cool? Not at all. During the time this Meetup was setup and appealing to so many out there, we never had one motherfucking meeting! I posted so many messages regarding options/ideas for meeting times/places on the main page, personally messaged many of these members, welcoming them to the group and asking about their specialties, opinions, schedules…NOTHING CAME OF IT ALL.

I got a few responders out of the 200+ members, but otherwise NADA. At one point I scheduled a meetup time and location and not one fuck showed. Reaching for the Stars! existed for over a year and not one thing happened? I guess most people prefer to reach for the ground.

I was so dumbfounded and distraught after this experience, especially after surviving through all the awful experiences I've had to endure with the online dating, networking, music scene horseshit already! Un-fucking-real how bad it is anymore, to simply connect with legit humans. And even after a connection is made, it's nearly impossible to take anything to the next level. SON OF A WTF???

IT'S THE GOD DAMNED FUCKING TIMES!!! **P.O.T.** IS TO BLAME!!!

Shit even politicians and former leaders of our country are vulnerable to **P.O.T.** Look what Barak Obama went through during his 8 years as the nation's leader. Gee, where did he obtain such a prominent shade of gray on his head in that short time frame? First ever African-American (black) President, duh, who also had to clean up the biggest shit-storm of a mess that W. (Satan) created and left for Obama to deal with. What an unfortunate batch of **P.O.T.**

Obama was dealt and forced to smoke from his pipe in the Oval Office.

Black, yes, like when hip-hop used to be referred to as "rap", this country had such bigger balls and was much more authenticated in a sense when we were all black, white, racist, (and without sarcasm), genuinely sane, and REAL.

The real "god" of our country, (and maybe the world in general), George Carlin, once again stated it perfectly that we as citizens love to put all the blame on who's in charge, or always blame the rich and powerful for the world's problems. This is validated finger- pointing no question, but the mainstream public is just as irrational, ignorant, and askew as the high and mighty out there, they just can't afford *to be blatantly insensitive greedy pricks as obviously as the upper 5% are.*

Being a member of a few online dating sites in recent years I read many profiles where women also relate to my concerns. Many women's profile introductions begin with, "I'm not really into this online dating thing and I'm sure nothing will come of it, but…"

It's great to know there are other realists out there besides me that tell it how it is and aren't just being unreasonably cynical or have any kind of a "bad attitude". No, the dating scene sucks and more and more people and trends within our culture suck. (Oh no, that bad attitude coming out again. Out of NOWHERE, because it's not an attitude thing, it's stating the TRUTH. It's all about the **P.O.T.**)

During the pre-Shit Show era you would exchange numbers with another and most likely end up on a date. But in recent years the odds have turned to the outcome of most likely nothing will come out of any meeting or number exchanges. Girls will give you their number then ignore your attempt to call, or ever follow through with an agreement to meet up. At least women used to be a bit more considerate and give out a fake number, or they might call or text you back to cancel after you left a message. Nowadays you're fucking ghosted.

It really is the *times* more than *people* themselves that are shit. Even with job opportunities and most any connections made there's inevitable setbacks, letdowns, failures after you think you're "in" and "set".

Just recently I beat out 14 other candidates for a trivia host job at a high-class restaurant in Boulder. The manager concluded, "You're perfect, and thank god you're not a Millennial." (Basically stating I'd be reliable and have good taste in music, so the trivia events would always run awesome and smooth.)

However, it didn't take but a week or so for the owners to back out on the idea for this trivia night to commence. (No biggie I guess, only paid $75/night each week with free drinks and meals.)

In some years prior to this letdown, I was offered a job as emcee/drummer guy for an open mic night at a massive establishment in Denver. This was that "dream job come true" *finally* presented to me after years of searching for these opportunities.

I was to host the open mic comedy session of the evening, then play drums in the house band afterward. Fucking perfect! NOPE, the establishment managers soon after decided against the idea and nothing came of it.

Oh, here's *another* perfect example how **P.O.T.** fucks everything up nowadays; many things that for so many years prior were achievements of success. Never before having to cogitate so many shitty components that make up the 2010s big shit show of failures:

I recently performed a 45-minute drum/percussion solo at the International Church of Cannabis, located near downtown Denver. This is a newer, up and coming establishment featuring an authentic old school church layout, enhanced by invigorating "THC-influenced" art and décor throughout. The church opens its doors to the public every Friday at 6pm, with a recommended $5 donation that includes entrance and free food! (All patrons much bring their own ganja.)

As the sermon kicks off, and well into and beyond the musical portion of the evening, *everyone* is allowed to toke-up inside the church! So I was privileged to be invited into this newfangled world and showcase my concept of "stoner-friendly, improvisational percussive jams" within such an exclusive setting. I was able to wail away at my discretion amidst their wonderful nave, which features amazing acoustics and awe-inspiring decor!

However, only one friend attended and was able to soak up this experience first-hand. *ONE* friend/acquaintance out of so many out there who would normally kill to partake in an opportunity like this. We're talking live drums being played in a huge nave within a wonderfully decorated, decked-out church that's 420 friendly, and only one motherfucker I know shows up???

Just utilizing this example as case in point how wretched these times actually are! Because weed has been legal in Colorado for a few years now and everyone's phones are constantly beeping and illuminating with a multitude of options for events to attend, I can't get anyone's attention to commit to something this unique and amazing that was unheard of before marijuana was legal and the Church of Cannabis existed. Any other time in history *many* friends/acquaintances would've dropped everything to be included in this sort of ritual; a sacramental that combines music, art, *and* pot all in one setting!

See what I mean? How my efforts, talents, and credibility is completely sufficient enough to get in with so many things like these examples and beyond? Yet people, circumstances, and so many scenarios within these times that be FUCK IT UP.

It's like an 80s pop song; where the final chorus repeats until the inevitable fade out. Most any connection made between humans these days starts off as a nice, promising foundation with potential for growth but eventually fades into nothing. How sweet it is.

PLACES OF REFUGE

I must go back in time and share with you some of the extraordinary experiences I've had with many of my living situations over the years. I have lived with so many unique individuals in so many interesting places of residence I could practically write an entire book based on these crazy scenarios alone.

I'm ashamed to admit that I have never lived on my own in my entire life! Never have I been financially stable enough to live in a one bedroom apartment or simple studio alone at any time.

For any type of logical reasoning for this, read the sections in this book dealing with all my dilemmas in life.

SoCal Times

FIRST Move to Cali (Summer 1996)

When the virtual world of the internet grew more popular, I began to surf through various musician ad postings in places where I could see myself living and playing music. I saw an ad from a band in Santa Barbara that seemed to have a perfect description to meet my musical desires. They were a three-piece outfit and listed influences of Rush, King Crimson, Primus, and the likes. Like Seattle in the early 90s, Santa Barbara had just recently signed some bands that made it big in the mid-90s; Dishwalla, Nerf Herder, and Ultraspank were a few of them.

I emailed this band Grue and proceeded to speak with them about further details via phone. I had just graduated college the previous year and I was ready to take a risky move with my musical goals. We all decided I should load up my drums and head out there, where I would crash on their floor for a month and see what came of it.

A few days later I arrived in Santa Barbara and parked my car near a pay phone on State St. (The main drag where all the action takes place in Santa Barbara). As I waited to meet the band leader, Barak, I noticed a small pickup truck drive by with a long, blonde haired skinny dude at the wheel. He glanced over as he passed me I then noticed the blue *Counterparts* sticker on his back window and realized this was Barak.

I followed him to the apartment where he and Tim, bassist, lived together. I unloaded my essentials into the living room where I would reside and we chatted a bit about music and stuff but they were antsy to get my drums set up in their practice space that night.

The space was a storage unit that was connected to a surfboard shop. It was quite small and reeked of surfboard material. I was feeling more uncomfortable as time led on due to my mind's high expectations and all that was being presented into my reality, but I was excited as well.

The next morning Barak headed to work and Tim headed for campus. I just lay there in my sleeping bag feeling a bit stressed about this situation I was now stuck in. Things were just not feeling comfortable from the vibe of the guys, to my living situation, and the cramped, dirty rehearsal space. Oh well, rock and roll!

This first rehearsal session was a disaster! My drum chops where below par and their music was much more technical than I anticipated. Even after listening to the tracks over and over and learning the parts off the CD, the actual physical exercise of playing them was over my head at this time. Everyone seemed concerned so we ended the evening and decided to crack at it again the next day.

They gave me a video tape of one of their performances to watch as they spent the day working and studying. I knew this was my final chance to step up to the plate and really show them I knew their material and I certainly had better drum skills than I displayed the previous evening.

The second jam session was still a bit reckless and I was very flustered with myself. After this jam concluded, so did the musical goal and relationship with these guys in general.

Only two full days and nights in Santa Barbara and I knew it was over for my opportunity with Grue. And the feeling was mutual. From that time on we really didn't speak much and I had to spend the days job hunting and nights in my sleeping bag on the living room floor. It was horrible for me.

A couple weeks went by and I answered another ad posted by a guy named Josh. I knew I had to get the fuck out of Barak and Tim's pad so the pressure was on to get re-situated fast. I met up with Josh and his best friend, Chris, for some Monday Night Football; the classic Broncos vs. Raiders rivalry. We played pool as the game was on and talked about music and life in general. Fortunately for me we really hit it off on a personal level so I was finally feeling warm and happier inside because of this. The hard part now was finding a rehearsal space to jam with these guys, as they didn't have one yet.

I continued to live on the floor of Barak's apartment, work crap jobs, rollerblade the boardwalk, and hang out with Josh constantly. My only savior for survival at this point was going out with Josh and checking out all the hip nightlife on State St. The *Wildcat* bar in particular became my favorite spot, especially during Halloween, oh my!

My drums were still stuck in the cramped surf shop storage space and I would jam on them alone from time to time but things were looking bleak for anything musical to happen at all. The best thing that did happen was I convinced my mom to get me an early Christmas gift; a brand new DW double bass pedal.

After many days had passed we finally set up a jam at an elementary school. It was me, Josh, Chris and some other chap. We didn't accomplish shit! Chris didn't even have a mic to sing with and we all just jammed some sloppy nonsense for a couple hours before we got kicked out.

And that was it, a month and a half in Santa Barbara and I had to bail back home.

SECOND Move to Cali (Summer 1999)

I ended up moving to southern California a second time just three years after my first attempt. Interestingly enough it was to try and get a band going with Josh again.

My first stop en route from Colorado to California was Los Alamos, NM to visit and stay with my college buddy, Jon. Second stop was Phoenix, AZ to visit and stay with another college buddy, Tom. I had some good times spending these two evenings with my boys and catching up, but the show had to roll on…

San Diego

Third stop for me was to visit and stay with my high school friend, Nathan, who had finished his Master's at Cal Poly in San Luis Obispo and recently moved to San Diego.

I arrived at his apartment, we catch up on stories, and then it's time to check in with the parents as Nathan skateboards off to get some beer. Nathan had the entire night planned; to hit a great burger joint and then proceed to a unique music club, all on foot. It turns out that this burger joint is the oldest bar in San Diego, The Waterfront. (Located where the actual waterfront used to be in the city.) The burgers were the best I have ever tasted! No kidding; cooked perfectly fresh with grilled onions and all the fixings you can add from a tray provided. There was also a live jazz band jamming during our feast.

Then it was off to a bar called the Casbah. It was voted the best alternative music club in San Diego. The place was set up just how I like clubs: A main stage with dance area surrounded by black leather furniture and mirrors on the walls. There was an outside smoking section in the middle set up like an ally with plants and trippy lights. Lastly there was a backroom that had a selection of 80's video games to play. Incredible sound and energy was a prominent feature that I was very impressed with as well. I remember the name of the band who performed that night, Smile. Where are they now?

The next morning we hit Jamba Juice in order to get our focus and energy flowing. We then drove to a frisbee disc course, cruising in Beef's 1964 VW hippie van and listening to our friend Tank's band, The Wontons. What a fantastic course! Leave it to Southern California to charge a dollar to play the fricking thing, but man is it nice.

Los Angeles

First stop was Santa Monica, where I stayed with Bay Area family friend, Mark, for the first time in years since I last crashed at his pad in Lake Tahoe. I pulled over at the nearest Vons market and began making desperate attempts to reach him; as well as any of the three Ciancia brothers I wanted get ahold of. Luckily he answered the second call and just happened to live a few blocks away from Vons, in lovely Venice Beach, CA.

He was living in a guest house attached to a home owned by a successful screenplay writer. We sat in his room and watched the Independent Film Channel (IFC), featuring a great scene with three hot lesbians! We then called his movie writer/producer friend in Venice and headed over to his place. We hit the bar scene for the rest of the evening.

The next day I spent driving around LA trying to make contacts for jobs in entertainment. I had a couple appointments, one that turned out to be a modeling agency run by total flamers. I had to take a piss so bad before the appointment that I just whipped it out and went in a 5-gallon trashcan located in the basement laundry room of the apartments this agency was located in. Did I have to share that? Maybe not, but you try and find a place to take a leak in LA. It's a fricking chore! In fact, I wrote a song that day in my head about this entire stress-filled adventure called, "Pissing in L.A."

One crazy story from a certain L.A. adventure was when a high school buddy was in town on business and scored a room at the Continental Hyatt "Riot House" Regency, located in the heart of debauchery on Sunset Strip. He had tickets to go see North Mississippi Allstars *one night so we pre-partied in his room, on the balcony overlooking Sunset Blvd, (where Robert Plant officially made the statement he is a "Golden God").*

We lost each other during the show and as I ventured back to the room I began conversation with a street hooker who ended up back in our room for a couple drinks. I pretended my ATM card wasn't working so she'd eventually "have to leave".

Woke up the next morning all discombobulated, friend gone to meeting, and just remained in the room solo the rest of the day pretending to be a hungover rock star.

Santa Barbara

The first night I arrived at Josh's we ate pizza and watched my Terry Bozzio video before crashing out. I lay there in bed amidst this beautiful city once again with my thoughts of pondering hope to succeed this time.

Josh and his guitar buddy, Patrick, had a rehearsal space in a warehouse section of the Isla Vista district, located right on UCSB campus. It was where all the bands rehearsed; including Nerf Herder before they blew up and Ultraspank who were just being signed at the time. It was all perfect for me; I could jam my drums any time during the day or evening and it was right in the main part of campus where there was a pizza place and cool bar to hang at. And let's not forget the beautiful scenery! UCSB is located right along the ocean with fifty foot cliffs leading straight down to the beach.

Once again I worked some crap temp jobs out of desperation then each day all three of us would meet up for a jam. Usually Patrick would already be there jamming on guitar with a huge weed buzz rolling. Many times we were blasted out by Ultraspank, who were really heavy industrial metal, while we were doing this Alice in Chains unplugged type of project.

A guy in the same I.V. rehearsal units as us owned one of Neil Peart's drum kits from the Modern Drummer giveaway contests Neil would oversee. He showed me the disassembled kit in his jam space and was getting ready to sell it. It was definitely Neil's early 80s era Tama kit. Yummy!

Things began to dissipate and show no progress for success with our band, now called SexExit. I found myself falling into a lonely depression; spending time at night just walking by the house parties filled with all these happy, energized, young coeds. One night there was a cover band playing outside on a porch at a crowed party and they were jamming "Beautiful Disaster" by 311. I sat there and analyzed the scene; noticing the cute girls checking out the band and me checking out the drummer and knowing I could do way better and how it's too late for me being that I'm already out of college.

I did however get a chance to play "Beautiful Disaster" years later in my band Slugworth. And it's also become the two-word phrase of how I describe my life; a beautiful disaster!

From this party scene I walked over and sat on the edge of the cliffs above the ocean, and I seriously debated about jumping. I was absolutely wrecked with pain and hopelessness at this point. That's the power of my depression and mental issues and where they can take you, to almost wanting to jump off an actual fucking cliff.

I had outdone my welcome at Josh's mom's place and had to spend a few last lonely, chilly nights on the floor of the rehearsal space. I didn't even have enough money to hang at the pizza place or bar anymore. I was crushed beyond belief.

One highlight I remember from this second short stint in Santa Barbara was watching MTV and the video awards that happened to be broadcast on 9.9.99. And then there was the local alternative radio station I would listen to each morning while I got motivated for something and at one point they were promoting the new 311 album, *Soundsystem*. They had giveaways and free tickets for their show in Ventura coming up. Although I was too tired and lazy to participate in any of these events for a chance at the free tickets, I did make it to the show.

Ventura

I left Santa Barbara and headed south to Ventura, just 25 miles away. The goal was to scalp a ticket at a very cheap price since I was almost dead broke. I parked in a garage near the venue and began my passive stroll around the streets in search of tickets. I can't stand having to wheel and deal so I just observed others making the purchases until I felt the right one was legit for me. I then saw a lady in a wheelchair holding a couple tickets for sale. I approached her and she was asking $20 for one, and as ridiculous as it sounds I couldn't even afford the $20 price, so I moved on.

Soon again I saw the wheelchair lady and she decided to give me a ticket at my pathetically low asking price of $10. It was a GA ticket so I made my way up to the balcony and took a stand in the way back corner so I could just be in my own world and take in the entire atmosphere of the show. It rocked! The crowd was pumped and the new songs were amazing to hear for the first time in big theater setting of a venue.

During the post-show scene I sat across the street from the venue observing all the tour buses and commotion surrounding them. There was a horde of screaming girls and I would occasionally see a band member get on the bus, then off the bus, and the crew scattered in between the buses in the back-lot area.

I was literally the last person standing on that street after all the buses drove away. My mind was so fucked up with envy, jealousy, and melancholy to the point where I just couldn't move. I wanted this lifestyle, and 311 are all my age and living it.

I remember the slow walk back to my car knowing that the band members and crew are on those buses continuing onward to the next concert location, and here I was about to sleep in my car in some parking garage. Fuck me what a pitiful shame.

The next morning I proceeded to drive towards the beach area where I parked my car and took a three hour nap in a big hole I found. After I awoke I had to find a phone and make some calls for my salvation. The two calls I made were to my San Diego connections.

First was Andy, the bassist I found on the internet who was interested in jamming, and second was my good friend Nathan once again. I spoke live with each of them and they both told me to get down there. For the first time in days I felt a fire of delight lit within my soul and I took off without any hesitation for the second largest city in state.

San Diego (revisited)

I pulled into Nathan's apartment parking lot, and as I am the most guilt-ridden, passive, neurotic on Earth, I climbed into his hippie van to go to sleep, using a beach towel for a blanket. As it turns out his girlfriend noticed my car that evening and I woke up to Nathan wondering what I was doing and brought me inside to the fold out couch bed that I would sleep on for the next two months.

Now that I had refuge and a little more stability and comfort in my crazy situation, I could focus once again to find some tolerable employment. The very first morning I awoke on that living room couch and searched the yellow pages for some jobs before hitting the pavement for more crap temp work or whatever. I called a few talent agencies and this lady, Tia, called me back immediately needing someone that fit my profile to be a businessman for a quick scene. She was all frantic and asked for my reliability to head up to Balboa Park and check in for instructions. This was perfect as Nathan's place was in Mission Hills where the film shoot was taking place.

I get up there, check in, and they throw me in a dressing room where I put on a suit and stood around for a half hour. I was never needed after all so they paid me for my two-hour contract, and here I was now involved with Tia Casting.

Next I began to stroll the Garnet Avenue scene where all the hip shops and businesses are located. Right off the bat I landed a job as floor sales guy at a bike shop. My job was simply to get people interested in purchasing bikes, preferably beach cruisers. This got me excited for the fact that so many hot beach girls would be stopping in there for bikes, as it was located right off the boardwalk. The only bad thing was I can't stand retail or sales work, and I hadn't worked a cash register since high school. The owner, BJ, was an older guy with an intense look and came across as pretty anal. This job, like so many others, would only last a couple weeks. What a tragedy that I couldn't tolerate the work or atmosphere there, even with all the benefits that came with the job.

Blind Melons Era

Back on the pavement I walked to the end of Garnet Avenue one day and saw a live music bar called Blind Melons. I went inside and asked about employment and the bartender went to the back office and out came this rough looking guy who asked me my experience and if I like blues music.

I was hired after he predicted another new guy wouldn't commit, and sure enough there I was working the back door a night later with this huge five band concert deal going on. It was madness during my first night. There was underage people lingering all over and trying to hop the back fence to get in so I had my hands full.

Worst part of all was I had to leave a gathering early that day before my first shift. It was with Nathan and his friends who were having a Coen Brothers movie marathon. The *Big Lebowski* had just started when I had to leave and watch everyone making their first round of White Russian drinks. I had not seen this movie before, so that mixed with the anxiety of a first work shift made for a difficult departure from the festivities.

I ended up sticking with this Blind Melons gig for eight months! A record amount of time for me, until this psycho bitch of a bartender purposely got me fired. A story so fucking lame I choose not to share.

The experiences working those eight months at Blind Melons were mostly gratifying. I was one of the door guys so it was pretty chill and we got tipped out after each shift. Then I would usually skateboard down the boardwalk to my co-worker buddy Brian's place to have some beers, tokes, and watch surf videos. I would then head back to Nathan's just before sunrise and repeat this cycle of living a few days each week.

Blind Melons also hosted open blues jams on Tuesdays and Hump Nite Comedy on Wednesdays. I was able to jump up on the drums and jam out during my shift and even had a jam with Kevin "Chevy" Rameriz from the Psychedelic Zombiez, the band I knew since high school in Evergreen.

Like most all open jam nights the music is almost always blues oriented and you must deal with the usual jackass guitar player trying to run the show and dictate everything. Fuck you old school classic rock blues guitarists! Shove that Stratocaster up your ass, it's an open jam!

During the Hump Nite Comedy I was also allowed to perform my funny little rants from time to time. One night it was a really big event that packed the house and somehow I got on the list to perform. The worst part was I had to take a shit just minutes before my routine! Usually I can bypass this urge and hold it until after but this one hit in full force. I had to push it out under time-limited stress in the employee bathroom with all the bartenders walking by the door and the sound of the last couple comedians finishing their set.

I happened to be drunk and wearing a Burger King crown that night and hit the stage flaunting that ridiculous thing as I ripped into the nightlife culture of San Diego. I analyzed and compared the night party scene and all the redundant rave music; how people were more into coke and ecstasy there as opposed to Coloradoans being into weed and mushrooms. Whatever.

The other great benefit of working at Blind Melons was the owners took us to Lake Tahoe for a Christmas break getaway. We piled in a Ford Expedition, I put my "couch days revisited" mix tape in, and we pounded beers during the entire 10-hour journey!

We were all treated to a day at Heavenly Ski Resort and during the two nights there in Tahoe we partied HARD. The Blind Melons owners ran another bar in Ocean Beach called Winston's, and we had that crew joining us as well. One of the Winston crew brought some liquid acid and we dripped it onto goldfish crackers and ate a couple each for the night out. We went bowling then prowled the snowy streets late into the night on this light acid trip. Quite a time I must say.

Jason

The greatest thing of all to come out of the Hump Nite Comedy was my introduction to Jason. I was working the door during a normal Wednesday night and this guy who looks like a cross between Larry from the Stooges and Steven Wright walks up to me and asked how to get on stage. Dustin, who promoted the comedy night, told Jason that he had to bring five friends into the club to get a spot-on stage. Jason immediately responded with, "Oh forget it there's no way". This remark intrigued me and I continued to talk with Jason about comedy for a bit before he bailed. Turns out Jason was a local from the La Jolla/Pacific Beach area who hits an occasional open mic night like I do.

After some whacky experiences hanging with Jason during my last year in San Diego, he continues to be one of my best friends over a decade later. We have become permanent phone buddies holding regular conversations, almost daily, that work as our mutual therapy sessions by hashing out all our unfortunate situations that torment our lives. We even take effort in organizing a visit for a few days each year; usually consisting of Jason visiting me out here in Colorado and continuing our outlandish adventures together. Man are we both a crazy mess of manic energy!

Slade & Trask

Talk about a couple characters and a couple great guys in general. These twins were introduced to me through Andy, who again was the original reason for me to head down to San Diego in the first place.

Andy is a fantastic bass player but unfortunately we only jammed together once my entire time out in San Diego. We loaded his bass into my Honda Accord and drove up to Santa Barbara where my drums were still set up at the time. We jammed that evening, crashed on the floor of the studio and left back to San Diego the next morning. And that was my experience being in a band with Andy.

Like me, Slade and Trask were diagnosed with ADD and this just fueled our crazy ambitions to conquer every scene possible whenever we went out. I was working just enough to have some money to socialize and booze up plenty with these guys on many nights in PB. I remember one place in particular we all went out to every week on a certain night when the drink specials were intended to get everyone sloshed. Of course I took advantage of this and proceeded to get so messed up one night that Slade, Trask, and crew watched me as I tried to hit on chick after chick during the entire evening.

The most epic time spent with Trask was when we both pulled a 48-hour, non-stop adventure with no sleep at all. We planned to go skiing at Big Bear and had the alarm set for the early morning hours, only to have drinks and play darts all night until we heard the alarm go off!

We skied hard all day and during the three-hour drive back

we began to see blurry visions of color on the highway. We figured it was nap time until Trask got a call from a girl he knew that was hitting the bars and a late-night party that evening. We said fuck the naps and complied to the invite. Somehow we managed to stay up all night and see the sunrise once again. 48 hours, rock on!

San Diego Night Clubs & Musical Experiences

San Diego became the first place where I got to experience the after-hour nightlife scene. While working at Blind Melons, they came up with a rave theme night after the Hump Nite comedy was no longer working. A young, hip bartender and promoter named Pili was the organizer for this event. I ended up writing an article about him in a local publication. We became tight and he introduced me to the after-hours scene, as well as ecstasy.

Knowing Pili and his huge posse of rave-hopping partiers got me *rolling* into a whole new world that would please my manic, adventurous Leo-ness. I hit some of the biggest rave nights around the city and soon began to end up at after hour parties. These late- night gatherings were usually hosted by rich guys at huge houses, just like you see in the movies. There was always plenty of pills, coke, and weed to indulge in for anyone who wished. And as the sun would begin to rise everyone would make their way to the Silver Fox, a dive bar in PB that opened at 6am.

HALLOWEEN

I thought of the goofiest costume ever while in San Diego. I decided to dress, paint my face, and spray my hair in all white to be the "walk signal guy". Yep, that illuminated stick figure we all see every time while crossing a major street. My group of friends were tripping out on the idea and how nuts I looked! We would ask people if they knew what I was trying to be and only one girl got it right. Everyone else we asked were stumped, and the comment of the night had to be, "Are you a retarded mime?"

My other idea for an interesting costume theme is to dress like Captain Kirk and have a sexy green alien babe as my companion. This would be so easy, classic, and I already have the perfect flip open cell phone as my "Beam us up Scotty" transmitter device. I just need the right girl, but it has never come about for the past few Halloweens that I've wanted to do this. Shitballs, maybe someday…

Costco Lunch

So many fantastic experiences and adventures lasted well over a year while living in San Diego, but things eventually took a turn for the worse. After being fired from Blind Melons the movie extra work also dissipated to nothing and I was going broke. It got to the point where I ended up maxing out a credit card just to live on the basic essentials. My friend Jeff was broke as well so we would meet at his apartment, take some hits off his bowl, then head out to Mission Valley Mall to check out MILFs and the Costco $1.50 hotdog and a Coke deal. Sometimes we would even cruise the store for food samples. We would later treat ourselves to dollar taco night and Coronas at PB Bar & Grill; the popular establishment where I would end up working my second door guy job, just down the street from

Blind Melons.

The Real House

I was waltzing through campus at SDSU and noticed a posted ad for people to live in The Real House. It was looking for interesting characters to live together in a house full of webcams, rent free, just like the show on MTV.

I applied, interviewed, and landed a spot in The Real House. I remember the founder, Gio, telling me I would have a roommate and it was going to be interesting. I really didn't care about anything except being part of this experience and living in an incredible house rent free!

The house was located right in the middle of the SDSU district and consisted of a swimming pool, huge living room with giant screen TV, and five separate rooms that were each painted a different color. There were 24 webcams placed throughout the house, even one in each shower.

During move-in day I began to put my stuff in the big red room with two beds, when a very hot, very dark, black girl entered the room. After the words from her mouth spoke, "Oh yeah I really like this guy." I realized I was in for an experience. (It turned out when she interviewed with Gio she told him of her infatuation with blonde surfer-looking fellas, so here I am so conveniently picked to room with her.)

It was July 4th weekend and I was the final of six roommates to move in. I had to grab a quick bite to eat and be ready for the open house rager that was already planned for inaugural celebration.

My new dark skinned beauty of a roommate took a trip with me up to Burger King. We were in line at the drive through ordering when she suddenly grabs my hand and sticks it right up her skirt.

From here we ate our junk food back at the house and I hopped in the shower. Apparently my new roommate hadn't had her daily shower either and decided to jump in with me! (I really wish I could please you all with the details of this shower experience but let's just say that a couple of the roommates happened to be online watching from the living room computers, and only they know of the events that took place.)

The party ended up getting pretty wild with people jumping into the pool fully clothed or completely naked, as George did. George was a huge 350 pound guy and oldest member of The Real House. He was also a sport-o-holic and a fellow Leo; three total in the house, with the two other tenants being Scorpios. Fire signs galore!

With crazy fun drunken George, two bi-sexual black girls, and a couple more inhabitants I don't even remember, it was some of the best five months living I've ever experienced. A great house full of wild personalities and no rent or bills to slow us down. Let's just say it was epic, except for the fact that it did only last five months.

We had an erotic Halloween party and I invited a bunch of my new film shoot friends to attend. The agreement to be at the party was to either wear a costume or some sort of skimpy bedtime clothes. I wore a stupid cowboy hat with a

Dracula cape and remember the house manager telling me to take my pants off, as he was in his undies to fit in with the undies theme himself. I kept telling him, “No way, I’ve got a costume.” But he was all in my face, so I walked out of the party where my full glass of rum and Coke just happened to slip out of my hand and crash onto the concrete front porch.

Mr. Manager tackled me down and we rolled all over the front lawn with a couple dozen guests watching. As we tumbled around in drunken disarray one of the guests I invited jumps in and starts fighting the manager! I got up in disbelief of all that was happening and basically got my notice the day after to leave within a week after this incident. I argued this and got thirty-days notice instead, only to move just down the street and live with four college dudes.

One more story during my times living at the Real House was when a buddy of mine, Brendon, visited from Colorado. He was out in San Diego working a bike expo and decided to crash at The Real House. (Anyone who entered the house had to sign a waiver that notified them of their presence in front of numerous webcams.)

We took a fairy out to Catalina Island to visit another friend who also worked with us at Schwinn back in Boulder. He took us on a sea kayak trek around part of the island, which was amazing as you could see down into the water where lots of colorful entities were living, including Leopard Sharks.

About half way into the journey Brendon tipped over into the ocean. Being that we were all pretty stoned it took him at least five minutes worth of attempts to get back in his kayak. This was not only entertaining for me and our other buddy to watch but also great for the other water sport spectators that were passing by.

Back in San Diego we decided to hit the beach scene for dinner and bar hopping. As I was taking a leak in one of the boardwalk bathrooms Brendon bumped into some girl he went to high school with. I know, what are the odds, but this is where the story gets interesting...

This girl cruised with us to my old stomping grounds, Blind Melons, for some drinks. I guess the liquor took effect as she began putting some flirty moves on me, and she was mega attractive. I'm getting into this girl at the bar as Brendon is pressuring me to go to Tijuana.

We parted ways with the girl and drove for the border. Meanwhile I'm all pissed off because I blew an opportunity with a hottie to rather get in trouble with a friend in Mexico. We drove across the border in my Honda Accord, which still had its Colorado plates attached. We were still a bit loopy and ended up getting lost on the highway somewhere in Mexico. Brendon was driving as he was a bit more sober and brought us into some tiki hut style village area. Since I was passed out up until this point I was awakened to see these small huts and a few dogs checking us out. Imagine two white Colorado natives lost in some part of a slummy, Mexican residential area. We both had to piss and did so very quickly then I got behind the wheel to get us the fuck out of there.

We were cruising along the vacant highway trying to make sense out of the road signs but having no luck. We eventually did find the border and were stuck there trying to cross back over into San Diego for well over an hour. I was so annoyed by this point I put in my Metallica/Megadeth mix and cranked it in order to deter the Mexican children from trying to sell us necklaces and shit as we waited.

The moral of this crazy story was that I passed up a fun opportunity with a very attractive girl to instead get lost in Mexico. It's a classic story now but we could've been mugged or even killed during that time we were lost. Two younger, drunk white guys driving around the roads of rural Mexico in a little Japanese vehicle sporting Colorado plates? Might as well drop a bar of soap on the ground, pull down your pants, and bend over willingly for the next "friend to be".

And speaking of my Honda Accord...

My Car

There have been a few occasions in my life where I lived out of the mobile entity that most people use to just get around in. Standing close to 6'3" and owning a Honda Accord during these pleasant eras was a bit of a predicament. As with all the other hardships I've lived through (and realizing other's more eminent hardships around the world) I figured sleeping in my car for a very short phase in life is hardly rock bottom. Although it was miserable and depressing to wake up in various parking lots and peeking out through my fogged-up windows each morning, I pressed on like always.

If I had all my belongings packed in my trusty hatchback I would have to sleep sitting up in the driver's seat. It's still unfathomable that I allowed myself to reach a phase as dreary as this. Who else with a college degree and such ambition in life could resort to living out of their car? Not many I presume, but shit happens.

The Basement Dweller: A Pleasure Prison

Three times since my graduation from college I've had to seek refuge in my parent's basement. Not that it's a torturous arrangement by any means but it sure reminds me of the messy reality I live. Twice I've had to move back into my childhood room in the basement of our Evergreen home, and now the latest move has been into the basement of the Louisville house my parents own; being here for the duration of my thirties and into my fucking forties!

Most people would look at this as a cop out or taking the easy road from responsibility and all but it's not anything like that. It's a forced option and I'm lucky to have sympathetic parents who understand my unhinged lifestyle and they keep me off the streets.

But again how can this be? With someone like me who has such character, ambition, a zest for life, and even a college degree? It's fucking asinine, and live in my head for just a few weeks and you'll get it.

Hence during my third term now spent in a parental basement I coined the phrase *Pleasure Prison.* I live in a very nice basement with great hospitality, amenities and all yet I'm trapped here with no means of escape. After all these years I have yet to make adequate money to afford a place of my own. Sure I've done well enough to live on my own with a multitude of roommates over the years, but as I enter further into middle age it's well overdue for me to finally live on my own. I can't keep the most tolerable jobs rolling long enough to stay ahead financially, so I'm trapped in this pleasure prison!

I "pay" my rent and utilities by helping with house chores and yard work when needed. I get to enjoy my mom's amazing home cooked food, love and support from both parents, but with my ambitious and stubborn, independent persona it's torture to have to live in a predicament like this.

Sometimes, if motivated, I will take a quick hike or even bike on a nearby trail. And if more focused motivation kicks in I will drive or ride my bike to my rehearsal studio and jam on my drums for an hour or so. There's also the occasional adventures to Boulder for recreational activities or hanging with friends, even Denver for promotional work or band rehearsals and gigs. Otherwise I spend a lot of time dinking around in my basement or wandering the streets and parks of the Louisville, just pondering and dwelling in my reality.

VACATIONS/ADVENTURES

The Hauges are road trippers at heart. As noted in the *Loogie Era* section of this book we, as a family of five, took many long excursions all over the country. It is now that I'd like to share some stories of a few of these family trips with you. (As well as some other excursions I took on my own or with select friends over the years.)

Syracuse/Lake Ontario

Being that most our relatives live in Syracuse, NY we took many trips (via road and plane) to visit them. One time I was privileged to join my dad for a quick trip out there to see a Syracuse vs Georgetown basketball game. They were huge rivals at the time and this game became the largest crowd in Carrier Dome history, nearing 33,000 in attendance.

I remember the Syracuse band playing "YYZ" by Rush during a break in action, which was really cool as I was just getting into Rush at the time. The final score of the game was Syracuse 70, Georgetown 71. Since I was born in Georgetown Hospital I was secretly rooting for the Hoyas.

Lake Ontario is a very nice place to visit as well. Some relatives own shoreline properties and we can sometimes stay in one of the guest cottages available. There was also a big plot of grass where we could play volleyball or croquet. As more years past my sisters and I could hang with the older cousins and indulge in their nighttime activities as well; card games, with booze and weed as the horsdoeuvres.

During one Syracuse vacation we Hauges trekked down to New York City and got to visit the World Trade Center. I bought a poster of the Manhattan skyline at the gift shop located on the top floor and wish I still had it.

I could go into more details of our experiences visiting

Syracuse and Lake Ontario but I must move on…

Note: (12/21/12, my last official journal entry before the end of the world.)

I sit here at Bittersweet Cafe in Louisville during the last day on Earth. Perfect name of a place to hang with my life being in a constant paradox anyway. If the world ends this book dies with me, if we survive I stick to my goal of not writing anymore content in the Spin Cycle *after this day.*

The biggest problem left in these remaining hours is not only am I craving adventure this evening but I must finalize my content. Being that I could/should be reading through some journals and other resources of my writings that could/should be included here, it's just too late and too much to perceive. Whatever material that is discussed in this book is finished at midnight and I will not add any more to it. I want this book to be just right; an epic piece of work that covers all the right elements, but we as artists are known for paranoid neurotic perfectionistic tendencies.

Anyway, the next crucial stage of my job as a writer are the more grueling tasks of editing, publishing, marketing, and all that scary business-sided crap I hate to even think about, let alone act on. I'm in a deep, lost depression phase of sorts so it's hard to do shit right now. I feel more like hanging with like-minded company but I can't dial anyone in these days.

Ha, I just now changed my deadline to finish writing anymore content in this book once my laptop battery goes dead. Fuck midnight.

Great Sand Dunes National Monument

My family and I have taken multiple trips to Great Sand Dunes National Monument. After so many years traveling the entire country, we simplified and embarked on many summer weekend trips to the Dunes. It became the annual event every summer to the point where we started to invite friends to tag along. After I got my driver's license I would visit the Dunes on my own every summer with a different friend as my companion. And for some reason the band that was always played during the road trip to the Dunes was Asia. Yep the same debut album from the poster that gets ridiculed in the movie *40 Year Old Virgin.*

Being that the Great Sand Dunes are the highest dunes in North America it's always a great accomplishment to summit the highest peak, some 900+ feet of climbing in soft hot as fuck sand. During summer the surface temperature of the sand reaches 120+ degrees and every step you take you're sinking in a half step back.

My first experience at the Great Sand Dunes was with my dad and family dog, Skipper. We drove the Loogie out from Evergreen and I brought my little one speaker boom box with a blank tape and documented the entire weekend trip. During the last stretch of the drive into the park Skipper was constantly whimpering, only to then smell the most wretched scent of shit I have ever experienced. Skipper had unloaded some brutal dog diarrhea in the back of the Loogie. Luckily the Visitor Center was only minutes away and I remember watching my dad spray the enormous pile of diarrhea out of the back with a hose.

Later in the evening my dad and I shared a movie moment together by lying down on the hood of the Loogie and gazing up at the stars. He showed me all the constellations, satellites, and whatever else was part of the beautiful night sky. Thanks dad!

Each night there is a campfire program with slides and information about the park. I remember one time at the end of the slide show presentation and the ranger asked if anyone had questions, so my guest friend yelled out, "Are there any bats?" For some reason this was very amusing to us hyper teenagers and this certain question became another annual tradition where any friend I brought to the Dunes as a guest had to yell out this same question at the end of the slide show program. I love silly little traditions like this in life, don't you? (In fact, stop reading for a moment and take time to reminisce over any silly little traditions you might have conceived throughout your life.)

Many people sled, ski, or snowboard down the Dunes. Being as adventurous as I am I've tried all three. It's a bit of a chore not only hiking up the steep sand hauling gear but it's also very sticky which makes turning very difficult. However I still recommend it.

Solo Dunes *Trip*

I had just recently purchased my "dream SUV" 1997 4Runner (Ltd) and we were ready for an excursion. No better getaway than another trip to the Dunes, although this trip contained an extra ingredient, LSD.

I was amidst a dark depression during this time so the real

reason for my escape to the mountains was to “soothe my soul” with my new 4Runner as the incentive to make the trip worthier. Camping was free as there was no running water and the toilets were closed. I liked this aspect as I’m always living on a tight budget and this saved me $30.

I grabbed a perfect spot at the end of the main camping loop which included a view of the Dunes. I threw some belongings on the picnic table to mark my territory and proceeded onto the four-wheel drive trail that went a few miles into the mountains. The first mile was all sand, and although it was a blast there were moments where I almost got stuck as my wheels would sink in a bit too far if moving too slow.

I drove for over an hour and decided to turn around as the sun was going down. After plowing through a few areas of water during the trek, I decided to set up my camcorder on a log on the way down and then run back to my 4Runner and capture footage of me blasting through the water like in a television commercial. I’m always acting as producer, cameraman, and actor in most all my excursions in life. It can be draining but what’s an ambitious, creative, Leo to do?

Unrest in the Forest

I awoke in my 4runner and drove off to a more private area of the Dunes where I could eat a quick breakfast and begin my ascent to the top with snowboard in hand. First hassle of the day was the constant attack of a few hornets that would not leave me alone and eventually followed me up the Dunes. This ordeal was unbelievable; I’ve never seen such persistent bees in my life. About halfway up the

Dunes I finally had to drop my board and take time to kill the annoying fuckers; over an hour of annoyance they caused me in total.

I made it to the top and surfed my way down, which again is a difficult task as the sand is sticky and you can't really move fast enough or make sufficient turns. I then proceeded back to camp, had lunch and took a nap.

I got up around 3pm and had to quickly organize for my late afternoon hike back to the top (without the hornets this time around). I parked my 4Runner, geared up, and then the unfortunate situation of having to take a dump kicked in. After wiping and exiting this wonderful porta-crapper I grabbed my walking stick, ate my "snack", and headed out.

I was agitated from the verity of racing against time and having to stop often in order to make sure I got proper documentation with still photos and video commentating. (I had purchased a disposable camera for the first time in years and had to be very selective on my 24 photos allowed, but this was a nice challenge rather than cheating with a digital camera.)

Almost an hour later I reached the perfect spot where I could watch the sunset over the Dunes, hoping to enjoy the beauty of my surroundings before darkness prevailed. It was just after a bowl smoking session that the acid began to take effect.

As my buzz kicked in I took some photos of the sunset and began to draw designs in the sand that were set to a story in my head. Then for my own pleasure I booted a soccer ball off the crest of sand where I resided and watched it roll all the way down to the bottom. (Again I filmed this event only to realize my lens was on tight zoom and didn't capture any of the ball rolling extravaganza)

It was now dark and I realized that I didn't get a picture of the sand calligraphy I drew with my walking stick, so I frantically turned on the video camera, switched on the night vision setting and filmed the entire area of artwork, covering about a fifty-foot area of sand. Too bad it didn't turn out because I had some very interesting messages and drawings mapped out in that big area of sand.

I watched the only other car leave the parking lot and began my descent downward following the trail of the soccer ball. As I searched for the ball I could not get enough light from my $10 Target headlamp. I accepted the fact that I could only see ten feet in front of me at best and began to panic after remembering two separate campers had spotted bears in the area earlier and the Park Rangers were warning people of more bear sightings than usual as they're preparing for hibernation.

With visuals of hungry black bears in my mind I went into full panic mode knowing that I was vulnerable meat. I began a full sprint in search for my 4Runner but ended up running in circles.

After about fifteen minutes of this frantic panicking running around the darkness trying to find my vehicle, I decided I better just climb up a tree. I figured I would be safer up off the ground and conserve energy. I realize black bears climb trees but I had a big stick and was up about ten feet in a smaller tree which is much safer than being on the fucking ground.

Now settled in this dead tree, my mind started going over

the best and worst case scenarios of my situation. Meanwhile I was completely sweaty and disoriented from the physical workout, anxiety, and LSD taking full effect.

While in the tree I kept seeing beams of light approaching over the horizon that appeared to be coming from flashlights, but as it turned out the light beams were headlights of cars from a distant town. Even though I was only ten feet up I had to keep reminding myself how unstable this tree was, and the cold autumn air was setting in as well. I had no choice but to stand in the same place hugging the trunk of the tree while constantly tapping out drum beats and kicking my feet against the main trunk of the tree to avoid frost bite. It's great being a drummer but never thought I'd be practicing my rudiments on the trunk of a dead tree for hours during a cold dark night!

Luckily being the boy scout I am I had a full bottle of water and Clif Bar in my backpack that would give me enough nutrients for the duration of the night.

I also began to see other visions; observing plants melting, red eyes of make believe critters looking at me and scattering off. I looked up into the night sky and noticed the stars all made a grid pattern that seemed to map out the structure of the universe. And worst of all the moon became the face of a skull, which I thought for sure was a sign of my demise.

I kept trying to enjoy some element of this "trippy" situation but the cold weather and unstable tree prevented this from happening. I would try and get songs stuck in my head as I tapped out beats with my hands and feet but nothing would numb the pain of the reality of what was turning out the be the longest, coldest, loneliest night of my life. All I could think about to give myself encouragement was how many other people have survived through ordeals much worse than mine. I was in familiar territory and only about a mile or so from the campground.

After surviving the eleven hours of cold dark night fun the faint sign of dawn's light presented itself over the mountain tops. I climbed down the tree, took the keys out of my backpack and began to push the unlock button, only to see the lights of my 4Runner come on just over this bluff about 100 feet away!

With mixed emotions of frustration and relief flowing through me I hustled over to my 4Runner, turned on the engine and cranked the heat. I made it back to camp and passed out until late morning, still amazed at what had just happened in all the hours past.

Canyonlands/White Sands (with the Evans')

The Hauges and our neighbors, the Evans, took two trips together within a year's time; Canyonlands, UT in the summer of 1987 and White Sands, NM in the spring of 1988. It was great times and we convoyed out together with our Loogie and their black Jeep Wagoneer named "Mud". We had CB radios so we could communicate while on the road.

At Canyonlands the entire gang went four wheeling but Len and I decided to go on our own excursion hiking into the vastness of the Canyonlands. We brought one big jug of water and headed out with the hot sun pounding on us. After a little while we reached a crevasse that was about four or five feet wide and had about a 100 foot drop below.

After Len jumped the gap I stayed back and debated taking the plunge for about five minutes. I tossed over the water jug to Len but it didn't reach his hands and plunged down into the crevasse. Being that it was my parent's water jug I insisted we hike downward to retrieve it.

We made it down to the bottom of the crevasse, picked up the stupid jug and proceeded back up to the same place where we dropped it. After making the second jump across the crevasse we had a long stroll back to the campsite in the hot sun with no water. It ended up being a four-hour adventure in the baking heat and our parents were terrified when they learned of our tales.

After the success of the Canyonlands trip we all took a spring break escape to White Sands, NM. With the Loogie, Mud, and CB radios at hand again.

I remember entering White Sands while driving the Loogie and Len was driving Mud. I had Pink Floyd's "On the Run" playing as we drove slowly along through the beautiful white sand and it served as a soundtrack for the journey. We all played on the sand for the afternoon and that was that.

We also hit Carlsbad Caverns where we witnessed a million bats that fly out of the main cave at dusk.

Las Vegas

With or without my family I've made numerous trips to Vegas, each time by car. Yes we would take the twelve hour drive there and back each summer to visit cousins and indulge in the scene.

Although I've never been much of a gambler there was one memorable time where I spent the entire night at Slots of Fun playing the $2 Blackjack table while consuming many Coronas until sunrise. I played for hours and funny enough I didn't know what I was doing. Once I learned the strategy for Blackjack I haven't hardly won at all since.

One event that changed my world was seeing Cirque du Soleil's production of *Mystere.* The performance blew me away. I bought the CD and a t-shirt and a year later I went and saw it again. I have seen a couple other Cirque du Soleil productions since but I still count *Mystere* as being the top dog of the pack.

There are so many epic stories of my times spent in Vegas, especially the hard-partying times friends or with my cousin Dawn and her husband Gary. We've all been to the City of Sin and partaken in the same debauchery as everyone else over the years.

I say again; what happens in Vegas should happen more often!

Moab

Moab, UT has been one of my favorite getaways for years now. It offers everything I crave minus skiing. Many who have been there know how epic the camping, hiking, biking, and four wheeling is around the area. It's only five hours from the Denver area so it's been one of the more convenient trips for me to take over the years.

I first stayed in Moab at a young age with my family, but after discovering my love for mountain biking I became infatuated and took yearly trips to Moab with a posse of friends. I've probably been there a dozen times and road almost every trail offered.

Snowcat Trips

I was very fortunate to be included in two separate snowcat ski trips; first one in 2003, the other in 2007. I went with my good friend Brian, and these trips consisted of a weeklong adventure to various ski areas throughout Colorado and into New Mexico. The gang of twelve professional engineers and me would "warm up" at Copper Mountain on the first day then head into Salida, CO and prepare for the snowcat expedition at Monarch Ski Area.

After the snowcat day we would venture off to a few more ski areas for the remainder of the week, always ending the trip at Crested Butte. During the 2007 trip we hit Taos for a couple days. The mountain was spectacular and had the option to hike up this ridge on Kachina Peak and indulge in some extreme chute skiing.

Me and Brian ended up skiing seven days in a row during the 2007 trip. A record I will most likely never break.

California (revisited)

Right after my departure from my mailroom job in the summer of 2007, my good friend Chad and I hit the road in his Grand Cherokee.

Chad got a speeding ticket right off the bat as we passed through Eisenhower Tunnel. It was soon after my turn to drive but I had just finished eating a pot brownie earlier. As I drove Chad noticed that I was cruising at a slow 50 mph just as I was making the comment that I didn't think the brownie buzz was kicking in yet.

Our mission for this week-long trip was to go surfing on the west coast while catching two Rush concerts along the journey. We began our quest by stopping in Fruita, CO to take a bike ride, the first one for either of us ever in this area. We rode a loop in the Kokopelli Trail and I remember being frustrated how technical some parts were and the fact that it was very hot out. Otherwise a fine ride with a fine friend.

Rush was on their Snakes and Arrows tour and one of my most memorable concert experiences ever was catching Rush at the Hollywood Bowl on my birthday! What a venue to see my favorite band at, and to make it more historical Danny Carey of Tool was there and met Neil Peart, his drum hero, for the first time ever. Fuck yeah!

The rest of the night, however, was a mess. We were staying with my friend Jeff and his girlfriend in Hollywood. We all went out to a couple dive bars and crossed paths with some chump named Diamond. He was going to set us up with some coke and I volunteered to ride along with him and a couple others in this BMW up to the Hills to score the coke. All the while Chad and Jeff took off separately to a strip club, where I should've gone instead.

I remember waking up in the backseat of the BMW with

the shotgun seat empty and one of the guys saying that we were had. Diamond took off with our money and never came back. I chipped in around $80 so I was pissed. And I don't even like coke much anyway. It was my birthday, I just saw Rush and was pumped up and ready for anything, so I splurged and regretted.

After the LA debacle we made our way to San Diego where we stayed with my good old friend Nathan. He took us out to breakfast on the first morning, a place where Whoopi Goldberg used to wait tables. He then dropped us off in Pacific Beach and we rented our surf boards for the day. God damn those boarder shorts are not good with chaffing issues to the nads! Why don't they have terry cloth or something where the crotch is rather than just stitching for your balls to rub on? Who cares, the surfing was spectacular and Chad could now cross off that mission from his bucket list.

Our last stop was Las Vegas to see Rush once again. I was skeptical of seeing a show at MGM but it turned out to be just what I needed. The sound was great and best of all, powerful!

Mexico

I had never been on an exotic beach vacation in all my life until I received a text from my high school buddy, Todd, that he was planning a trip to Playa del Carmen. As usual I had no money, but also no life, so I committed. Todd covered the travel costs to allow me just enough spending money to enjoy the trip. (I would pay him back later.)

During the flight we were seated in the very back rows of the plane with no one else near us and the two young stewardess served us free drinks the entire flight. I vaguely remember landing or even passing through customs after many mixed drinks and some fun partaking in the "mile high club". (Right, even if I had the opportunity I would turn it down, it's not worth the anxiety and surely isn't a bucket list priority for me at all.)

We stayed in a cool villa that was all inclusive. The only problem was we visited off season and there was no girl action. We just drank by the pool during the day and went out at night. Again with little spending money I was limited on how much fun I could have in the evenings. Although we did take a boating/snorkeling trip as well as rented wave runners at one point during our stay. I was hoping to hit a nearby island and rent scooters to tour the island, but we slacked on that option due to grueling hangovers.

Michigan

During the summer of 2010 the entire family took a trip to Michigan to meet up with some in-laws. I traveled alone by train; a 24-hour trek in its entirety. The worst part about the train was when I booked my ticket the lady on the phone said there were no power outlets in coach seating. This was bad news in the fact that I wouldn't be able to bring my laptop and watch DVDs during the long haul. However this lady was full of shit as there we're outlets located at each seat. So without my distracting laptop entertainment I was forced to hang in the bar cart area most of the time checking out the scenery. This was quite an experience, even though it was dark during half the journey which made for a torturous number of hours with nothing to do or look at.

Although it was a long and boring trip I was glad that I traveled this way for the experience. And to tell you the truth I prefer it to air travel. Fuck airports and planes!

My few days in Michigan were wonderful. Since it was around the time of my birthday and Traverse City was hosting a film festival my sister treated me to the showing of *Rush: Beyond the Lighted Stage*. Michael Moore was in attendance for this wonderfully produced documentary based on the world's greatest band. I highly recommend it.

There was also time spent on Elk Lake where we all went waterskiing, wakeboarding, and my favorite activity of kayaking. The entire group of us also played some miniature golf and I road go-carts with my nephews.

Desert Rocks/Powellpalooza

During the last couple years of my 30s I attended two music festivals with a few of the KGLR pirate radio crew. We drove out to each event in my 4Runner packed with radio transmitting gear and my full drum kit.

The first Desert Rocks, 2010, was located just outside of Moab, UT and consisted of about 3,500 attendees. It was set up in a large open area of land with scattered trees and bushes so everyone made up their own campsites throughout. There were multiple stages with music playing all day and into the night. This was a great time, despite my one mishap with the festival hottie that I described in the

After the Fact portion of this book.

The second Desert Rocks, 2011, was located in an open desert scene and windy. My band Dillusiac met me out there and we set up our gear right outside the main stage area so we could be the pre/post show entertainment.

But instead of any epic eye catching performance that night I fell asleep in my 4Runner and never awoke until the next morning. I had to walk over to the jam site that following day and talk with my two bandmates to explain my bullshit. I felt awful as we had all planned this, made the long drive, set up so much gear under a huge tent we brought, and we never jammed. This was one very rare case where I was full blame to create such a fiasco.

Powellpalooza, 2011, was located in Lake Powell, UT. We had a hotel room this time and were allowed to party with the bands on house boats in the harbor. I met a couple cute girls who were promoting Camel cigarettes and made a great impression on them with promo talk and whatnot. The rest is history.

And now I move on to the grand finale of all trips I took to wrap up my 30s, the inevitable European Vacation. (Underrated movie with Chevy Chase as well)

EUROSCURSION (Spring 2011)

Before I started writing this book I had been itching to go to Europe. For *years* each spring would bloom and I would think about the option to hit Western Europe but it would never happen. I finally had to make a pact with myself and go before I turned 40. The funny thing was, like all the previous years of little work and lots of procrastinating, I still never had any money saved to go. But I did have an IRA savings account...

My IRA account had $11,500 in it and I decided it's time to live it up and cash out at least half of it for Europe, as well as pay off a loan that was eating at me. Well instead of half I withdrew it all! I cashed out the entire amount of my retirement, paid off the stupid loan and began to plan my European adventure. I kept this plan very quiet and never allowed anyone to know about it until just days before my departure. And the greatest part about this decision is that my departure for Europe would come in perfect timing after being on the road with my friend's band, Morsoul.

Dan and I had met while working at Dog House Music in the summer of 2009. We bonded as stoner drummers and within no time after we met Dan invited me on the road for two weeks in his converted veggie bus for an east coast tour. I would also play the role as band documenter and roadie during these two weeks. Many fine shows were played and the experience was priceless. Although I wasn't touring with my band it was still great to be on the road with like-minded musicians and able to visit many fine cities in the northeastern U.S. We even made a stop in Syracuse, NY and that gave me a chance to see a few relatives!

The two weeks on the road with Dan and band was a worthy experience. I departed from the gang the morning after a show in Philadelphia. I'll never forget that call to my mom, sitting on a park bench in downtown Philly as I was having my laundry done nearby, informing her I was about to board a plane for Europe.

LONDON

Day 1

I had to start my European adventure in London, no question. It is the main hub of Europe and I wanted to spend a few days there to get my grip on reality of being in another country.

After I landed in Heathrow, and taking a much-needed dump, I hopped on the Piccadilly underground tube en route to the main area of London where I would try and find a hostel. I loved the female English accent on the train announcing all the stops that were coming up, especially Cocksburg. And yes I minded the gap.

One of the first stops during the ride was the town of Hammersmith. This was the location of the famous Odgeon Theater where Rush and many other bands have performed at over the years. I got off the train and took my first picture of an amazing tree that was directly in front of an ancient building then made my way to find some juice or water for the trek. I did see the Odgeon but it was under a highway and wasn't that spectacular from where I was standing so I got back on the train to get to where I needed to be.

As I exited the train for the second time at Victoria Station I noticed how busy this place was. First priority was finding an ATM or money exchange station. After this I immediately found a pub to have my first official European meal. I sat at a typical London style pub and ordered a burger and a beer to revive myself.

Next I had to venture back into the station to find out where any hostiles were and which had availability. Turns out only one was adequate for me and this lady gave me a map and pointed the way. I put on my iPod and jammed out to the Sex Pistols in homage to where I was; my first time ever in Europe, starting off in London England!

It took me over an hour to find the hostel, all while holding in a brutal beer piss. This would not be the last time I would end up roaming around aimlessly to try and find many featured landmarks in London. It is so much harder to make your way around this city as compared to the easy grids of American cities, so I realized my ADD and awful sense of direction would be tested to the max for many days to come.

Day 2

My first morning up I enjoyed a nice cold shower then dressed up for my first adventure to the Camden district square. This is infamous for the London punk rock scene and I wanted to start my adventure there. I was very excited to take my first ever ride on a double decker bus! The top level is the way to go as the view is splendid. The bus ride took quite some time but it was well worth it from all the amazing architecture I observed and captured photos of.

As I exited the bus into the Camden district I strolled by a punk rock band that was playing in the street and they had quite a crowd gathered around them. Then I proceeded into the market square that had so many vendors and so much going on that this would keep me occupied for at least a couple hours. I couldn't decide on what food to order so I settled on pizza and ate it on seats that were made from scooter parts and overlooked a nice little canal. For this lunch break I became a MOD.

I then ventured around to try and find a punk rock style pub and get a drink. I failed to find a good pub but was burnt out and ready to return to the hostile. I did see a bunch of local punks hanging about and I was observing them as I engaged in the grueling task of finding the right bus to take back to the hostel and how to purchase a ticket. I was beginning to realize that Londoners aren't the best at friendly help when needed. It took me an hour to finally get on the right bus for the journey back to the Victoria area.

I had a ticket booked for the Jack the Ripper tour but missed it completely, as once again it took me way too long to get around and find the place. For the rest of the day I just road the double decker buses and roamed around various areas of London taking in the sites.

Later that night while I was lost in route to my hostel once again, I ran into these two younger girls that were sitting on some steps and drinking vodka. They were in pre-party mode for a rave that night so I hung with them for about thirty minutes before I had to hail a cab to get back to my hostel.

Day 3

After another fine breakfast of juice, coffee, and toast I headed out to find Abby Road Studios. I got lost and covered so much ground on foot before having to hail another cab to get my ass there. I was so annoyed and fired up until I finally reached Abby Road Studios. This was a bit surreal just knowing all that has happened in this place. Everyone was taking photos crossing the street where the Beatles did for their *Abby Road* album cover, so I asked this girl to take my photo crossing it as well. This was quite a task as so many cars kept zipping through there honking at all us stupid tourists. I took off my shoes to be barefoot and borrowed a cigarette to become the character of Paul McCartney.

After this experience I had intended to take a tour of the city, a castle, or something but wouldn't you know it, I was too late and missed all the tour buses. I did find a bus that would take me to the Tower of London so I was psyched to stroll through that attraction instead. It was very cool roaming around all the areas of the Tower and thinking about the violent things that occurred in that place.

Two hours later I was once again on an endless stroll to find the right bus to get me back to base camp. I walked around for at least an hour and a half not wanting to give into a cab ride and spend more money than needed. I did find a bus that took me back to Victoria and celebrated with a nice big plate of fish and chips.

London reminds me of Las Vegas in the fact that you really don't need anymore than three days there. It's an energy draining city after a while of sight-seeing and whatnot so don't prolong the adventure longer than necessary. I recommend taking some of the tours that are offered, if you can catch the right bus. Too bad I missed seeing Leeds Castle and the White Cliffs of Dover.

AMSTERDAM

Day 4

On board the Eurostar en route to Amsterdam! I sat next to this cool Aussie who was heading to Brussels for some sight-seeing.

When I reached Amsterdam I tried to reconfirm with some regulars about where to get off. Well some local jackass told me to stay on the train until the end, which took me about ten minutes past the main city into the airport station. This was a drag as it was getting late and I still had to find a hostel. My savior ended up being an American lady who helped me back on the correct train with her and she gave me a big can of Heineken to enjoy as we traveled. She even used her smartphone to help me find a hostel for the night once I reached the main part of the city. Bob's Hostel.

I got off the train and immediately noticed thousands of bikes parked at the train station. It was unreal, and I was also being gazed upon by a bunch of cab drivers who were hoping I would give in for a ride to my destination. Nope, stubborn me decided to venture into the city by foot at what was now one in the morning.

Just like London I had the worst time finding my way around Amsterdam. I walked around until three in the morning, passing through the many canals and the Red Light district with all these ladies in windows trying to get my attention.

Day 5

I ventured out of the Bob's Hostel towards the Torture Museum. Best part about this is I could carry around a big can of beer without being harassed. I hit my first coffee shop along the way and purchased a joint for the adventure.

I picked a nice spot to relax and enjoy my drink and smoke, just before entering the Torture Museum. (No rehash needed here, you can imagine what awful stuff a torture museum displays.)

Back at the hostel everyone was smoking up and chatting about whatever. I observed one guy who was so messed up he was shaking and starring at the floor. Then I looked over to see these two attractive girls sitting alone and had to make a move. They were both from Italy, just visiting like me.

We talked for a while and as one wanted to take a nap the other decided to join me at the coffee shop just behind the hostel. A barista who went by the name Yellow served us. We proceeded upstairs into this artsy area with benches and we were surrounded by amazing wood carvings. We smoked up and tried to carry on conversations but it was hard for her to grasp my English over the loud music. There was a group of guys in the other corner who couldn't take their eyes off her and this made me feel proud that it was finally my turn to be the lucky guy with the hottie for once.

Day 6

I had no plans for this day except to smoke out a bunch and venture the Red Light District in the night hours. I met a young couple from Connecticut who had been traveling Europe together for eight months! We chatted for a while then went our separate ways.

By nightfall I was on foot to the Red Light District and ran into a few American dudes. We ventured around together analyzing all the girls checking us out from the windows. They informed me that the windows that display purple or blue lights are those that are comprised of transvestites or transgender folk. Good to know, thanks for the tip my lads.

Like London it's so hard to find things when you need them. I was walking all over just trying to find an ATM so I could get a hooker--I mean cash for food and booze.

Day 7

After I finished another crappy hostel breakfast I sat in the lobby smoking my joint and noticed another guy sitting alone smoking as well. We started talking and turns out he was from Canada. I was relieved that I had someone who would be easy to converse with. I told him my plans to get some magic mushrooms and roam the city for the afternoon. He liked this idea and mentioned there was a huge park on the other end of town that would be great to trip in, so the plan commenced.

As we were gearing up for this adventure the two Italian girls walked by us and they became part of the plan. Then another young guy joined in who was from Oxford. We sat at a table and planned our route, where each of us was assigned a nickname for what our intent was during the journey. I can't recollect how a few of the names came to be, but here is the list:

Prozita, Plettra, Zaino, Tom Tom, Scatter Boy (Guess who

was Scatter Boy)

We proceeded to the nearest mushroom shop and the nice fellow behind the counter gave us a menu and described every type of trip we could take. It was overwhelming but we settled on some mushroom rocks as they were called. Four of the five of us munched down the chunks of rock and it tasted so bad that the one Italian girl who ate some ended up puking them right back out into a trash can.

We strolled along through the city with us three guys starting to trip and the giggly girls just venturing along with us. Thankfully we had the Canadian, Tom Tom, who had navigated through the city to the big park the previous day so there was little worry about getting lost. But as the buzzes kicked in more it became a bit nerve racking to deal with the reality of our surroundings. We were amongst all sorts of amazing architecture and lots of other people roaming about; many of them on bicycles whizzing by us constantly. We kept pausing during the journey unsure whether to stop and enjoy the trip or just get to our main destination.

We reached the main entrance of the park and had a quite a time getting across the street as tons of cars and bikes were constantly moving all over and we could not figure out the street light system. We did make it and were relieved to finally be in the park and able to enjoy our trip.

We were immediately greeted by a couple homeless vagrants; one guy was dressed like Mad Max and kept making passes at the girls, and the older guy was roaming around in circles just checking us out as he talked to himself. Tom Tom was focused on Mad Max and I was keeping an eye on this older freak. We told them we needed to bail and moved on.

They followed us for a bit until they got the hint that their company was not invited. Then the girls decided to head back to the hostel, which made me and the guys nervous as we were so paranoid on how vulnerable they were being alone. But they assured us that they were going to get a cab and be fine.

Me and the fellows found a bench to sit at and took in the scene of amazing vegetation, water, and park animals amongst us. At one point a huge bird flew right at us and the other guys freaked out and leapt off the bench in fear. Then they had to piss (somehow I didn't have to go for once) and it took them about ten minutes to get the nerve to find some bushes and release their bladders, as none of us knew how harsh the penalty might be for public urination.

We remained on this bench for about an hour and I noticed the sun was already going down and it was getting cold. We were not too psyched having to deal with departure from our trip so soon but it had to happen. We ventured back through the park and hailed a cab as our savior. The cab driver took us on quite a ride, driving fast and aggressive. Since I had shotgun it was like I was in a live video game.

We found the girls at the hostel and invited them out to eat. While the gang ate dinner I hit a pub down the street. I grabbed a table, got a beer, and just sat there observing the atmosphere. While sitting at the bar this wild Aussie guy jumped up from a couch and gouged his head on a hanging lamp. He had a nasty gash in his bald head and was bleeding all over but refused any help and continued his storytelling.

After about an hour went by the others still hadn't come to the pub so I strolled back to the hostel. They were all hanging out in the lobby and the three of us guys were pondering the reality that we all had early flights the next morning. I had to get on the internet and book a flight to Oslo.

OSLO (A Day from Hell)

Day 8

I slept through my alarm and had to frantically get out of the hostel. I was running through town towards where I thought the train station was but headed in the wrong direction. I tried asking for help a couple times but my ADD was in overload and once again had to settle on a cab.

I exited the cab and ran into the station to buy a train ticket but my credit card was not reading properly. I was in such panic by this time I had to have someone lend me a couple euros to get a ticket and run onto the train just before departure.

I arrived at the airport, made it through customs, and literally jumped into the plane as the gate was closing. I was rewarded with the fact that the scenery looking out the window was amazing, observing all these drifting ice chunks in the Norwegian Sea as we approached Oslo.

As I exited the plane I noticed a bunch of guards with sniffing dogs at the end of the terminal. I passed by them only to suddenly feel a hand grab me on the shoulder. "This way sir." a stern voice said.

I was escorted over to another area of the airport and the guard said that the dogs detected drugs on me. I was very surprised and wondered if all the weed and drugs from Amsterdam were still lingering on my clothing, so I was not very concerned. They told me to empty out all my pockets and searched through my backpack. Then suddenly in my left cargo pocket I found a smashed up "space cake" that I had purchased in Amsterdam the day before. It was half a chunk all smashed up from being in my pocket as I slept on it the night before. I gave a look of "oops" and all eyes gazed upon me as I held the chunk.

They took me into a small holding room with one steel bench to sit on. I remained in this room for about an hour, all the while different people kept coming in and asking me more questions. I was still not too worried as I figured they would understand I came from Amsterdam, was cooperating, and it was such a small chunk of cake in the first place. That was until they insisted on a strip search. I had to get fully naked in front of about three officers and they had me squat over a mirror to check and make sure I had nothing stuck up my ass. This is when I started to get agitated.

I was led down to another room in the airport and told that I owed a huge fine. I had to go into the airport bank and try numerous times to have money transferred from my account so I could get enough to pay them. Turns out there was no way it was happening so they had to settle on the few hundred I had on my debit card. (At least I got to flirt with this cute Norwegian blonde who was working the bank window.)

They threw me back into another room where I stayed for a

torturous three hours. I demanded food and they instead gave me a blanket so I could try to nap on the comfy steel bench.

I was transferred again to yet another room where a few others were being detained as well. This really sucked since there was barely any room to sit and this one guy could not stop pacing back and forth and kept asking if he could smoke. At this point I was getting depressed and realizing I might be more screwed than I thought, and then the really bad news hit. I was to be deported back to the States in the morning.

They took a few of us from the airport, loaded us into a police van, and drove us a short distance to a nearby refugee camp. We all sat in a detaining room as they locked up our belongings. One by one we were strip searched again and led off to other rooms where we would stay the remainder of the evening, locked in a room for the night. Each room consisted of four beds and I was put in a room with three Middle Easterners. They stared me down and the guard made a comment, "We don't get many Americans in here."

Turns out my roommates were cool and offered me an apple and asked about my story. One older guy acted as the room leader. He had supposedly been in this place for over a year! They gave us a toothbrush, toothpaste, and deodorant then locked us in the room for the night, with a guard sitting outside in the hallway in case we needed the restroom or something. I was so exhausted by this point that I thankfully fell asleep.

Day 9

In the morning we were treated to a nice hostel style breakfast and watched some television until they were ready to transport us back to the airport for our deportation. I was escorted through the airport by two undercover officers and put on a plane to Newark, NJ.

I recall so many thoughts and feelings during the long flight; all that I went through and how overblown this whole ordeal was from just a small chunk of space cake. As if this wasn't painful and degrading enough, once I landed it took the shuttle about an hour to come pick me up and bring me to the sleazy hotel I would be staying at for the night.

Then I had to use the computer in the hotel lobby to book a flight from Newark back to Denver. After all this I just relaxed on my hotel bed, ordered a pizza, and watched television until I passed out once again.

And that was it, my European adventure cut short by over two weeks due to a simple, innocent mistake by me and the unjust laws of Scandinavia. I was banned from all of Europe for two years. (Aside from the UK which is exempt from the rest of Europe.)

The worst part about all this was I had a hot date with a girl to see Rush in Stockholm the day after my Oslo bust. Instead I was hanging out in a hotel room in Newark. She was one of the people I had to touch base with using that lobby computer about not being on my way to Stockholm but rather stuck in New Jersey for the night. How sweet it is.

The outcome that should've been was to spend one more day and night in Amsterdam and skip Oslo. The two Italian girls from Bob's Hostel were planning to see the sex museum the same day I traveled to Norway. I could've just slept in and had an extra 24 hours of fun in Amsterdam rather than putting myself through the frantic chaos of getting to Oslo. But like my dad I'm on a mission to take in as much as possible on any excursion I embark on.

When I think and write about the outcome of the trip it really stabs me in the heart how much pain that small chunk of space cake cost me. The opportunities lost are disheartening and who knows when another chance will arise to hit Europe again.

intermission

Back home I was privileged to share my European tales with my family at a dinner gathering for Mother's Day. Then as I finished sharing the stories about the Oslo incident I realized I still had the original round trip flight booked back to the States. A lightbulb went off in my head and I decided to book another flight back to London where I could finish up my original Europe excursion. I was not going to give in and live with the fact that I only experienced one week in Europe; London, Amsterdam, and a night in Oslo?
Fuck that I'm going back to finish what I started!

SCOTLAND

Glasgow

I was on the train to see Rush in Glasgow. The ride took hours to get from London to Glasgow so I entertained myself once again by staring out the window with my tunes rolling and appreciating all the landscape. I was darn proud that I didn't give up and was back in Europe!

At the end of the ride I ventured back to the bathroom and noticed a couple other guys wearing Rush shirts. I spoke with one, Dave, who was from Boston, MA and studying abroad. We hit it off and journeyed to my hostel quickly to stash our belongings and then hailed a cab to the venue. Funny that we got there too early before show time and walked back to the hostel for a beer before our adventure back to the venue once again.

Upon arrival at the concert location the second time I came across a sign that pointed to the venue and someone had written "CUNT" on the sign with a marker. How European is that! (Yes I took a photo)

Dave and I were not sitting together for the show so we decided to meet at a landmark afterward. The show was spectacular, cameras were allowed, and the locals around me were fun to socialize with.

By the end of the show I was determined to buy a souvenir of some sort and settled on a nice hoodie for $65 Euros.

I met Dave at the entrance and we proceeded back to my hostel for post-show celebration beers. We then agreed to meet in the morning and take a train into Stirling and venture the castle district.

Stirling

Dave and I hit the streets where we wandered through a trippy graveyard and began the long haul towards Stirling Bridge. I was so excited to be strolling through all the history from the days of violent battles in this area.

We crossed over the Stirling Bridge and had another hour-long trek to the William Wallace Memorial. The monument was spectacular and had over 200 stairs that led up to the top where the chilly winds kept us from staying up there too long. After we descended downward we ran into a character dressed as a classic Scottish warrior and he put on a solo skit for us and a small group of tourists. It was great as he was full of information and really animated in character.

We made our way back down to town where we had a couple brews at the William Wallace Tavern. It was so authentic with all these football fans watching a match and the older locals enjoying some fine whiskey. (Or "whisky" as the Scots spell it; as like the difference between the American spelling of "theater" and the European version "theatre") We had to get back to the station where we said goodbye and I headed on my own to Edinburgh.

Edinburgh

When I exited the train I was stunned at how breathtaking all the architecture was. This was what I was hoping for to experience that authentic European vibe. I waltzed along to my one and only hotel for my trip and settled in. Although I was exhausted from roaming castles all day I decided to venture around the city at twilight and take numerous pictures of all the fabulous architecture. This would turn out to be the best decision of my trip. I took so many amazing photos with the darkening sky that gave a real intense, gloomy effect to all the buildings. Even the Edinburgh Castle was all lit up.

I covered a lot of ground once again and took a break at this interesting tavern with purple lighting and a DJ spinning tunes. There was also a big screen behind the bar that was showing all these weird cartoons. It was the perfect scene I needed that evening.

Back at the hotel I took a long bath, utilizing the amenities of a nice hotel for once. In the morning I checked in my backpack and strolled through town up towards the castle. It was surreal to enter the main gate and take in all that made up this grand castle. I spent over an hour in there and was hungry enough where I had to eat something before my departure to the airport.

As I exited the castle I discovered a whisky distillery that had an hour-long tour. I had just enough time to kill and jumped on this opportunity. You start out riding in a fake barrel of whisky and video screens that tell the tales of brewing whisky from scratch to finish. Then you end up in the tasting room and finish the tour in another room that holds the world's largest collection of whisky bottles. There were a few bottles that peaked at over $1000 each.

From there I headed back into town and found a place to eat. I had the perfect window seat so I could observe all the action on the cobble stone street. However as I looked at my phone clock I realized time was ticking and I had to get back to the hotel, catch a bus, and make my flight to Belfast.

The airport was a distressed mess. The lines were so long and they had us empty out all our belongings, which sucked for me since I have my small backpack organized just right with all my crap for traveling. Long story short I barely made my flight once again, the shortest commercial jet flight in history clocking in at 35 minutes total.

IRELAND

Belfast/Bangor

After exiting the plane I had to begin the task of finding the right bus into Belfast. I lucked out and got on one fairly quickly and was dropped off in the middle of the city. There was a heavy drizzle and I had to make for a fast walk to find my hostel, only having to stop once to ask directions this time.

The hostel was Vagabonds. It remains my favorite of the European trip. It was three stories comprised of all sorts of cool rooms and a lounge area with a television, couches, and a multitude of instruments to play at will. The place was managed by a couple young Aussie girls and they set me up with internet and a beer. I was the only one who checked into the room I was in that had about fifteen cots in it.

I ended up back in the lounge area where a few others had congregated and we had many drinks together. Then someone spoke of a popular bar that everyone was going to hit later that night.

Paul would end up being my one roommate for the

evening; a dread-locked Jamaican who was raised in London. We hit the club together and it was full of other black people. Paul made the comment that it was the most black people ever seen at one place in Ireland's history.

Back from the bar later that night Paul rolled a spliff and we shared stories until the early morning hours.

The next morning I was clueless on what to do so one of the kind hostel workers mentioned this Black Cab company that takes people on tours of the city. This was a no- brainer because I wanted to learn more about the violent history of Belfast. This cabbie picked me up at the hostel entrance and proceeded to drive me around the city for almost two hours, telling me all about the history of Belfast. If you're ever in Belfast definitely partake in this Black Cab tour!

The next day I was on a train for Bangor. My mom's Irish heritage is from here so I was excited. I began my trek around Bangor taking photos of this great park full of spectacular vegetation and then walked all over the city trying to get to the port for more photos. Along the way someone had written over a "ONE WAY" sign to make it read: "BONER WAY". I thought this was the greatest thing ever to come across after being so annoyed from all the bloody walking.

Dublin

I took a bus ride to Dublin and on the way the time hit 21:12. That moment was not only a great connection to the band Rush but it was displayed in red digital numbers above a television screen that showed live video feed of where the bus was heading. Cool.

The arrival in Dublin was perfect as my hostel was located right by the bus station. For once I would not have to roam around asking numerous people where the fuck my hostel was. It was Isaac's Hostel which was located on the main drag near the huge needle that pokes into the sky at nearly a football field's length.

I entered my room and immediately headed out to find some authentic Celtic music and enjoy a Guiness of course. Dublin is a bit more expensive than the rest of the UK. My Guiness cost 7 Euros! And I think they even expect tips in Dublin. Oh well I enjoyed the music then ventured back to the hostel to wrap up the night.

The next morning I enjoyed breakfast in the cafe that was connected to the hostel and proceeded to take a video tour with my camera around this unique hostel. The basement was awesome! It was an abandoned wine cellar with huge leather couches. I settled on one and wrote in my journal while I listened to the entire U2 *War* album.

As the Queen of England was in town there was security all over the city and lots of attractions were closed, including the Guiness factory. I ventured out anyway, took a quick stroll through the university campus, and ended up at a huge wax museum.

After some time spent in the museum I proceeded to the Brazen Head, Dublin's oldest pub dating back to the 1100's. While I was ordering my beer I noticed a couple girls from my hostel and approached them. Turns out they were both from Sweden, but not the usual blonde, blue eyed divas you'd expect but rather dark skinned with black hair. We had some drinks and I enjoyed some soup. We exited the bar and there on the street were many football fans dressed up for the big game taking place later that day. I decided to get one of my infamous pictures of the group looking down into the camera. I then strolled onward and just took in the city sights.

Back at the hostel it was happy hour in the beer garden so I took full advantage of this. I met another Aussie, we had a couple brews together and I informed him of a pub crawl happening that evening. We both agreed to partake and walked a long way to the place where the kickoff for the crawl began. These two younger, small Irish brothers led the crawl and they got the group of over a dozen riled up and ready to hop.

The first pub featured a great acoustic Celtic band so I took some photos and bought their CD. The brothers noticed I was taking photos and nominated me the documenter guy for the rest of the evening. We hit about 4-5 pubs in all and I got very liquored up, enough to where I was flirting with all the Irish girls I could and taking more photos of me with them.

The next morning I had a vicious hangover and had to spend about an hour on the internet trying to plan out my quest back to England. I had quite a long walk to the port where the ferry would take me to Wales. I ate some greasy food and walked forever to find the port. It must have been a two-hour trek total and I barely made the ferry.

ENGLAND

Manchester

I caught another train that would take me into Manchester. I was supposed to see Rush on tour here as well but with time and money becoming more of an issue I decided to bypass this option. I ventured on to find my hostel but it turned out that I had not written down the correct address so I got off at the wrong station and walked all through town to end up nowhere. I had to go into a hotel and ask the desk personnel where I was. Luckily they had heard of my hostel and called it to get directions for me.

I ended up back on the train to the correct address and walked down a dark and gloomy street to where the Grapes Hostel was. As I entered it I noticed how trashed out it was; the carpeting was all torn up, walls unpainted, but the reward ended up being that I was given a private room all to myself with a big bed and shower! The owner found out I was the "lost guy" and bought me rounds of beer in the pub area. He and his friends were the classic Englishmen. We all talked about weird stories and this younger guy from Dublin joined in who was staying there. He had bi-polar disorder so we could relate to each other. In fact the next morning I ran into him again at the train station and he told me he was on his way to a shitty filing job. I could fully relate!

Liverpool

The best thing that happened to me during my journey through the UK was missing my train back to London, and rather catching a last-minute train to Liverpool. How was I going to let myself live with the notion of not seeing the home of the Beatles?

I was amazed with the amount of great architecture. I would rate Liverpool just behind Edinburgh for scenic ambience. Amsterdam was the most beautiful but we're now talking about authentic buildings and that sort of stuff.

Just after I checked in my backpack at the train station and ventured out the English rain came storming in. I had to run back and get my rain jacket to enable me to finish my tour of the city. I saw a cool outdoor amphitheater, a giant tomb, and an enormous cathedral. Along the way I ran into these two girls I had met on the ferry the day before and they pointed the way to the Beatles Museum.

It was a worthy stroll to get there as this museum features endless amounts of Beatles memorabilia. I spent a couple hours roaming around the place, without the stupid audio guide option. I never utilize that option as I am more of a visual person and like to move through things quickly. I rarely have time or patience to read information let alone listen to some voice on headphones telling me about things along the way.

I wrapped up the Beatles Museum portion of my adventure and strolled back to the station, grabbed my pack, and boarded the train for my last ride from Liverpool to London. To celebrate pulling off a semi-successful European trip I drank a couple more beers during the train ride and took my very last picture looking out the window during the sunset. My final salute to Europe. See you again someday!

NIBLETS & TIDBITS

Let's finish off this book with some amusing randomness.

TOP LISTS

Everyone has a list of their favorite things in life; you name it, we rate it. The concept of picking out a top five list for anything can be a bit formidable to anyone's thought process, so I will now rack my own brain with attempts to narrow down some of my favorite things into small lists of five. (Well let's make it five-ish.)

Holy shit here we go…

BANDS (by genre)

Progressive: Rush, Yes, Pink Floyd, Genesis, Porcupine

Tree

Classic Rock: Led Zeppelin, Police, U2, Who,

Scorpions

Alt Rock: Primus, Smashing Pumpkins, Tool, Weezer,

Rage

Grunge: Alice in Chains, Soundgarden, Nirvana, Pearl Jam, STP

Metal: Megadeth, Metallica, Pantera, Slayer, Ultraspank

Punk: Bad Religion, Sex Pistols, Agent Orange, Ramones, Pennywise

Rap: Beastie Boys, Tribe Called Quest, Public Enemy, Grandmaster Flash, NWA

Jam: Phish, Ozric Tentacles, whatever else, gahenga

Top 11 Bands (As influenced by Spinal Tap)

1. RUSH
2. Primus
3. Alice in Chains
4. Smashing Pumpkins
5. Tool
6. Yes
7. Led Zeppelin
8. Rage Against the Machine
9. Weezer
10. U2 (or Police?)
11. Pantera/Megadeth/Metallica

Top 11 Albums (most inspirational since childhood)

1. RUSH - "Exit...Stage Left"
2. YES - "Fragile"

3. CARS - “Cars”
4. RAGE - “Rage”
5. RHCP - “BSSM”
6. WHO - “Who’s Next”
7. U2 - “Unforgettable Fire”
8. BEATLES - “Rubber Soul”
9. LED ZEPPELIN - “Physical Graffiti”
10. SCORPIONS - “Love at First Sting”
11. METALLICA - “...And Justice for All” / MEGADETH - “Rust in Peace”

MUSICIANS

Drummers: Neil Peart, Tim Alexander, Stewart Copeland, Jimmy Chamberlin, Danny Carey, Will Calhoun, Philip “Fish” Fisher, John Fishman, John Bonham, Dave Weckl, Nick Menza, Brad Wilk, Pat Wilson

Guitarists: Alex Lifeson, The Edge, Steve Howe, Tom Morello, Matthias Jabs, Jerry Cantrell, Tim Mahoney, Marty Friedman, Dimebag Darrell, Adrian Legg

Bassists: Geddy Lee, Les Claypool, Michael Manring, Jeff Berlin, Chris Squire, John Patitucci, Paul D’Mour

Vocalists: Maynard James Keenan, Layne Staley, Brandon Boyd, Angelo Moore, Chris Cornell

Chicks: Breeders, Veruca Salt, Tori Amos, Liz Phair, Sneaker Pimps, Bjork

MOVIES

Epics: Almost Famous, Braveheart, Gladiator,

Goodfellas, Shawshank Redemption

Action: Departed, Beverly Hills Cop(s), Lethal

Weapon(s), Conan the Barbarian, Jaws

Comedy: Fletch, Big Lebowski, Vacation(s), anything

Chevy/Murphy or John Hughes

Sci-Fi: Star Wars, Starman, Fifth Element, Tron, Dark

Crystal, Time Bandits

Horror: Halloween(s), Saw(s), Evil Dead(s), Ring,

Exorcist

Indie: Pulp Fiction, Clerks, Across the Universe, American Psycho, Hot Dog

Directors: John Hughes, Quinten Tarantino, Cohen Bros, Martin Scorsese, Cameron Crowe, Terry Gillian, John Landis, Kevin Smith, Mike Judge…

Actors: Jack Nicholson, Robert DeNiro, Jeff Bridges, Samuel L. Jackson, Christian Bale, Philip Seymore Hoffman, Tom Hardy, Chevy Chase, Eddie Murphy, Morgan Freeman, Adam Sandler, Will Ferrell, Jason Lee, Ron Pearlman…

Hollywood Crushes: Olivia Newton-John (first ever), Milla Jovovich, Mila Kunis, Naomi Watts, Uma Thurman, Heather Graham, Amber Heard, Megan Fox, Jennifer Connelly, Jennifer Lawrence, Halle Berry, Kate Beckinsale, Elizabeth Hurley, Elisha Cuthbert, Jessica Alba, Evan Rachel Wood…and most any of the 90s era girl rockers out there, (Liz Phair, Gwen Stefani, Sheryl Crow, Veruca Salt…) and any of the many Sports Illustrated swimsuit models since it's conception. (Especially the 80s era divas!)

Quotes Galore:

My insightful, poetic analogies on life.

"The one true thing about destiny in life is that there is no destiny." (bathroom stall)

"My life is like progressive rock; most people just don't get it, yet I still progress and ROCK."

"Yet another magical thought instantly lost from my mind. When? Where? Why? How? More and more arrive and flow, neato neato, this BLOWS!"

"Here I sit, such greatness of wit, dynasty the emotion carries, but dwell on hope and thou shall perceive. Engulf the lengthy mold, the enchantment, the Golden Globe."

"Bless me oh Lord for this is my year. Let good things come and the misery disappear."

"I can say that although I've rarely kept a steady job, relationship, or established much structure throughout all my years, at least I've *experienced* life!"

"I'm constantly trying to live a life combining the personalities and ideologies of Keith Moon, George Carlin, Hunter S Thompson, Jack Kerouac, Ben Franklin, and a small dose of Charlie Sheen. Anyone want to trade?"

"Life is good, my reality sucks."

"I'm a FAG." (**F**reelance **A**rtistic **G**uy)

"To have an interest or fervor for arts & entertainment is one thing, to try and live it is a whole other ballgame."

"I'm not even skating on thin ice anymore but rather searching for ice to skate on!"

"I have the thickest skin of anyone I know, just no balls."

"Most people stress trying to find a sufficient living with a career that pays adequately for their skills offered. Artists are struggling and *paying* their way through life until their skills get noticed, appreciated, or god forbid compensated."

"I'm like the Bruce Jenner of the arts & entertainment world; a jack of all trades within the industry yet *only* really good within all these sectors and not excellent at one."

"The glass could/should be 80% full."

"Being an artist is a lot like working a dead-end job, in that there's little room for expansion beyond the lowest form of reward for effort. Except artists rarely earn any compensation for their sagacity and are forced to work a dead-end job to compensate."

"I'm a LEO; a god damned LION, not a fricking MANATEE."

"If most people say they are swimming against the current, then I must be swimming up a fucking waterfall."

"My mind is like a clogged drain; full of all kinds of interesting stuff but none of it ever loosens up to allow things to flow."

"If you look at life in relation to the edifice of a spider web, then my web is that of a Black Widow; still representing a structural element like all webs, but in more disarray."

"It's like I'm permanently stuck skating in a half-pipe; back and forth with bumps and bruises along the ride, while most everyone else is chilling in massage chairs; relaxed, pampered, and can get up and move on with their day at will."

"Living with minimal or no human connection and interaction is painful for the heart and soul, however dealing with humans can be such an injurious pain in the ass it ends up draining your heart and soul."

"Life is like The Wizard of Oz; we all have this path to follow and receive help from various sources along the way. It just helps so much more to have a Toto as your companion along the way."

"Life with a mental disorder is like having a fever, but unlike the rest of the world's inhabitants we only have the option to have our temperatures taken rectally, rather than orally."

"Life with a mental disorder is like having mild form of some chronic disease; medicine and therapy gives us some relief but there's no definitive cure."

"Life is like a flowing river; it offers various ports and stops as 'opportunities' along the journey. Some you pass up and regret, others you stop at and WHO CARES?"

"Artists who obtain fame and fortune from their accolades represent the planet Jupiter, whereas the rest of us are stuck in the distant abyss representing Pluto."

"An optimist likes to filter out the bad and focus on the good, while a realist wants to fix the bad and make things more genuinely good."

"I have too many balls in my court, just need others to grab whatever ball is there's and not leave it with me. Step up to the plate and reciprocate motherfuckers, before I kick you in the balls!"

“Really sucks when you have the talents, perseverance, and everything required for the arts & entertainment world, but the industry itself, along with certain people, trends of the times, and no legit connections or monetary backing, FUCKS YOUR FATE.”

“Before your artistic proficiencies are discovered and appreciated you’re constantly being fucked in the ass by the industry and world in general. When you do get that lucky break into fame and tremendous accolades for your craft the world suddenly changes its mind and wants to suck your cock.” (My asshole is closed for business. Who’s ready to start opening their fucking mouths?)

“My mind is that of a circus tent full of performers and spectators high on cocaine and LSD.”

“Conservatives will always be assholes, Liberals will always be pussies. Where’s the cock and balls in this country?” *(We desperately need a Common Sense Party)*

“I prefer women like my skateboard trucks; TIGHT.”

“Do as much as you can with what you got.”

“Shaved pussy is #1” (bathroom stall)

“I don’t dream big, I dream medium.”

“Doing nothing is underrated.”

“As if floating around on an ice burg it’s nice to let life take its course, yet at some point we all have to take the plunge into the frigid water and swim to land.”

“People seem more stressed and depressed dealing with these hard times. I’m stressed, depressed, and *always* dealing with hard times.”

“Korn is Tone Loc meets Faith No More” (Stoner moment, but a friend agreed with this?)

“Your wife is HOT. Time to fix your AC.” (billboard)

“Everyone in America says they work their ass off, then I ask how come we have so many fat asses roaming around the land?”

“My life is a metaphor relating to a cracked bowl; I seem to hold everything together for a while but shit constantly leaks out or the bowl eventually breaks.”

“American Spirits represent the purest of all cigarette brands, just too bad the American spirit and our purity has been dumped into an ashtray.”

“Everyone says I’m so nice, genuine, and awesome, yet so many of these same folks diss me, leave me hanging, back out on promises/plans…Here’s a concept; practice what you preach! Commit to what you say, follow through with more things, and be nice, genuine, and awesome yourself.”

“I’m either going to kill myself pursuing it or get killed while accomplishing it.”

"No need for tattoos, bracelets, or any bling. My aura

speaks loudly enough."

"Life is a never-ending internship of trial and error."

"Working dull pointless jobs for a creative-minded individual is like what kryptonite is to Superman; they constipate momentum and eat away at your true powers in life."

"I sure have *done* a lot, just haven't *accomplished* shit."

"For me a hit of good weed is an immediate launch into Heaven, followed by a nose dive right into Hell.

"At least we still have heart to support our troops, otherwise we only support and over-worship our athletes, entertainers, or anyone with high status and fame."

"Funny to live in a world where you can make a living sucking dick but might not ever make more than pocket change exploiting innovative capabilities you possess."

"With an overwhelming abundance of ideas flowing through my mind and so many projects unfinished, it's to the point where I need jumper cables (connections/help) to jump start my aging engine (head/ass) to get anything completed."

"Funny that I hate people and circumstances that make my life a miserable challenge, yet I seem to make my own life a miserable challenge."

"America is a one of a kind entertaining shit show set in an amazing theater."

"So sad to live in a world where honesty gets you in more predicaments than lying."

"I get why the homeless prefer booze and drugs to food, because being stuck in a bland, lonely, hopeless, painful reality is much more tolerable when intoxicated, DUH."

"It's like I'm taking the SATs with a gun pointed at my head while fighting the flu."

"I'm sick of the 80s always being overpraised after all these years. I don't want any more sugar poured on me, I don't want to be shook all night long, I don't want to run so far away. Let's move the fuck on!"

"More creative when stoned, more focused when sober. Notice more interesting things and details when stoned, remember more when sober. What's a guy to do?"

"It's like I've been given the world's most awesome dog that I never get to pet."

"Most seem to cruise along in life pretty consistently, some just need to get their tires rotated and balanced more often."

"I've got balls of steel and Red Bull for blood."

"Become the CEO of the life you live."

"I'm like a stick of dynamite with no fuse."

"I'm a Punk Rock Hippie Jock."

"My life progresses at a pace that can be compared to the agonizing time it takes getting a large pot of water to boil at high altitude. I just want the water to boil so I can start adding in all the flavorful ingredients and finally eat!"

"My lifestyle is about as consistent as Oprah Winfrey's

weight."

"Hail to the butt-crack professions!"

"The glass *is* half full…of bullshit."

"My life is that of a twisted film; mixing the constituents of a John Hughes production, Quinten Tarantino script, and directed by Stanley Kubrick."

"It's my birthday, think about that a bit. I'm forty years old? HOLY SHIT."

"My life is like vegetable soup; it's healthy and full of goodness, but every so often you bite into a lima bean or something yucky."

"I have the amazing tendency to procrastinate with many of my objectives for months, yet I can configure out a practical solution or miraculous idea within minutes."

"Most people experience marginal amounts of pain throughout their lifetime, while I experience marginal amounts of pleasure."

"My appearance is vanilla, but I'm really a Baskin Robbin's store full of flavors."

"If the world is that of one big moldy cupcake with the frosting covering up the unpleasantness of the world, then I'm the master at adding colorful sprinkles on top, to at least keep things vibrant and interesting."

"Just as it's nearly impossible to find the perfect item of clothing (the right fit, comfort, style) it's equally as hard to find the perfect combo of ideal traits in another human."

"It would be great if you could replace a dysfunctional brain like you can replace bad transmissions or engines in a vehicle."

"My space shuttle is all packed and ready for launch, just need the rocket boosters."

"My struggles in life are that of trying to conquer Mt. Everest. Yet I'm trying to summit with a hangover and no oxygen along the way."

"I feel like I've been handed the most forgiving prison sentence possible."

"If it comes to burning a bridge with someone, don't bring

a match, bring dynamite!"

"I'm sick of collecting tadpoles all my life, it's time to

catch a Marlin!"

"In this world it's more worthy to be great at one thing rather than really good at many."

"Most people deal with that occasional bad day, whereas I

anticipate that occasional good day."

"Drama is great, unfairness sucks."

"The Earth is beautiful, too bad humans can be so vile."

"I'm too much for this world and it's too much for me."

"Everything in the Universe is amazing. Except my life!"

"I'm on a path like everyone else, except mine still contains wet cement."

"An artist without an agent or any management is like Popeye without his spinach."

"An artist without management is like a bathroom stall with no toilet paper. You can get the main job done then there's always gonna be more shit to deal with."

"Life is random. Some people get through it easy; riding on a plane, train, or yacht, whereas most get by with a car, truck, or bike. And the least fortunate are stuck with scooters, skateboards, or their own two feet."

"My life is about as predictable as a coffee-induced poop; it's going to commence and be something each day but what actually prevails is never foreseeable."

"Will the stories I write and things I document be a reflection of the adventures I experience, or a prelude to my demise?"

"Suffering takes more courage than dying." (Napoleon, I concur)

"I'm writing on a soap dispenser, take that society!" (public bathroom)

"If you're going to ban steroids from sports, you might as well ban Pro Tools from music." Zack Wylde (Revolver interview, April 2005. Too much digital BS in music.)

"The privilege of a lifetime is being who you are. Follow your bliss and the universe will open doors where there were once only walls." (Joseph Campbell)

"Destiny, protect me from the world." (Radiohead)

"If you get the inside right, the outside will fall into place."

(Eckhart Tolle)

"Well if the inside is wired properly no problem, but for many there's a lifelong battle to fix the inside and henceforth might not ever get the outside fall into place." (RGH)

"NOTHING is set in stone anymore. Most things are set in quicksand. An agreement is made, a handshake and/or business cards exchanged with a smile of anticipation and excitement, but what that smile really says is, 'Sounds great, but I'm going to fuck you.'" *(Agreements or simple plans are established, but rather than any type of solid foundation for further progress it's usually all set in quicksand and disappears before the outcome of the agreement or plan is ever able to exist in the first place!)*

"I'm made up as a comparison to the layers of the Earth. The Crust is my outer shell; the healthy appearing physical package that all people see. The Mantle is the most prominent layer; representing my inner emotional issues and reality of my surroundings. The Outer Core represents my true persona and multitude of ideas and talents, and the Inner Core is my soul/spirit. I must fix the Mantle and relish more in the Outer Core, as the Inner Core remains deeply hidden with anticipation to shine." (Whateverness.)

Facebook Status Updates

I couldn't leave you hanging without having you read through some of my more infamous Facebook update postings over recent years. These are more random quotes, thoughts, opinions, and goofy statements of mine that made it into the virtual world for many to ponder over:

2112 DAY, YEA

Looking for something to do during the late hours of the evening? Get high and watch American Psycho in Spanish.

Happy Birthday Jesus! Please come back from the dead and slap our brainwashed faces out of this technologically dependent world of iHELL.

New Year's; a classic American holiday full of booze, fights, hangovers, DUIs and "resolutions" that no one ever has the will power to live up to. Oh sure, quit smoking (again) and no more daily porn surfing of course.

Whether you ski, board, or go both ways like me (huh-huh) nothing on the slopes is as demanding and gratifying as ripping through a tight line of bumps. Twice the effort and fatigue as steeps or powder, with twice the rush. Hail mogul skiers and Mary Jane!

NO MORE TIPPING!!! Every time I order a regular coffee (and sometimes a scone or other overpriced carb-sugar-filled shit) I always tip a buck, and I'm the last person that believes in karma, superstition, or any of that BS, someone bitch slap me!

*Brendon- Consider yourself slapped.

A Groupon for ballroom dancing. Sounds beyond enticing.

Vegan Entrepreneurs meetup group? Is this a joke? Must be

Boulder-based, LAME.

What happens in Vegas...should happen more often!

Holy shit it's amazing what thrilling news you can discover through one of our many wonderful mediums that feed us information. Just learned the cello player for ELO died in a freak car accident: A bale of hay struck his van and killed him in England.

I passed the 'Are you a Megadeth fan' quiz with flying colors. I am just that cool, and now Dave will hunt me down as his 8th or 9th drummer, just wait.

A quote you'll never hear someone say while on their death bed: "Sure wish I spent a little more time at my dead-end job."

Don't worry there's still a movement happening, it's just very slow and scattery, like my bowel movements." (In response to a friend criticizing the current music scene)

After watching the season finale of Metal Evolution on VH1 Classic, it's unleashed the notion how sorry I feel for all these vanilla coated suburban Boulderites. Being how open-minded, artistic, and intellectual this region is it's unfortunate that no one gives metal any credit! These stoned out jammy tweaked freaks are innovative and talented but could never handle the audacity and extreme intensity that goes into playing \m/etal.

Strange that most all my favorite bands have the most annoying singers: RUSH, SMASHING PUMPKINS, RADIOHEAD, MEGADETH, PRIMUS...yet the proud beauty of this perception is that the musicianship is beyond worthy to even care about the vocal element anyway. Amen.

A true, authentic friend is someone who will take time from their schedule to help you with a simple task. A modern day friend can't even respond to a call, text, or email asking advice of anything. Fuck you very much to the modern day fickle, flaky, self-absorbed bullshit “friends".

Awesome breakfast at Sunrise/Sunset, Broncos game with a friend, then band rehearsal. All followed by Stanley Kubrick movies into the early morning hours.

Colorado drivers can suck it. I'm gonna start ramming thy annoying wussy inconsiderate nimrods if they don't wake up and MOVE IT. Driving a vehicle is one of the world’s easiest tasks, yet so many suck at it. Just fucking drive bitches!

Besides appearance, how can you easily decipher a GenXer from Boomers or Millennials? Those other's voicemail box is full. (HaHa get it? As Boomers don't know how to check their voicemail and Millennials don't know that it still exists.)

Two Week Flu (February 2011)

I caught the flu which kept me horizontal for two full weeks, and rather than miserable it turned out to be two of the most fulfilling weeks of my life! I spent all this time viewing a plethora of inspiring documentaries on Netflix "instant watch". I was feeling just crappy enough to keep me away from work and other obligations but okay enough so I could "enjoy" this time of sickness with undistracted, relaxing entertainment. The flu gave me uncompromising freedom to become that much more educated in life from viewing all these fine films. Thank you flu!

Here's a list of the documentaries I digested during this

two-week period:

Exit Through the Gift Shop
Beautiful Losers
Monster Camp
Super High Me
Gonzo
You're Gonna Miss Me
Moog
Blood Into Wine
Inside Deep Throat
Confessions of a Superhero
Parking Lot Movie
Bukowski: Born Into This Champion

Man on Wire
Skid Row
I'm Still Here
Don't You Forget About Me
The Last Dispatch
Frontline: Storm Over Everest
Tales From the Script
Bangkok Girl
I'm Trying to Break Your Heart
Wilco
American Grindhouse
After Innocence
Rising Son: Christian Hosoi
Stress: Portrait of a Killer
Hoop Dreams
It Might Get Loud
LoudQUIETLoud: Film About the Pixies
Van Halen Story: The Early Years
Frank Zappa/Mothers of Invention: 1960s
Flaming Lips: Fearless Freaks
Chain Camera
Fire on the Mountain
Jimmy Hendrix
Stupidity
Stripped
Bad Religion: The Riot
Edgeplay: A Film About the Runaways
Heavy Metal in Baghdad
I Need That Record!
Put the Needle on the Record
Rock Prophesies
Girl 27
John Entwistle: An Ox's Tale
Cream: Classic Artists
Scott Walker: 30 Century Man

We Jam
Econo: Story of the Minutemen
Radiohead: OK Computer
Barenaked in America
Face to Face: Shoot the Moon
New York Dolls: All Dolled Up
Bela Fleck: Throw Down Your Heart
Air Guitar Nation
The Industry

I kid you not, I watched all 55 of these wonderful documentaries during my two weeks on the couch. Well maybe I skimmed through some of them, but either way it was the best experience I've ever had while feeling like shit.

COMEDIC INTENTIONS

Now we reach the portion of the *Spin Cycle* where I dump all sorts of random nonsense into one chapter that will have you in a whirlwind of emotions. This is the true nature of how my brain thinks and how I can come up with such an array of uncanny thoughts.

Random Thoughts (Derived from my crazed mind)

- How much wood would a woodchuck hump, if a woodchuck could hump wood?

- What color is a smurf's poop?

- I'll bet a fig newton could kick the crap out of a Twinkee.

- When you make a snowman completely out of yellow snow, do you get bonus points?

- If you collected all your naval lint during one lifetime how big a ball would you have?

- If you masturbate with Lava hand soap will you have an "erupting orgasm"?

- What if your penis came with various settings for urinary fulfillment: spray, stream, massage, mist…a nice way to enhance "golden showers" as well.

- I recently took a piss in a toilet only to have the bubbles form a near-perfect rendition of the North & South American continents! I kid you not, this has actually happened to me *twice* before while pissing. (Take notice as to what cool shapes your piss bubbles make.)

- Buggars, farts, and vomit, OH MY!

- Why is *gray* spelt two different *weys*?

- Why do some people pronounce orange *arange*? Well if that's the case then I must have two *orms* not arms?

- #1 demented sex fantasy: To be sodomized by a troll.

- What is going through the mind of a Goth?

- Shit Dick (title for a gay porn movie)

-

- If I had my choice to do it all over again, I'd come back to Earth as an Omish bum.

- Funny to tell a fly to eat shit and die, that's exactly what they do!

- A nice relieving piss beats an average orgasm (add a fart to the mix, sumptuous)

- How about segregated graveyards? (WHITES ONLY, GAYS ONLY)

- Ever fill in the enclosed letters and numbers on a sheet of paper during a boring seminar or lecture? (o, 8, d, p) I sure do.

- I love when you cough up a loogie so dense you can chew on it like a piece of gum.

- Not a good idea for any dad to offer his son a Blow Pop sucker: "Hey son, wanna *Blow Pop*?"

- Ever notice the subliminal sexual messages that Nestle, Hershey's, and Mars companies put in their candy? Mr. Goodbar (the Gigolo), Snickers (necking/foreplay), Pixie Stick (dip and suck), Gobstopper (diaphragm), Jolly Rancher (all animals must hide!), Baby Ruth (not only sounds like incest, but looks like human excrement as well) Blow Pop, Milky Way, Zagnut, Almond Joy, Oh Henry!

- Guys, never use black condoms. Black is a thinning color.

- When is the BET (Black Entertainment network) gonna get with the times and become AAET? (African-American Entertainment network)

- Ever notice when talking to someone you can only focus on one eye? Then you go berserk trying to pick which one to look at, or get a headache trying for both.

- Haven't you always wanted to go up in one of those hydraulic telephone pole repair boxes? I have.

- Wouldn't it be funny if our culture said, "Fuck you" instead of "Bless you" after a sneeze? Maybe not.

- Ever notice when trying to pass someone while driving your old, small, gutless car that we have the urge to press as hard as we can on the accelerator, as if it makes a difference on your speed when the pedal has already reached the floor board with normal pressure. *(I don't particularly like this observation, although true it's also dumb.)*

- Why is it that almost every fricking nature show is hosted by some old, white foreigner?

- Horses are scary animals. Think about it, one of these things paralyzed Superman for Christ's sake! Christopher Reeves spent the remainder of his life on wheels with tubes stuck in him due to one of these creatures. Kryptonite? No. A FUCKING HORSE!

- Wouldn't it be funny if we talked to dogs in human voice, and humans in "dog".

- Remember getting in trouble as a kid and your parents

said you were in trouble with a capital T? How about a *lower case* ‘t’ for once mom?

- Imagine some famous people taking a difficult dump:

Arnold: "Get out!"
Adam Sandlcr: "You will exit my anus now you stubborn shit!"
George Bush: "Barb, I'm having some trouble in here…"
Chris Farley: "Oh my god! It's stuck! Son of a…"
Dan Quale: (singing) "I'm taking a shit, taking a shit, C-H-I-T shit."

- Ever wonder who and where the original people are that were recorded as the background laughing for sitcoms and stuff? Mostly dead by now, but still.

- Here's an idea for a doll: The Manute "Smoke-a-Bol" doll.

- Think how fucked up a gay bulimic is: They got stuff entering and exiting out of the wrong holes!

- Don’t you hate it when you are walking across a hall or quadrant and you see you’re about to veer into that other person’s path, and you can’t decide whether to speed up or slow down before you bump into the other person? No? Fuck you.

- How about a TV/radio show where all the language is bleeped out *except* the cursing?

- Farfeinugan: Something that occurs when you sneeze and fart at the same time.

- Bathroom “Guest Books”: Okay, how about a “Defecation Log Book” that you write in and describe your dumping experience: size, texture, number of wipes/flushes…

- Gag Scratch ‘n Sniff stickers: Teva Feet, Armpit Odor, Inner Cheek Fungus, Sweaty Socks, Puke, Toe Jam, Belly Lint…

- H&R Block? How about T&A Block: Topless women doing your taxes.

- How about a game for a Bachelorette Party: “Pin the Cock on the Hunk”

- Would you fuck a Gelfling? (Ha, and reasoning for my Facebook URL: fizzgig

- Don’t you hate that jackass who feels the need to take the stall right next to you when there’s others open. Like he needs a poop buddy for security or something.

- Always a treat to be talking about someone and get caught by *that* person.

- Ever blow your nose and you hear that little squeak noise like a leaking balloon?

- Next time you gas up your vehicle, notice what the ending price is and think about what happened there at that exact location on that date. Example: $17.86 total, so what was happening right there during 1786? Now gas is so fucking expensive these days that you can only predict what will happen at that location years from now: $65.39,

6539.

- Funny moment in life when you hear the entire song from a blurb you heard during an infomercial or as background music to a commercial. It's hard to accept it as a whole song, sounds weird at first, but life goes on.

- While in the restroom at certain restaurants they teach you a foreign language over the intercom. If taking a piss, one might learn a few new words or even a sentence. So imagine what can be accomplished during the average dump. Great concept!

- Why do some public restrooms put the urinal right next to the sink? Smart call.

- I think God is gay. (The rainbows prove it.)

- Do Mexicans celebrate the 5th of May? (As we Americans celebrate Cinco de Mayo.)

- Microwaves: Notice how they always have the pre-settings; Popcorn, Beef, Defrost, etc. What are the pre-settings in Asian countries? Dog, Cat…

- Why do household fans always have a toggle knob that turns from "Off" to "High" and then "Low"? This goes against all logic! Off, Low, High is the way.

- Talk Show: Like Jay Leno's "Headlines", how about "Bad Moments in Karaoke".

- Why does it seem more honorable to grab a beer out of the garage fridge rather than the kitchen fridge?

- Death: When I die I want my ashes dropped in a series of shot glasses. Just add water and whatever part of me you got will grow back. (Girls, then you may actually get to take a true "blowjob shot" after all.)

- Ash Vase: Big clear glass vase that you collect family member's ashes in; mark the layers of individuals as the years go by for all to see.

- Silence is Golden. (Especially if you're deaf and being pissed on.)

- Ever notice how dogs drink their water in broken time? (This question was mainly intended for musical nerds, but all should take notice from now on.)

- Unlike girls, guys have no major faults at all. (Except being alive and having a penis.)

- Life's philosophy of a starving artist: Do Drugs, Create Art, Hump Hotties

- TMI? How about NEI (**N**ot **E**nough **I**nformation) I fricking hate vagueness!

- What ever happened to all those John 3:16 signs at football games? I guess Jesus don't matter no more.

- Pizza: One person always gets stuck with the smallest piece, or the one piece with the big air bubble on it. Lame.

- Imagine Snow White masturbating while watching her 7 dwarfs sodomize each other.

- Imagine each phase of Michael Jackson being all your

siblings in one fucked up family.

- Imagine a U.S. President sticking a cigar up some fat, pasty white intern's pussy.

- Ever shake someone's hand and their wrist "clicks"? Yuck!

- WFL (Women's Football League) "Bull Dykes on Parade" for opening music.

- Reality Show: Lock up 5 people in a mansion compound for 12 hours, each on a different drug with helmet cams included, follow their adventures.

-How about a Cat Dome. Like a Dog Park but rather a dome with a bunch of cat toys and carpet obstacles all over the place, and the ground is sand to act as one giant litter box.

- I hate how our alphabet is set up so you have to emphasize certain letters with examples as you talk to someone: B as in "boy", D as in "dog", M as in "mortuary". Fuck this, I want a new alphabet!

- How about a cookbook called *Stoner Snacks* (Actually it would be a one page pamphlet with giant bold lettering stating: 7-11 IS YOUR CALLING)

- Barf bags should have the scent of BBQ, hotdogs, baked beans, and such to get the person to vomit without any hesitation or uncertainty.

- Lamest things included in any drum kit: wind chimes, fake 'clap' noise effect, 14" floor toms.

- Love it how in each household there's always as least one clock that never gets reset for the time change. Fuck yeah!

- Speed bumps piss me off just enough to where I drive faster than needed in between each one. Not cool.

- I hate it when you're leaving work on a Friday and the boss stops you and must go over the game plan for Monday. "Fuck you! The week is over and I only have two days off, which just started now, it can wait, prick."

- INSANITY? Next time you listen to music with headphones on notice when the singer gasps for air before singing each line. While watching a basketball game close your eyes and listen to the squeak noises made from the shoes on the court. Go into a WalMart, hang out by the checkout lines and compose a shitty song out of the broken melodic pattern derived from the continuous beeping noises made from the register scanners.

- My poop smelled so bad the other day the auto toilet flushed twice!

- Why can't people just put a new roll of toilet paper onto the roller? Rather they always plop the new roll onto the back of the toilet, sink counter top, or balanced on top of the roller itself. Really?

- How come the driver's side windshield wiper never works as good as the passenger's?

- LAME: Paying for a customized ring tone. Just let the

fucking phone ring with the number of options for ringtones the phone already comes with.

- LAME AGAIN: White dudes that use the term "bitch". In fact, let's 86 that term forever, it's only good enough if used by bitches.

- With how much damage a hurricane causes it's a wonder why we give them such boring, innocent names: Andrew, Fred, Katrina... (Oh dear, not them!)

- I love it when you play the game of "pass it on" and the sentence becomes all distorted by the last person in the circle: "Timmy's shoes are red." Then by the last kid in the circle it has become: "Jimmy wants to fuck my head".

- I hate when after saying "Fuck an A" and someone needs to be clever and say, "Fuck a B it's got more holes." Well FUCK U, as U seems to be the perfect shape for a cock to fit into, like that of a vagina, so I will fuck that letter. Or maybe an O, but not A or B.

- PDA is inconsiderate and kinda nasty. Kiss and fondle out of public view already.

- GOLDDIGGERS football field (Idaho Springs, CO) I've *never once* seen football players or anyone on that field any time after passing it on I-70 for YEARS now. Why? How?

- I hate how gay people refer to their significant others as their "partner". It's not a business, you're just together and fucking each other. It's your "lover".

- Racial Inequality: How come in laundry we still separate the colors from the whites?

- Hey ladies, I will leave the toilet seat down for you, but I'm going to piss on it as well.

- How about a Skype meetup group? *(It probably already exists in this cheese-douche culture of ours.)*

- How about *Skype Tank*? Fuck all the hassle of trying to get on Shark Tank, just sign up for a time slot and a conference room panel gives you 5-10 minutes to pitch your idea over the internet. Why all the grueling process of time, money, efforts with registering, flying to location and shit to get on the actual show where you'll most likely have your ass handed to you? To then go back home feeling defeated. LET'S CHANGE THIS STUPID FUCKING AGE-OLD CONCEPT FOR PITCHING IDEAS.

- We got the MAC, so when are the Irish going to come out with the "Mc" computer?

- iGrad *(the next computer program to get an online degree)*

- iMaxipad *(combo cell phone and maxipad for girls. Perfect.)*

- Funny when a neighbor is interviewed on the news after another neighbor was caught killing his entire family. They always say, "I don't understand, he was so nice, quiet..." *Well now he's a murdering asswipe, so deal! ANYONE can crack, it's part of life and happens all the time in quaint suburban neighborhoods by that "nice quiet guy".*

- I hate it when smokers toss their cigarette butts out the window of a moving car. And I really hate chewers that leave their chaw in public drinking fountains. Fuck both ya'll.

- Moment of true anxiety: When the teacher picks students by random selection.

- You know how we are always doing something for a *good* cause? I want to start being an activist for *okay* causes. (Mediocrity; The American Way)

- Funny that Black Friday has become so commercialized that we must add in a Black Friday Eve. Fuck this, I'm ready for the Black Friday Plague!

- I hate when a bartender makes a Car Bomb shot without Jameson included. Or when they make a White Russian with too much cream rather than Kahlua. Cheap fucks, now I just ask for a Black Russian with a touch of cream. OR when bartenders can't fill a pint glass to the brim. I don't care to receive my drink appearing as if someone already took a big gulp out of it. Head or no head, TOP IT OFF FUCKERS!

- Awesome Blossom: Like the wave but everyone in the stadium stands up row by row all the way to the top, then they all sit back down row by row to the bottom.

- Car Horns: Funny how we utilize various honks to represent certain situations; the cute and quick "beep-beep" for goodbye, or the overwhelming "beep-beep-ba-beep-beep- beep..." for the exciting goodbye as you drive down the neighborhood street.

- Since Americans like an endless variety of options for their products of preference these days, (flavored coffee/beer/cigarettes…scented toilet paper…) I'm waiting for the day we come up with flavored oil for our vehicles: "Please give me the Blueberry Delight oil, my Mazda runs great on that stuff".

- I will not die satisfied unless I have a chance to spin that big fucking wheel on the Price is Right!

You know you're getting OLD when...

- You're drinking tolerance changes from "pound many and get psyched" to "sip a few and get sleepy".

- Hangovers also become inevitable and are sure to be twice as damaging from half the consumption anymore.

- You start reading books *without* a highlighter.

- Dress clothes no longer gather dust.

- A remote control and computer mouse become more important than going out with your friends (or to any social event for that matter) We all turn into unmotivated, excuse giving, whining, lazy, comatose slackers of sorts.

- You no longer have a beer gut, just a *fat* gut!

- We utilize slang in different forms: "That band was *bad*! The drummer was *phat* and the show was *killer*." NOW: "My job is *bad*, my boss is *fat* and I want to *kill her*!"

- You actually care when you go to bed.

- You leave musical festivals early.

- Start watching network shows like CNN, Discovery, prime time news...instead of MTV, COPS and the likes.

- You take time to make a salad to go with your Macaroni or Ramen.

- Men's motto in life (especially in relation to women and booze) makes a very subtle yet somewhat effortful change from *quantity* to *quality*. Well we try dammit!

- Women's views and complaints on their body changes from, "I need to diet or start a workout regimen." to "Cindy, how did that Liposuction surgery work for you?"

- You switch from "Let's start the night with a six pack, then club hop, chase chicks..." to "Let's chill out at the local coffee shop, sip on some lattes, and talk about the not-so-finer things in life."

- The walls in your room switch from adolescent booze and girl posters to artistic scenery or mature posters of poetic optimism.

- You definitely know you're getting old when the neighborhood Boy Scout asks if he can help you cross the street.

THE ONION

Anyone who knows of or has read a copy of *the Onion* will get a kick out of this section. I possess the perfect aptitude to write for a satirical publication such as *the Onion*, and since they had a headquarters based out of Boulder I jumped on the opportunity to try and get involved. Only problem was that all they offered was promotional work for no pay and they never accept writing offers from anyone.

Well fuck this notion, here's some samples of writings I submitted to *the Onion* back in the late 90s.

NEWS IN BRIEF:

"CHILDREN FREAK AS TEACHER TURNS INTO MEDUSA"

CONSHOHOCKEN, PA- A scary scene took place in the town of Conshohocken, PA yesterday as several elementary school students stormed out of their classroom, frightened and screaming. According to one of the students their teacher, Ms. Steppelpling, was teaching Social Studies as normal when all of a sudden, snakes started growing out of her head and her eyes lit up. "I've seen Clash of the Titans many times, and Ms. Steppelpling became Medusa!", said Josh, 8. "I was scared she might turn me into stone and I ended up pooping in my Toughskins." When the school's security questioned the students further, one of them mentioned they were waiting for the bus before school when a strange man wearing a leather "Pennywise for President" jacket and sporting a mullet haircut gave the children a sheet of paper. "We love to shoot spit wads during class and this guy gave us a cool sheet of paper that was already cut neatly into tiny, colorful squares. We thought they would be perfect to chew and spit out of a straw", said Alex, 9.

The proper authorities confiscated what was left of this sheet of paper, only to find the paper contained some of the most potent concentration of LSD known in existence. When Ms. Steppelpling's classroom and desk were searched nothing else drastic was found.

Although one officer did find handcuffs, a whip, and a 9-inch dildo in the top drawer of her desk.

REAL 'CROCK OF SHIT' FOUND

NORTHERN CALIFORNIA- Finally, after countless years of people referring to some "crock of shit" and comparing it to statements and assumptions they feel aren't worth a darn, an environmental research scientist discovered what is being described as an actual crock of shit! Dave Bushman of the National Park Service, and well-known explorer and researcher for northwestern territories in the country, stumbled across a discovery that will be set in the records as one of the most unusual and amazing findings in history.

While hiking around some of the thousands of acres in Northern California's dense forestland, Bushman ran across something he never would have expected to see; a giant bowl of shit. The pile of crap is said to be at least 50 feet in diameter and 20 feet in depth. "That's enough crap to spread across an entire football field", testified one expert. "The smell was unbearable!", said Bushman. "I figured this poop-hole could have been one of Paul Bunyan's old natural bedpans or something." (small chuckle)

Scientists and environmentalists are conducting intense research at the site trying to come up with conclusions on how the enormously disgusting crockpot-like pile of shit came to be, and what type of feces it contains. So far the only possibilities researchers have come up with is that the shit hole was built by alien visitors as the follow up to the well-known crop circle patterns, which could be the blueprints for the makings of more crockpot-like shit holes or who knows what. One scientist, who refused to be identified stated, "Crop, crap, whatever. This shit-pile could be the means to preserve a mass dumping of alien excrement for reasons unknown. The truth is that everyone who uses the phrase 'that's a crock of shit' can now point the finger to this." (Massive chuckle)

HOROSCOPES

Aires (March 21-April 19)
Shit it's too late! Now that you have begun to read this you are cursed with a spell that will turn you into a blind aardvark in exactly one hour!

Taurus (April 20-May 20)
Today you will take one of those messy shits that requires a dozen or so wipes to finish the job. Good luck!

Gemini (May 21-June 21)
Screw Scope! After brushing, I recommend swishing around some Beluga whale semen in your mouth for 33 seconds. Results will be the whitest, healthiest teeth on Earth! (Followed by projectile vomiting, in which I recommend brushing your teeth again.)

Cancer (June 22-July 22)
Today your doctor will inform you that you have cancer.

Leo (July 23-Aug. 22)
Your porn star career will end as you become paralyzed from the waist down after a terrible car accident. (The day after you are informed you have HIV.)

Virgo (Aug. 23-Sept. 22)
Later today your shiny, freshly waxed car will become a pooping target for a flock of seagulls flying overhead. Ironically enough, a song by the band A Flock of Seagulls will be playing on the radio at the same time.

Libra (Sept. 23-Oct. 23)
"Zit Juice Art". Utilize your severe acne problem by taking close-up photos of your zit juice that splatters out onto your bathroom mirror during a regular popping session. I guarantee worthy results!

Scorpio (Oct. 24-Nov. 21)
Big problems will arise in your home as you discover your dad is a satanic worshipping, animal necrophiliac. (I don't know if any counselling will help in this matter, try homicide.)

Sagittarius (Nov. 22-Dec. 21)
Today you shall worship hippos, tomorrow ants.

Capricorn (Dec. 22-Jan. 19)
Little do you know your life is heading towards great success. You will one day become the world's best pogo-sticker.

Aquarius (Jan. 20-Feb. 18)
I recommend changing your name to Fred. (Unless your

name is already Fred, in which case change it to Taintface.)

Pisces (Feb. 19-Mar. 20)
It's time for a big change. (Get back to me in a couple decades and I'll tell you what it is.)

Palm-Claw Technique

When taking a dump there's sometimes a leftover chunk o' poop that gets caught up on the anal rim region of one's ass after the main log(s) have passed through successfully. A small turd-chunk that was originally part of a bigger shit-log yet broke off at the last second; a small turd-plug that remains stuck at the opening of one's butt-hole.

This turd-plug is not to be confused with a "dingleberry"; as a dingleberry is a turd-ball that hangs from one's butt-pubes. The turd-plug is leftover remnants of an actual shit-log that was exiting your anus, but (no pun, you silly assholes) sometimes the anus clenches up prematurely, forcing a stoppage in natural bowel movement procedures and a break in the main log. From here the main portion of the shit-log (that's already exited the anus) will torpedo downwards into the toilet, while the disastrous leftover chunk from the original log is either vacuumed back up into your rectum, or (if the shit-chunk is small enough and on the softer side of life) it remains stuck at the anal opening of the shitter's ass.

Like that of what you see left hanging out of the soft-serve frozen yogurt dispenser just after the clerk has filled your cone and turns off the nozzle. There's always that small amount of frozen yogurt-goo leftover at the end of the dispenser opening. The leftover goo-chunk is stuck there and hanging out of the exit hole just a bit, yet too small, soft, and sticky to allow gravity to take effect. This smaller chunk never drops off but rather becomes the beginning of the snake-swirl of yogurt that will fill the next person's cone. And so on...

One can compare this annoying little leftover poopy chunk to that of a slightly melted Hershey's Kiss. Although small in size it can wreak havoc during the wiping process.

Hence it is necessary to utilize the Palm-Claw Technique:

The Palm-Claw Technique entails ripping off 2-3 squares of toilet paper, folding them up into a nice rectangle, then placing it onto your palm. The occupant then contracts his or her thumb and fingers inward (shaping the folded toilet paper into the letter U) and then proceeds to grasp and divest the Hershey's Kiss from its clinging position stuck to the anus. (Like that of a hydraulic claw used by heavy excavating machinery to dig up chunks of Earth, only the human Palm-Claw is used to grab off one nasty chuck of annoying sticky shit.)

After the Palm-Claw has done its job, it is then safe to commence normal wiping procedures, as the main culprit has been removed from the equation.

*Wet wipes highly recommended!

Another fun fact about when I poop is sometimes I have taken it upon myself to hum the theme music from The Vikings *starring Kurt Douglas. I perform this task as the brown being is in the process of exiting my cavern. Why? Beats the shit out of me.*

There's also the infamous *Cum-Plug*; that dried up leftover spooge that collects and dries up over your dick-hole after you've blown your wad. This causes your post-sex, diminishing-boner piss to spray out in odd directions for a few seconds. Eventually the force of the pee-stream completely clears the plug and you finish off normally; pissing *in* the toilet rather than all over it.

*No wet wipes needed for this mess, but definitely lots of toilet paper! (Or a towel.)

UNDERRATED:

Things I view as underrated in life.

Palm-Clawing
Cum-Plugs
Ant Farms
Blimps
Sponges
Umbrella Hats
Popcorn Ceilings
Thumbhole Shirts
Tripping in the rain
Sinclair gas stations
Pyroxivors
Contrails

Mello Yello
Pogo Sticks
Cloud gazing
Bathroom fans/windows
Underwear skid marks
Procrastination
Erasable pens
Clicker pens
Invisible ink
No. 3 pencils
Flip Phones
Rugby Scrums
3/4 sleeve shirts
Drive-in movies
EPs (mini-albums)
Disposable Cameras
Air Dancers
Subaru Brats
Daiquiri Ice
Clusterfucks
Sun Showers
Paper Airplanes
Generic food isles
Playing Kick-the-Can
Staying up past midnight
Speeding through school zones
Hold music (c'mon it's amusing)
Hot Air Balloons
Hocking loogies

Popping zits
Real books
Aglets
GORP
Near empty ketchup bottles that make funny fart noises when squeezed
Taking a dump in a port-o-potty
Jerking off with sandpaper
Instrumental music
Shuffling music
Harpsichords
Rototoms
Hay Rolls
Manatees
Flowbees
Dashes
italics
Gourds
Sinkholes
Clean, solid shits
Lyman-alpha Blobs
Shoulder shrugging
E.F. Hutton commercials
Onside kicks that succeed
Kicking people in the balls
Bands that sing about Satan
The dull side of aluminum foil
Dogs with plastic cones around their heads
Leaving last year's calendar on the wall for

another year (or more)
Leaving one clock in the house untouched whenever a time change persists
Getting naked and taking a swan dive right into a pile of cactus
Running barefoot through a field full of goat heads
Marquees that are only partially lit
Boise St. blue football field
Electronic Football
Bubble Hockey
Bloody Noses
Glow Worms (aka Black Snakes)

Allowing an ant colony to migrate up your urethra and nest up in your bladder

Observing that middle-aged drunk guy with no shirt and cutoff jean shorts dancing all erratic at an outdoor music festival

Hollywood Dreamer

(Some nifty ideas I've come up with)

Unfortunately I cannot reveal any of my product invention ideas or a few other items of sensitivity; only because that big fat "you never know" factor. Otherwise I'm all about sharing anything and I'd

LOVE to collaborate with others on any of my many creative happenings, and theirs. But if I list them here we all know what the potential results could be. It seems a bit self-important, paranoid-lame I know, as **Life in the Spin Cycle** *is intended to be a "share everything memoire" with no holds barred, but still.*

I've been stuck in ruts so many years throughout my life, contemplated suicide, and been flaked on and fucked over far beyond any rational comprehension. I'm also aging and running very low on "do it all fuel" anymore, so I can't take certain gambles at this point. I'm well over-due for this "karma" to apologize, suck my cock, and I get on with my "real life" that could/should be.

I'm just one of those rarities whose forte or "purpose" is having endless creative ideas, numerous ambitions, and natural "Hollywood skills", that's it. I'd love to be a successful musician and leave it at that, but no, I have too much else to offer that could also be something! The music part for me is mostly jerking off; naturally easy and satisfying but the shortage of lube out there and so much bullshit involved it's never "the shit", so big picture shit o' mine is what needs to be implemented.

Ironically drumming, one of my best skills and certainly favorite craft in all this artistic mayhem, should be the hobby or "avocation" in my life, and the many other ideas and talents I have could branch out further and make for a healthy lifestyle for me to live, out of their discoveries and into an actual "vocation" of sorts. And for the record, even all my filmmaker friends who are stressed and struggling say they're "glad they're not musicians", because they know the mightiest of all the arts also comes at the highest cost and most sacrifices within the confines of the same fucked-up circus.

After reading though Life in the Spin Cycle *I'm sure you the readers can now grasp some justification on how my life is what it is; as a performer, rather than observer, within an over-saturated circus of constant stimulation and chaos. It's pretty obvious with a mind as creatively wild, open, empathetic, flustered, distraught, and stubbornly determined as mine I belong in entertainment, and NOT in any 8-5 bullshit schemes of the "real world", period.*

Get it ALL out there in one book; sharing ALL Rolf Gunnar Hauge stands for, does, and comes up with. It's endless and mostly all possible, just in this industry we freaks need adequate help to get so much shit off the back burners of the stove and onto the buffet table out there!

I've shared plenty *already but* again *the irony is the bigger dream ideas and artistic talents should be whored out to the world as much as possible, and NOT sit in the dugout of my laptop files for more years to come. Unfortunately I must be careful and not release too much that still has potential for "Hollywood success", without first having proper legal backing and all that crap to keep the package deal legit.* **THEN** *I whore out more ideas and creations to the public and not have to track down any fuckers who take without asking.*

The ideas never stop, it's the funds that do. (Or really funds never expand enough beyond "getting by" in life). My brain is always in rapid-fire mode and the creative ideas and twisted thoughts constantly spew out of my pores. It's like living in humid climates; you dry yourself off yet more sweat keeps emerging, and I can't afford anymore towels!

Hence need funding. Aside from more networking and endless tenacity from my end, it's also back to hounding those mega-stubborn investors, over-priced lawyers, continued negotiations with flaky bitch society, **then** *move forward with the "dream team" out there.*

Any way you might look at it all, title of book beyond validated.

FILM/SHOWS/DOCUMENTARIES

"***LORG***" (**L**ife **O**f **R**olf **G**unnar. You've read the *Spin Cycle*, now there's L.O.R.G.)

"Undiscovered Brilliance" (Documentary on 'starving artists')

"Desert Trip" (Group of friends take psychedelic road *trip* to Moab)

"WTF" (A movie featuring constant fucked up nonsense. Hence WTF. *WTF?*)

"Vomit Dome" (Short film where a bunch of people are locked into a big spinning dome-like room and shown clips of disgusting things until many start puking. The twist is they begin using all the vomit to create art and put it to use in interesting ways)

"Siafu" (Horror film about killer ants, with a modern twist)

- Picking the size of ants for this film is a tough call; as large is scary but just tiny enough to crawl up someone's pant leg is creepier. So, I choose each ant to be 5.5" in length. (Cause I like odd numbers and it's the average size of a man's erect penis.)
-
- I also choose the epic music of Apocalyptica as the soundtrack to this film. Just imagine...

TBC Films **(To Be Continued):** Very short films with a crazy plot, shock value, then abrupt ending with To Be Continued… at end of clip. To then never have anything ever continued, leave audience hanging. (Shown in theaters before main feature begins)

"***SNN***" (Stoner Network; show full of trippy, bizarre

entertainment. *Adult Swim ish*)

"***Real Talk***" (Talk Show; me as host AND drummer,

interview basic people)

"***Background***" (All about the 'extras' on a film set. 2000

my idea, 2005 it was *Extras*)

"***Khaki Pants***" (Low budget film or documentary based

on promotional industry)

"***Is Pepsi Okay***?" (Another low budget film or documentary based on service industry)

"What's the Password?" (Film revolving around the

barista world)

"The Password Is…" (Documentary, behind the scenes

of barista world)

"***ish world***" (Documentary based on flaky/fickle

standards of 21st Century)

"Overwhelm-Nation" (Documentary on current

trends/stresses of the country)

"***Tree Branch Tales"*** (Theatre play with stories from

each tree branch. Huh?)

"IDEALology" (Documentary or sci-fi based on an ideal world for us)

*How about a movie that releases a deluxe DVD package with option for a 2nd or even 3rd choice of soundtrack when viewing the film again. Make things interesting!

*Or if I became a serial filmmaker my lame "subliminal trademark" in all my films would be books/magazines always held upside down; as most filmmakers try to deliberately showcase some known historical publication in their films I'll just leave the audience hanging with, "Why is that actor holding that book upside down? This happened in another scene just minutes before." "Oh that's a Gunnar thing, he's just fucking with us."

*I also propose the "7-ish minute short film" concept; as many of the greatest songs throughout history are composed as a 7-ish minute piece, I also feel short films made in this same length of time can do enough justice.

SKITS

(First 3 already complete, need willing female for 4th)

"Singing Bush" (Copy of infamous "singing bush" scene during *The Three Amigos*. Ask plant to stop singing or I piss on it. I start pissing then bush bites my dick off and I run towards camera screaming; blood squirting out, bush laughing then back to singing)

"Diarrhea Sunscreen" (2 guys sitting outside up against a building wall. One unloads projectile diarrhea in his shorts, it runs out of his shorts, other guy dips his hands in it and covers his face and arms with it as sunscreen. They continue talking/eating)

"Poop Shoe Cleanse" (Jogger enters frame, steps in dog shit. Sees homeless guy pissing behind tree, runs over to the bum and has him spray off the poop with his pee stream, jogger jogs off) *completed and viewable on my YouTube page! www.youtube.com/scarpie33

"Carrot Run" (One constant shot following a girl from behind; out her house, into car, to grocery story, buys one carrot, back home, scrubs clean, masturbates with carrot)

"That Shit" (SNL style skit featuring unappealing food product in a can, tube, or whatever called *That Shit.* So people at dinner table make comments, "You gonna use *That Shit*? Pass me *That Shit*." HaHa, neat)

"Sobriety Check Point" (Guy pulled over and suspected of smoking reefer. Cops give him sobriety check by having him stand still and taunting him with junk food, scary masks, puppets...anything to see if he will crack and give in from an intoxicated high)

"Post Office Parade" (An actual parade where the postal workers run around pretending to shoot at each other as their session rolls by the crowd)

"The Interview" (Guy with no arms applying for data

entry position, clown applying for front desk position. Candidates who are obviously unqualified but determined to get through discrimination)

"White Lies" (Like any sitcom but focused primarily on 2-3 pathetic dudes constantly lying to get out of annoying obligations in life. Multiple quick skits or actual sitcom?)

"Stereotypes" (Skits or full-on sitcom based on stereotypical situations, duh)

"Airline Crash" (People rated on jump technique/style while exiting the plane onto blow-up ramps; 360, spread eagle, twist-spread…)

"Baggage Claim Entertainment" (Juggling clowns, stand-up comedians, etc. while people wait for their luggage)

"B-Rated Infomercial Guy" (Speaks for itself...or does it?)

"Monster Truck Rally" (Event hosted by soft-spoken wussies)

"Ice Skating Event" (Hosted by tough talking guys)

"Songs to Poop To" (SNL infomercial takeoff)

"Bad Moments in Karaoke" (Like Jay Leno's *Headlines*)

"Ant Hill" (Film an ant hill, add voiceover dialogue)

"Lipstick" (Animated drawing over real dog that pops wood, but it's actual lipstick)

"Mr. Over-reactor" (Guy who constantly freaks out over stupid little things)

"Disgruntled Temp Employee"

"Extras *Premier Party"*

ANIMATION/CLAYMATION

(First 2 in the making)

"Pink Blob Squad" (The "pink" element of this is a secret, to eventually be revealed) A huge, slimy chunk of pinkish goo splats onto a stage and breaks up into 3 Blobs (Curdy, Naple, Jim) who land at instruments and start playing a 40-second theme song. There's 4 other friends who are introduced and make their appearance during the song's quick break: (Vasor; fart cloud, Slosho; naval lint, Snika; snot rocket, Grote; ear wax)

"Blue Bear Nightmare" (Short animation/claymation where the giant Blue Bear at Denver Convention Center comes alive and wreaks havoc in the city. What he does during his limited minutes alive is priceless.)

"Gnome Dump" (A daily animated series via computer/tablet/phone where some funny gnome character is placed in a different setting/scene each day and viewers guess where he's going to poop after he finishes his coffee and cigarette. Get sponsors involved and viewers with the most correct guesses each week wins things from that sponsor.)

"Blackhead Brigade" (Blackheads are squeezed out of someone's nose and the white worms that are produced from this go on adventures all over that person's body.)

"Here Cums the Sun" (Beatles song plays as the Sun jerks off and ejaculates into space. "Those aren't solar flares!" Scientist zooms in with telescope and notices Sun is jacking off and blasting out his fire-cum.)

"Best Buds" (Sitcom, consisting of various strains of marijuana nuggets living together, each with personalities relating to type of strain they are.)

"Buds vs Tots" (Marijuana Buds vs Tater Tots, like Jets vs Sharks)

ANIMATED CHARACTERS

(First 3 close to birth)

Clit Missile Diva (Female superhero who shoots tiny

missiles out of her clit, like Pez)

Buggera (Scuzzlebutt-like creature that kills people by

flicking its buggers at them.)

ToxiSplat (Interesting character who kills people with his

toxic semen.)

Ass Clown (Costume of an ass dressed as a clown, or
clown with ass face?)

*An action film where main character (bad-ass hero type) uses a big electric guitar or bass as weapon: Play the strings and it shoots bullets, use whammy bar to launch grenades, flip the toggle switch to get flame thrower. (And yes I thought of this a few years before *Mad Max: Fury Road* was released.)

BAND NAMES (Up for grabs, bitches)

Naked Mole Rats

Bupple Rum

Pipe Dust

Omnipiupus FLAX
Grevillia
Nasal Drip

Butt Fungus
Oncidium
Agapanthus
Intergrefolia
Billy Balls
Hyperthymia
Pyometra BCM
Bovine Sperm Tent
Scrotal Squashers
Perpetual Folding Hut
Chocolate Covered Urinal Cakes
Indistinguisha-BULL
Liquid Acid Enema
Cockhole Mold
Camel Cum
Amplitude
Fungle Spore
Funkwads
Meth Sex

SONGS (Ain't no songwriter, most of these suck)

1) *"FARMER TED"*

*Rawhide, shuffle beat (Primus vocal style) My name is

Farmer Ted
I always wet my bed

I have a friend named Ned He seldom gets good head

We hang with this guy named Pete He hangs with a bunch of geeks…

2) *"PISSING IN L.A."* (pop-punk style)

Verse 1: I need to pull over and take a piss right now, but LA is hectic I haven't got a fucking chance…

Chorus: C'mon now I really need to piss
But charging 50 cents, what's this shit? I can let it flow in an alley
Behind a dumpster's not too shabby…

3) *"Bell Chime"* ¾ intro

*fast, funky, heavy (Primus 'Is It Luck' style)

4) *"For Those Who Don't…"*

*song for the unfortunate: abused, homeless, disabled, etc.

5) *"Bloodaxe Stomp"*

*song about Erik Blood Axe (idea conceived on dad's birthday 10/4...maybe that's the time signature? 10/4) Heavy stomping tom groove (da da da da da da-da, da da da da da da repeat) then into HH groove; slow raspy half-time (2 bars) then into normal time, then Rush 'Double

Agent' break, then into rest of song basic hard rock

6) *"Greased"*

*parody-mock on musical: "You better be wet, bah-bah-bah
Cause I need a lay-I need a lay And my boner's set on you."

7) *"My Sorry Life"*

*Tenacious D style: "My underwear is dirty, my socks do really stink, I think there's something wrong with me, My favorite color's pink!"

8) *"Sketchbrain"*

*song about sketchy chicks and their psychotic tendencies

9) *"Blissful Stroll"*

*instrumental; based around "kind" adventures of sorts (thought of during 33rd B-Day)

10) *"Contemptuous Realism"*

*based on the reality I live, and how many deal with today's unfortunate standards

11) *"Neurotic Perfectionism"*

*another fine descriptive piece relating to my life

12) *"Shackleton"*

*song about the bravest, most determined man in history (Inspired from IMAX; Blasting intro groove, Rush 'Alien Shore' style)

13) *"The Wheel"* (3-part conceptual piece)

*defining the connections within a force, unity, band…
HUB= foundation,
SPOKES=ideas, arranging, produce
TIRE=essence, performing, touring

14) *"After the Fact"*

*song that explains torment of not closing a deal in the moment and regretting it later

15) *"9 Planets"*

*instrumental conceptual song that 'travels' to each of the 9 planets; with each suite reflecting the vibe of that planet (Pluto could be like a bonus hidden track I guess?)

16) *"uhh"*

Rapid thoughts cross through the mind,

Regret not having paper or pen at the time…

(ha ha the cliché meaningful song with no point)

17) *"Centennial Peaks"* (written while in the mental hospital)

News in the morning, news at night
Fucking American Idol, can you dance alright?

Nurses checking vitals, meeting our needs
Grabbing us snacks of choice, very good indeed

Strolling down the gauntlet, observing all the realm
Chilling in the lobby, or napping in the room

Arts and crafts UNO, fuck it I'm outta here SOONO

18) *"About a Girl"*

I need her mouth, I need her tongue, I need her LI-IPS
I want to penetrate that hole, Between her HI-IPS

19) *"Pink Blob Squad"*

We're the Pink Blob Squad, so pretty and gooey

The Pink Blob Squad, so luscious and chewy
The Pink Blob Squad, righteous and delightful
The Pink Blob Squad, amazing potential

Curdy, Naple & Jim

And don't forget our friends: Vasor, Slosho, Snika & Grote

The Pink Blob Squad (4X)

20) *"Satan 7"* (6-6-6-7 time, get it now?)

*reggae groove over odd-time (bass line like in sports anthem song 'Hey' fashion-- da, da-da, da-da...da da da, da-da, da-da...da, da-da, da, da HEY...)

21) *"CCFs" (Cookie Cutter Fucks)*

*years of supporting, giving all the benefit of doubt, yet never reciprocated back to me…

22) *"Wish I Could Be Me"*

*song relating to my torment of not having the balls to really show my family and friends who I really am; which is an amped up pleasure/thrill seeking creative madman, but my stubborn emotionless "this is how I've been presenting myself to most of the world for most all my life" persona, is who I've become.

23) *"Weeks to Years"*

*song describing how most humans would only need a few weeks as me to completely validate my internal pains and stresses, yet I've endured it for a few DECADES.

24) *"Acid Laughs"*

***ALBUM** relating to funny incidents/scenarios during LSD adventures.

Songs:
Bare Bodies
Gurgling Tube
Crack n Cheeks
Concerning Lurch
Botanical Jerk-Off

25) *"Mid-40s Boner"*

Hidden Track: Alarm clock goes off, guy hits snooze, goes off again, guy grunts, gets up, takes piss/farts, gets in shower, sings while washing himself, gets dressed, leaves apartment in frenzy, door shuts, hear footsteps down stairs…footsteps back up the stairs, barges back into apartment, curses, grabs phone shuts door again, back down stairs, car engine starts, loud music blaring, peels out and vanishes. (Why not?)

Poetic Justice:

Cunts and Clits, Nipples and Dicks, big juicy anus and a face full of zits.

BOOKS:

PERFORMANCE: *An Evening at a Rock Show*

The house lights fade, fog machines ignite, as the intro music kicks in. The excitement of the crowd rumbles loudly as the band members finish their round of shots backstage and are then guided through the hallway corridors to the stage by the arsenal of yellow event coats and their flashlight beams. The stage crew frantically gets set into place with headsets intact and communicate last check-ins with the sound and lighting crew. The band members reach the stage and head towards their respected instruments. As the intro music fades to a close, the stage lights come alive and the band kicks into their opening song as the roars of the crowd plummet to volumes that shakes the entire venue.

This introductory paragraph is the beginning to a book I'm contemplating to write; concerning all the happenings within an entire evening one goes through while attending a rock show. From picking out the perfect attire to wear and into the early morning hour's breakfast gathering with friends afterward. It's always a huge spectacle with stories of worthiness to reminisce about.

SHIT SHOW: *An in-depth analysis ofAmerica in the 21st Century*

Summer in the Shed: *Dark Stories from a Schizophrenic Mind*

Bathroom Stall Protocol (Quotes/photos of bathroom stall graffiti)

Emails to a Friend (Disgruntled emails sent to a friend over a long duration of time)

Scrapbook Sanctuary (Book of my photos/drawings/crafty nonsense)

Cigarettes & Porn Mags (Road trip adventures; title relating to cravings we get along the way)

Green Room Escapades (Stories of musician's backstage experiences)

The Permanent Intern (Life of a struggling artist; we're all stuck, working for free)

Gray Area Perspectives (Finding the realistic happy medium within topics of debate)

Frozen Moments of Pragmatism (Screenshots of my social media rants)

Quotes, Analogies, Rants, OH MY

Viewing Life from the RIGHT *Hemisphere*

Looking at Life through the Tinted Eyeglass

Journal Entries from a Tormented Mind

Stories from the Crock Pot of Life

Neurotic Undertakings Galore

The Spontaneous Hopeful

So Far, So Good, So GAY

Metaphorical Stew

Suck My Ass Juice

If Only…

BUMPER STICKERS/T-SHIRTS/ZIT PUSS

Many of these listed are already printed, others are in the making…

BRING BACK 20th CENTURY AMERICAN VALUES

21st Century: Welcome to the Global Shit Show

2010s: The Great American Shit Show

2010s: Decade of Doucheyness

Modern Day Society: In The Moment, Nothing Beyond

Experience Life! Flush Your *i*Shit Down The Toilet

Proud to be an American. NOT proud of what America has become.

The Glass *Is* Half Full (of BULLSHIT)

The Glass Could/Should Be 80% Full

United We Aren't

Common Sense...Not So Common Anymore

Cynical Pessimist? Nope. Frustrated Realist

Need more bullshit in your life? Just add MALE

Need more insanity in your life? Just add FEMALE

Forgive & Forget? BullSHIT

Don't Debate, Just Do.

LIFE: One Big Bowl Full of Twisted Irony

Life is Beautiful (Too Bad People Can Be So Ugly)

It Is What It Is...And What It Is SUCKS

Mediocrity; The American Way

Screw HOPE, got ACTION?

Screw the 1%? How about the 70%

Save Humanity! Kill A Tech-Nerd

8-5 Slave? Not me.

Abolish Slavery! Emancipate citizens from dead-end hourly jobs.

Make Life Exciting

Do As Much As You Can With What You Got

Become the CEO of the life you live

Don't bitch about your job, make the job be your bitch!

Life's Unfair (Because I'm A Whiny Bitch)

I Don't Pray, I Jerk Off

Political Correctitude is RETARDED

Oval Stickers: 26.2 for proud marathon runners
(0.0 for my car)

If Jesus were black would he have moonwalked on water?

Jesus Pooped

POOP RULES

got ching? (with PDGA basket logo)

Keep Tahoe Green (the blue lake sticker with a Calvin sticker pissing into it)

I'm in it for the Art (put on the back of a shitty car owned by an artist)

Waking up is overrated

Doing nothing is underrated

Same Shit, Different Bunghole

Drama is great, Unfairness sucks

I think, therefore I think. Ya think?

Anti-Organic/Pro Carbs

In My Opinion, Opinions Suck

If you think education is expensive, you're fucking right!

Happiness is...being happy?

I Love Wet Underwear (heart symbol for "love")

I Love Hate

MUGGER, DRUG ADDICT, NUDIST, etc
(Colorado green/white "Native")

Jesus fish mounting Darwin fish ("The *Real* Truth")

Welcome to Boulder! Home of Yuppies, Hippies, and Freaks

I love animals too, but I'll still EAT THEM

Get high on life? No thanks, I'll stick to POT

Life Sucks/Death Swallows

I'm proud of my Animal Necropheliac son!

I HATE LOVELAND (instead of 'ride' or 'ski'. Ha, get it?)

Tom Shane...Please DIE

got jockitch? (herpes, crabs…)

Visualize My Bare Ass

WWJD for a Klondike Bar?

Homophobia is GAY

Get Stoned and Wander

Get High and Hump

Republican, Democrat: Same Shit, Different Pile

Republican, Tea Party: Same Shit, Different Pile

Beohner, Boner - Both pricks, Different spelling

Evolution of Humans (t-shirt featuring caveman to human then human hunched over with cell phone; progression right back to digression)

I'm With Stupid (t-shirt with arrow pointing down to crotch)

Than Q (t-shirt with photo of Q, for those Trekkies)

Procrastinative Tendencies (STs band logo font)

Bachelor, Not Soccer Mom (sticker for musician's minivan)

My driving habits reflect my personality ~ BI-POLAR

My other ride is a cymbal (for drummers)

My other car is a Matchbox (best as license plate frame)

POSTER: "Yes ladies, it's all of us." (Showing dude looking back at a hottie after passing her on a sidewalk)

Coca-Cola Commercial

Setting: Local coffee shop in hipster college town

Actors: Customer: White male 30-something with backpack over one shoulder Barista: Attractive, innocent, hip, decorated 20-something female

Scene 1 (wide shot) Showing male strolling down sidewalk towards coffee shop. It's a nice day and the patio is full of others working on their laptops while sipping lattes.

Scene 2 (wide shot) View from inside coffee shop looking towards glass door entrance, male pulls open door and enters, closing in on camera view. (Underground world music playing in background)

Scene 3 (wide shot) From behind towards counter as male walks up to order. View of large menu overhead and smiling barista behind counter.

Scene 4 (tight shot) Waist up shot of barista girl.

Barista: "Hey there what can I get you?"

Scene 5 (tight shot) Close-up on male's face with look of confusion.

Scene 6 (wide shot) Panning in on menu board, showing the many options available.

Scene 7 (wide shot) View of both actors from side, beverage coolers in background on customer's right.

Scene 8 (tight shot) Front view, waist up on male. With eyes still widened, slowly turns his head towards coolers.

Scene 9 (wide shot then zooming tight) Panning in on coolers we see many choices of beverages. Camera zooms in on bottles of Coca-Cola.

Scene 10 (tight shot) Waist up shot of male who's look turns into a happy smirk and slight nod of assurance. Close up of hand grabbing bottle of Coke, plopping on counter.

Scene 11 (tight shot) Waist up of guy, "Just this please."

Scene 12 (tight shot) Waist up of barista girl, "Okay then." and rings up order.

Scene 13 (wide shot) Looking at entire patio area from outside, male enters scene.

Scene 14 (tight shot) Waist up showing male holding bottle of Coke. He puts on a look of annoyed concern; slightly turning his head and moving his eyes around.

Scene 15 (medium shot) Camera jumps around to a few different tables with people working on laptops and sipping lattes.

Scene 16 (medium shot) Male takes a seat at empty table amidst all the laptop using coffee fiends, puts on headphones, and swigs a drink of Coke with look of total satisfaction. Sets bottle down, nodding head and tapping hands on table to his music.

Camera slowly pans out and from male, showing more and more patio scene.

Voiceover:

"Keep your caffeine tasty and simple. Choose Coke." (as Coca-Cola emblem fills screen)

THE END (fade to black)

Ultimate Threesome

Denver's beloved hard rock radio station, KBPI, used to have a lunch hour "threesome" of themed music. I submitted my request via email:

Hey Susie! I have the ultimate threesome request. It involves a bed with satin sheets and the accompaniment of Gwen Stefani and Angelina Jolie. Oh wait, this is for music…

My threesome request involves 3 tunes from 3 of the greatest 3-piece bands of all time; Rush, Police, and Primus. Think about it, not only is each band made up of outstandingly talented musicians, but each also has a lot in common as well. All three bands consist of a lead singer with distinct vocal tones and tremendous bass playing abilities, three of the most creative and technically awesome drummers of all time, and guitarists that all have very unique, innovative playing styles that adds that needed spice over the busy rhythm sections. And if this isn't enough, these are my 3 favorite bands! And just to be a bit more meticulous about all this, I have selectively picked songs by each band that has something to do with *driving*. Cool eh?

RUSH – "Driven"
POLICE – "Driven to Tears"
PRIMUS – "Jerry was a Racecar Driver"

I might have other threesome fantasies, but for the music world I would love nothing more than to hear you play this threesome request for my beloved ears during the lunch hour. Thanks so much Susie and GO CSU!

Rolf Gunnar Hauge

*Give Uncle Nasty a "what's up" for me!

TracBall Tournaments

Games take place on a basic field with rules like that of Ultimate Frisbee.

Time of game derived from playing one full rock album on my Panasonic boom box until album is over. Halftime commences after Side 1 is complete, then flip tape and continue 2nd half and game ends after last song concludes.

If a tie, then who knows. Haven't thought that far ahead with this concept yet. Fuck shootouts, maybe each team chooses one member to engage in a moonwalk race against the other chosen member and whoever gets across the field of play first, wins.

Sponsors: Puggs eyewear, Buff headbands, Yoo-hoo chocolate beverages.

R.T.T.S.F.S.G.Y.D.G.F.A.

Random Thoughts Tips & Suggestions From Some Guy You Don't Give a Fuck About

My soon-to-be online venture posting daily thoughts, tips, suggestions and such. Look for this to become the next hipster-weird sensation! (In the next life.)

One great idea for a party favor, where everyone brings a certain dish to add onto the buffet table of goodness; be the dessert guy. Go to the end of the table and plop down an actual cat's litter box full of sand and lay out a bunch of Twix bars on top of the sand. (Oh yeah, shits and grins of wonder on that one.)

ALSO, stay alert and look out for other brilliantly whacked-out proposals I'm offering to the world. First, a chain of vampire/goth-themed strip clubs (or at least occasional theme nights of this idea in already existing clubs out there), AND a café (to become a huge chain?) that serves fresh brewed coffee with a micro-dose of LSD dropped into the mix. Just no sufficient funds yet and many hoops to crawl through in order give birth and acclimatize these concepts into a reality this world desperately needs!

Online Survey

These are always fun to receive in an email from a friend (or stalker). I responded to this one some years ago:

Okay, here's what you're supposed to do...and try not to be LAME and spoil the fun. Just give in. Copy (not forward) this entire e-mail and paste it onto a new e-mail that you will send. Change all the answers so that they apply to you. Then, send this to a whole bunch of people you know *INCLUDING* the person who sent it to you. The theory is that you will learn a lot of little known facts about your friends. It is fun and easy!

1. LIVING ARRANGEMENT?

All over the fricking place! (commonly residing in parent's basement, friend's couch, or sometimes my car if needed)

2. WHAT BOOK ARE YOU READING NOW?

Does magazine count?

3. WHAT'S ON YOUR MOUSE PAD?

It's a replica 8" Zildjian splash cymbal my dad gave me!

4. FAVORITE BOARD GAMES?

Chutes & Ladders, Mouse Trap, Operation, Life

5. FAVORITE MAGAZINE?

Modern Drummer

6a. FAVORITE SMELLS?

Cinnamon, Coffee, Weed

6b. LEAST FAVORITE SMELLS?

Vomit

7. FAVORITE SOUND?

Anything musical that puts you in a deep trance.

8. WORST FEELING IN THE WORLD?

Anticipated Anxiety; i.e. The night before a new job you are starting that you don't even want anyway.

9. WHAT IS THE FIRST THING YOU THINK OF WHEN YOU WAKE UP IN THE MORNING?

Oh yuck.

10. FAVORITE COLOUR?

Dark Blue (and all “Earth tones”)

11. HOW MANY RINGS BEFORE YOU ANSWER THE PHONE?

SCREEN! SCREEN!

12. FUTURE Child's NAME?

Haven't even considered marriage yet, but maybe Milton?

13. WHAT IS MOST IMPORTANT IN LIFE?

Happiness! Which I have yet to find in my hectic life.

14. FAVORITE FOODS?

Italian, Mexican, American Grill

15. CHOCOLATE OR VANILLA?

Usually chocolate, except when it's "one of those days”.

16. DO YOU LIKE TO DRIVE FAST?

Oh yeah, I can't stand slow Sunday driving rubbernecking wussies!

17. DO YOU SLEEP WITH A STUFFED ANIMAL?

Matoog

18. STORMS - COOL OR SCARY?

Cool. Mother Nature never ceases to amaze me.

19. WHAT TYPE WAS YOUR FIRST CAR? “Stay Puft”

(1984 Nissan Sentra - white)

20. MEET ONE PERSON DEAD OR ALIVE?

George Carlin?

21. FAVORITE ALCOHOLIC DRINK?

White Russian, thanks to The Dude

22. WHAT IS YOUR ZODIAC SIGN?

LEO! And yes we're fricking crazy!

23. DO YOU EAT THE STEMS OF BROCCOLI?

Yep

24. IF YOU COULD HAVE ANY JOB YOU WANTED WHAT WOULD IT BE?

ROCK STAR, TV/Radio Host, or basically anything in music/film/entertainment.

25. IF YOU COULD DYE YOUR HAIR ANY COLOUR?

I CAN dye my hair any colour, so when I do I'll let you know.

26. EVER BEEN IN LOVE???

Thought so, maybe, whatever

27. IS THE GLASS HALF EMPTY OR HALF FULL?

Depends. If the glass is empty and you fill it half way it's half full. If you have a full glass and drink half it's now half empty. Aren't I a pain in the ass.

28. FAVORITE MOVIES:

Pulp Fiction, Fletch, Shawshank Redemption, Almost Famous, Braveheart, Big Lebowski, Across the Universe, Office Space...and the list goes on!

29. DO YOU TYPE WITH YOUR FINGERS ON THE RIGHT KEYS?

Who cares? But yes I do that.

30. WHAT'S UNDER YOUR BED?

The floor.

31. WHAT IS YOUR FAVORITE NUMBER?

3, 33, 333, 33.3...so pretty much 3's

32. FAVORITE SPORTS TO WATCH?

Football, Basketball, Hockey

33. SAY ONE NICE THING ABOUT THE PERSON WHO SENT THIS TO YOU.

Josh is an interesting friend going through the same shit as me; a dreamer with lots of false promises and bullshit presented in our paths...but we keep on pushing along! The one nice thing I would say about him is...he's nice.

Las Vegas 40th Birthday Bash

I arose out of rock bottom a little while after my stay at the mental hospital and noticed Soundgarden was performing in Las Vegas on my 40th birthday. If that wasn't enough to entice a quick trip out there, it was a good friend's birthday as well (same exact day and age) and the band was playing at The Joint venue located in the Hard Rock Casino. I have always wanted to catch a show at The Joint, and being that it was both our 40th I convinced my birthday friend, Rick, and one other, Mark, to head out there with me.

This plan got even better as I was booked to work at Comic Con in San Diego just days prior. I would fly out to San Diego, make some easy money by strolling around the scene dressed as a ninja, hang with my friend Jason during my off time, then fly out to Vegas for the real fun.

Mark and Rick picked me up at the Vegas airport and we proceeded immediately to an all nude strip club. I wanted to grab drinks and walk around downtown, or better yet hit our hotel first to freshen up, but they were amped to go.

The strip club scene was exactly as anyone can imagine so no need for any recap stories here, sorry. Although one disheartening part of the night was when I got really frustrated from having no money as usual so I couldn't indulge in full Vegas strip club activities. I spent the last remaining hour of my 30s lying down on the pavement of the club parking lot. I had a few drinks in me and my depressive tendencies set in so I lay down on the ground by our rental car like I was a drunken bum. That's how psychotically stubborn I can be; this ability to convert what should've been a great end to an evening into something dark and disturbing instead. Un-fucking-real.

Bus Stop

From the handful of times I've visited the Bus Stop Gentlemen's Club in Boulder, CO, I have one rock star story to share. Most guys will lie and say they hardly ever go to a strip club but I am one of the few who is telling the truth. I rarely visit a strip club due to various reasons, the most prominent being lack of money. I hardly ever get lap dances and mostly just sit there observing the dancers from the far away darkness. Plus the drinks are a fucking rip off, so I usually just get high in the parking lot before I go in. I get off more on the outfits the dancers wear than the nudity. I like sexy style as much as sexy naked bodies.

I went with a couple friends one evening and spent an astonishing $500. It was the rare night where I engaged in the "normal" activities being at a strip club; buying numerous drinks, sticking dollar bills in the girl's thongs, and partaking in a couple private lap dances.

I followed one girl into the private room where the lap dance commenced. To make it more of a rock star experience she added in some blow that we both snorted as she was grinding on my boner! We even discussed meeting up afterward but like I analyzed in the *Chicks* chapter she pulled the typical girl move and ignored me the rest of the evening, probably because we had finished our time and she needed to hustle more money from other guys. But most girls have been pulling this shit on me too much lately, strippers or not.

I don't really give a hoot about her or the money spent as it ended up as a rock star story, the type of stories I'm supposed to have much more of anyway. I enjoyed the evening and accepted the outcome, I guess.

Back to Vegas... The next morning, after the long evening at the strip club and my wonderful nap on the pavement, Rick put on a stark white t-shirt that read: I LOVE VAGINAS and wore it all throughout the MGM casino. Talk about comments! At one point we entered a crowded elevator full of children and Mark had to bail right back out before the doors closed.

We changed gears and hit the pool. It was mega hot so we spent most of the time under the shade or in the lazy river with our drinks. I went to go take a piss and order another drink and during my stroll I walked by a group of three younger divas. I happened to be walking by right as one of the girls was saying, "It's your birthday and you have to get some loving tonight". I stopped immediately and said, "Hey it's my birthday too, enjoy your day."

These girls were in their mid-20s and very cute, so it was only inevitable that I chalked up ANOTHER regret by not seizing the perfect moment. I was handed this opportunity in front of my face, on my birthday no less, and should've said: "Well let me give you my number and if you don't luck out with any pursuits for the evening give me a call. We're both staying in the same hotel anyway."

You know, just fucking lay it out there, go enjoy a great rock show and if I don't meet any other girls during my birthday escapades than at least I have a good chance for something afterwards with the pool girl. Why do I never take advantage of these moments and continue to cock-block myself time after time? And this painful story happened while on vacation in Las Vegas, the city of sin, on my fucking birthday!

(After the fact regret #333)

The Soundgarden show was fantastic! Funny thing about the venue was that it was very loud yet the cleanest place I had ever attended a show at. There was work crew constantly sweeping the isles and busing empty drinks.

After the show we didn't do much and I just dwelled on the notion of not dialing in the birthday girl from the pool earlier, as well as the realization I was now 40.

Into My 40s

Even though I promised myself not to write about any more of my life's stories past my turning 40, this little tale is just too important and classic not to include. This ordeal happened within the first few weeks after I turned 40.

I went up to the mountains with a couple guys from the KGLR radio crew in early August. We set up camp at 4th of July campground just outside of Nederland, CO. This was the same camping area that me and another couple of the radio crew camped at the previous summer. Just like the summer before we brought mushrooms to eat and enjoyed a hiking adventure through the woods. Well this time things went AWOL.

After we ate our shrooms on our peanut butter and jelly sandwiches, just like the previous year, we took a stroll into the vastness of the woods. We came upon a sign that said PRIVATE PROPERTY and as the buzz was beginning to set in I got extremely paranoid that we were within the property and should just head back to camp and enjoy the trip.

Well as we trekked back towards camp I began to have a hard time breathing and started feeling nauseous. As we kept walking and stopping to look around I was getting sicker and filled with more anxiety. I thought I might puke but couldn't and told the guys I need to get the fuck back to camp immediately.

At camp I was still in severe panic mode and couldn't control my symptoms no matter what I tried. I was pacing around, trying to relax and lay down, drinking water, but none of it was calming me. I began to stroll all over the campground and found two middle- aged guys who looked like mountaineering types and asked if they had anything to "fix me". One guy was a paramedic and saw my threatening signs of anxiety and said he could radio for help but it would put me in a huge predicament. Instead they gave me some energy powder to mix in with water and I wandered onward to my 4Runner. I planned to lay down in my 4Runner and ride out the anxiety but remembered the back of my vehicle was packed with firewood and crap, so instead I hunched down by the driver's door and tried to control my breathing.

A couple stopped by to check on me and by this point I felt so bad I asked if I could get a ride back into town. They complied but every time I stood up I felt faint and sick so I had to decline. There was no way I could handle a moving vehicle traveling down a bumpy dirt road; a trip that takes about twenty minutes in total.

I then proceeded past the parking lot and into another camping area where I saw this older hippie guy sitting alone at a picnic table. I tossed him my phone and wallet and told him to call my mom. Since it had been about two hours of these symptoms I had decided it was too out of control to ignore and I honestly felt fearful of my livelihood. It was so bad that I could feel the blood pumping rapidly through my body and I was overheating. All I could think about is if I went into cardiac arrest or something and didn't want to end my life this way, and I began to just completely break down from here.

With the mushroom buzz and my anxiety in full effect I then started yelling and crying. More people stopped by to check out the escalating drama as the hippie guy kept telling me to just chill out and enjoy the trip. One lady was a nurse and I told her I had Bi-Polar disorder and was having a panic attack meltdown. Unfortunately she moved on and I was left with the hippie guy and a few scared bystanders staring at me in fear.

I became so out of control that I started rolling around in the dirt, yelling and crying out of control by this point. I even tried to uproot a huge tree! From there I crawled into a stream, stood up and started to rant out loud at full volume. And if that wasn't enough I decided to piss myself right there, standing in the middle of a stream near all these people.

A little while after this scene took place I noticed that there was no one around except the hippie guy. By this point I had yelled and cried my guts out so much that he told me an ambulance was on the way. I kept asking him if he called my mom yet so I could justify my behavior but he never did. I had no signal anyway so I had to ride out the rest of the storm in isolation of my own horrific feelings.

The ambulance and one police officer arrived about an hour later, and of course by this point I had calmed down and didn't need the help anymore, but it was too late. I was sitting in the middle of a field covered in my sleeping bag and the officer drew his gun because he didn't know what was going to come out of this sleeping bag. I assured him I was cool and he escorted me to the ambulance.

In the ambulance I refused any medicine or help of any kind. I just lay on the gurney for the long haul back into Boulder. Along the way I saw the lights of cars following behind us and it reminded me of a film where they show the pre-recorded scenery out the rear window of a car. And it seemed to be in black and white like in a Quinten Tarantino film. I was finally enjoying my trip. The head medic even looked exactly like one of my high school buddies and I couldn't stop tripping on that.

Long story short I spent the night in the hospital moaning and cussing because the nurses who would not check on me much or call my fucking parents. It wasn't until the next morning that they finally contacted my parents and I was finally picked up and saved.

The highlight of the hospital room was looking at a scenic picture on the wall that came alive like I was observing an actual nature scene, except that this nature show ended up costing me about $1800. And if you tack on the ambulance expense it all added up to $3300 accrued. Oh to not have health insurance.

The point of all that I shared here was not to tell another tale of a drug binge but rather the reasoning behind my huge meltdown during the event. Since I never show emotions of any kind and my lifestyle is so depressing, all my emotions burst out during this one experience. The mushrooms can be credited with "allowing me" to release so much pain and anger that I wouldn't have released if sober. This sounds nuts to credit an illegal drug for helping me but it's true. I have not had a major meltdown in years, nor a bad trip ever, and I've felt so pent up and sad inside for far too long, it happened.

What made for my anxiety induced panic attack from earlier during the trip was the fact that I was on a prescribed medication; Lamictal. I never factored in the prescribed drug as all the times I've tripped on mushrooms I've never had a bad experience. I realized this a few days later and was so outraged that all the trauma and expenses incurred from this event was the result of mixing two different drugs. And as most people would blame the mushrooms for the mishap I blame the Lamictal just as much. The mushrooms triggered the Lamictal and caused the panic attack and nausea that I had to bear for hours, which included a dramatic, humiliating breakdown in front of a packed campground. It was a combo platter from Hell. I had to live through this awful experience because I'm messed up just enough for the need to be on meds in the first place. And because of all this I have racked up a huge debt expense and more frustrations in my already horrific life.

Funny how I can get by alright after mixing five illegal drugs in one evening some years ago at a Jane's Addiction concert but lose my shit after mixing one illegal substance with one legal one. You think I would've learned my lesson from the Las Vegas incident when I mixed substances with sinus medications but I didn't.

See kids, don't do drugs! (Legal one's that is.)

On a brighter note, I recently participated in the 34th Bolder Boulder race. (I missed the 33rd as I was working at the event that previous year.) After years of debating I finally registered and ran the infamous 10K race. I hate running but the Bolder Boulder is known more for being a fun experience than a serious race. People dress up all goofy, bands are playing on some of the street corners, spectators are handing out jello shots, as well as many other surprises the runners encounter along the route.

A fun moment during the race for me was when I dove head first into a Slip 'N Slide! I happened to be wearing my helmet cam and recorded this move, as well as a few other moments along the race course I deemed worthy of documenting. I also kept my promise that if I ran the race I would end it by doing the moonwalk across the finish line. As I entered Folsom Field for the final lap of the race I turned around and began my moonwalk. I made it the entire way through the stadium in moonwalk stride, filming all the other runners cruising by me wondering what I was up to. I tried to have someone up in the stands film me during that final lap but no one could commit, so all I have is my crappy POV footage. (Hey at least I can say I'm the first ever moonwalker to cross the finish line in any Bolder Boulder race to date \m/.)

(Footage of the head-first Slip 'N Slide dive featured on my YouTube channel.)

2014: Summer of Darkness

For lack of a more colorful title describing my summer of

2014, it was dark. I had no social life or a clue what to do. This was the worst funk experience ever.

I was out of work for the most part, isolated and confused, still playing drums with Finger Pie but always hoping for cancelled rehearsals and pause on gigs…I was so down and out it was the first time I had to back out of a band obligation due to depression. I couldn't be lively enough to partake; had one really good rehearsal then I called it. And it sucked, these chicks were into it and it would've been a good thing. (All-female Guns n Roses tribute, with me as token drummer boy for what was planned to be *Guns n Bitches.*) Fuck, sorry it didn't happen.

I spent most of the duration of this summer wandering around the neighborhood, into town, sitting alone on benches amongst the elements staring around with thoughts racing. I couldn't find any spark, get a grip.

For many reasons it all led up to this and I'll recall my only "blessed weeks" during that long, hot, secluded summer (like I'm Robert Frosting you…) was Shark Week. I'm one of those suckers that catches it every season, every show possible during this week. I literally chilled on the couch all that week absorbing sharks; as a passionate interest for most part (not as much as Astronomy for me but hey) and to deter myself from reality. One week of this, a cancelled Pie rehearsal, parents out of town, was GREAT. (WHITE, haha)

But the most glorious of all was the few weeks following my Shark Week vacation when I joined my immediate family and nephews on a week-long excursion to the southwest portion of our beloved state and into Utah, my favorite!

A week spent with adventurous, fun, loved-ones alike hitting the road and checking out amazingness. Traveling by minivan with me following in the Camry, (which gave me full reign on musical selection \m/) stopping in Moab, Arches, Mesa Verde, Four Corners, and finishing in Telluride. YummY.

This week-long getaway was phenomenal and cleansed my darkened soul.

ROAD TRIP YOUR SORROWS AWAY!!!

A classic moment during this trip was on Day 1 during a hike to Delicate Arch. *I didn't hike but rather discovered an ant nest at the trailhead. So instead of pressing on to the arch, I sat behind and fiddled with this ant nest for at least an hour!*

There was a hunger battle going on; a group of ants carrying a freshly killed carcass back to the nest, and I fed them any other specimens I could find. And best of all had to be the young, extremely cute Ranger girl joining in, after wondering what I was up to. (Later, I wish.)

Fuck yeah, and now quick rehashes on a few other self-induced getaways I "enjoyed":

3 Getaways

During the first couple years into my 40s I embarked on three solo excursions. Each one lasted about a week and entailed me driving to a number of locations and sleeping in my 4Runner along the way. There's not much to be said about these getaways but they did reflect the dark times I was in just after I convinced myself that my 40s would be great. These getaways were my time to reassess many thoughts and goals and keep me from killing myself. I had to be alone while staying on the move. But leave it to me to still make the times fun and memorable as well; visiting interesting historic sites and taking many photos along the way.

Aside from sleeping in my 4Runner, I made sure to end each getaway with a hotel room on the last night of the excursion, just to feel "spoiled".

And there is amazing photos from these 3 Getaways! Disc golf at Dillion, Leadville, *others*; *pitstop in* Vegas *for a bachelor party, then* Flintstones Bedrock City *the day after*; *crashing at* Wal-Mart *by night, venturing around by day and grabbing spectacular sunset photos at* White Sands, NM. *Come on…where's the photos in this digital* Spin Cycle?

(Next version readers, right about the time Tool releases their new album.)

Top 3 Shows/Publications I'd love to be featured on/in:

1-Any Talk Show

2-That Metal Show
3-Modern Drummer

If I could just achieve the right success and status in my life there's no reason why I shouldn't be interviewed on at least one of these programs or publications. (Among others out there) I often fantasize about being on a talk show and all the questions, responses, analogies, and stories that could be discussed. I'm an interesting person in conversation to say the least and I belong interacting with like-minded, artistic freaks like me. My quirky yet intelligent responses could be very entertaining for the world. I need to be heard. I deserve to be heard.

That Metal Show is so bad ass, check it out and see why it's understandable I'd fit in great with that crew for an episode (or season). As for Modern Drummer, this is the one magazine I've subscribed to regularly since my teenage years. My dream for years has been an article about me and my musical career featured in this publication. A correspondent from MD comes to my place for an interview; I offer him a Yoo-hoo, and we get down to business. Simple, and it's so fun to talk music and drums!

Another fantastic documentary series regarding the history of hard rock and metal is *Metal Evolution.* The same two filmmakers that produced and directed *Metal: A Headbanger's Journey, Iron Maiden: Flight 666, Rush: Beyond the Lighted Stage,* and a few other winners, also gave birth to *Metal Evolution*; an 11-part series that covers the history of metal through hour-long broadcasts that examine all the main genres of metal that morphed into existence since the beginning of rock n roll.

And let's not leave out another fine music publication I highly recommend for anyone who's into heavier-edged rock n roll; Revolver.

This Just In: While attending another Syracuse game watch event at Blake Street Tavern, after attending an exciting high school hockey match with my dad and nephew the other day, it really dawned on me how great my family has been for me throughout the years. I sometimes hesitate to attend these events as it seems that all I do is hang out with my immediate family anymore, but as I was watching this great hockey game I realized that I'm fine having my family as the main source of my livelihood. I'm perfectly okay with having my parents be my best friends. With all that we have experienced together I couldn't ask for better friends in my life anyway. Thanks so much mom and dad!

This also in: Oh come on, you don't want this book to end! (As I can't stop adding more niblets and tidbits to it anyway.)

I brought in $3,505 of income in 2012. How did I pull off surviving an entire year on just $3,505? No rent, minimal bills, and not doing much. I was isolated and have been for the past three years while living on four-figure incomes. Some extra income was made under the table during these times but let's not tell that to the Feds. But even with extra income on top of a measly $3,505 its mind blowing how an intelligent human being like me could survive and live a life like this!

Even funnier is to publish this book and get it launched properly will cost around $3,500. So I can say that it takes me a year's salary to publish a book! This amount also represents the total cost of my ambulance and overnight hospital stay earlier in the year. I spent a year's salary to take an hour-long ride and spend the night at a three-star hotel.

Holy shit that puts it all in perspective how little I've earned throughout most of my life, as well as the degrading lifestyle I've endured for far too many years of my adulthood.

To factor in the worst scenario of all this past year is I spent $600 on a fucking overrated smart phone, making it the worst decision-turned-regret of the year! Think about it; $600 out of the $3,505 I earned the entire year, for a fucking phone. Talk about a stab in the heart on so many levels, especially when I don't utilize the "smart" elements of my phone anyway. Bring back the flip phone!

I've skimmed my way through numerous years surviving on four-figure salaries. Years where I've just paid bills and roamed about the Earth; snacking on granola bars, nuts, and apples.

During warmer months my favorite afternoon treat is an iced coffee. When I have a bit more pocket change than usual I can "spoil myself" with an iced latte! Or I have the option of a regular iced coffee accompanied by a chunk of gluten free pumpkin bread!

Wow I sure live a life of luxury. My 40s really have been an ongoing nightmare of so many negative, humiliating, soul draining components involved it's unreal. The end of the world might have been the best thing to happen to humankind in 2012. Well, at least for me maybe. After reading through all these pages of my insane tormenting stories, gripes and grievances, and seeing all the dreadful events take place in this world since 2012, I'll take an alien invasion anytime at this point. Maybe not as to completely destroy us in all, but to "bitch slap" our pathetic asses back into morally sane, competent humans we could and should be!

As much as I appreciate this beautiful world, amazing Universe, my family, select friends, who I am, what I have, and all I've experienced in life, I've also suffered too much. Suffered beyond what I ever imagined or deserved. And to witness how bad so many drivers there are on the roads out there is a reflection of how incompetent and stupid so many people are in general. The whole big picture of preposterousness in this world can surely *drive* one mad.

ALL my bumper sticker slogans, metaphorical comparisons, quotes, analogies, and nifty little acronyms I come up with are ALL (unfortunately) true. As most people watch Sci- Fi programs, sitcoms, and reality TV, I watch and read up on *real* reality and factor in the big picture with anything I doubt and deserve some clarification.

Henceforth I *then* go off on tangents and allocate how it is, *without* biased opinions, jumping to conclusions, or possessing delusional propensities that most other people tend to within their rants of protest.

Almost everyone is still a good-hearted, worthy person. It's the times and trends that alters human perception and behavior. Society is not purposefully a bunch of fickle, flaky, fucks as I call them out to be, they're just conformist bitches that inadvertently adapt to whatever's going on within the confines of their cultural surroundings. There's only a small percentage of humans that don't hop on the bandwagon and rather choose to abandon this ship of conformity.

Again, one on one most people are basically genuine and

are who they really are, but as a society and culture it's a whole other deal. The small percentage of us say FUCK THIS NOISE and jump ship, while most others stay onboard, as the ship takes them closer and closer to Shitville Beach.

It's *not* irrational, negative bashing. It's truth. Truth hurts, that's why we lie and resort to optimistic cover-ups so we can all "get along". (Do I have to incorporate the Jack Nicholson quote from *A Few Good Men* here?)

I just love the visual I get with so many of you readers having to roll your eyes constantly throughout reading this book; as I've griped about so much and repeat my statements of truthful disgruntlement *so many times*. For no other reason than too many things are insanely retarded in this world and so many things have reeked unnecessary havoc on my life. So it takes psycho-reiteration to get things ingrained into the average person's slow, foggy, stubbornly biased brain!

Fucking wake up people! Take colder showers, do more coke, whatever it takes to finally shake your head with more reasonable agreements of "I get it", rather than rolling your naïve, piss-soaked eyes and ignoring the negative pragmatisms of the world that need to end!

Water under the bridge...the big lake at the end of the river must be overflowing with putrid rubbish that so many middle-class, conformist morons have let flow onward and chosen to ignore. To allow so much bullshit to drift under so many bridges that all ends up in one fucked-up Lake of Hell.

Nice going; you glass half full, good enough, is what it is, just deal DIPSHITS.

Cynical Pessimist? NOPE. Frustrated Realist.

Putting on the Condom:(The Wrap Up)

This is the final segment of *Life in the Spin Cycle* where I wrap up the big cock of topics into a generalized recap/summary of sorts; by reiterating some of the key constituents that eventually developed into the very first narrative I've now wrote about my life.

You've all made it this far and lived vicariously through the many wild adventures and daunting experiences I've endured. Maybe it's still hard to comprehend how I'm so unsuccessful and "tortured" in life, but it is what it is and I'm forced to live with it.

From all the stories that have derived out of numerous experiences and endless adventures throughout the first half of my life, it's amazing I have kept myself together through it all to be able to press on and write an actual book about it. Anyone who knows me well enough can vouch I'm not a lazy no good fuck-up who complains or rants away for no reason, but rather an intelligent, respectful, ultra-creative, multi-talented being who's lived a remarkable life. (Yet has more going against him than one would imagine.)

I had a fantastic upbringing and excelled in many activities over so many years, but my post-collegiate life has been mostly a tragic mess. It's too bad, as I truly do have a piquancy for life and so much to offer, so I really hope to overcome my demons and at least strive forward and progress better for the remainder of my life's existence.

I will continue to carry on and march through the mine fields of unpredictable impediments along the way, as long as I can. (Before I completely lose it and I'm writing my next book while staring out a window of the nearest loony bin.)

You've read about some prime examples I shared where I screwed myself with jobs and girls over the years, yet I never expected the few substantial late 90s "after the fact" regrets to still be haunting me two decades later. I mistakenly assumed the country was on a never-ending roll of positive growth and favorable times to continue. (Like it had been for decades prior.) I turned down some key job prospects in the late 90s with the notion that I was still young and there'd be plenty more opportunities that would present themselves along my "fateful path". No worries.

During my 20s I wasn't ready to commit to a "career-type" lifestyle, and what a painful outcome that has been the result of from this judgement call. Factoring in all my mental disarray, perfectionistic tendencies, bad luck/timing scenarios, and the times/trends changing so drastically in the 21st Century, the 90s were definitely the opportune times for me to leap into any of these prospects offered to me, and never look back.

My mishaps have not all been a product of my mental issues or regrets, but more so from too many outside factors screwing me more than necessary throughout the years. I am angered that I've allowed so many people and situations to ruin my stride and "force me" to walk on eggshells and hide who I really am. I have absolutely no feelings of ignominy from anything I've written about. I believe anything that was analyzed or scrutinized in this book is not only truth but fully deserving and justified for me to rip into and gripe about.

In recent years I've put forth many more times the effort to better my life in so many ways, on so many levels, and go figure the "opportunities" are not presenting themselves much at all like they did back when they just appeared and *I* turned them down. (Shitballs to this shit.) I'm hitting dead end after dead end from hopeful connections with people and their "promises gone sour" for something good to come out of (what should be) our collaborative efforts thriving together!

Population keeps increasing which creates more competition and stressful conditions for too many people working harder than ever to earn a decent living. Economic hardships are prevalent in an unstable, unforgiving job market, too much is being spread thin as we're smothering ourselves with so much social media rubbish and endless online distractions. There's hundreds of channels of television programs to choose from, sequels/prequels/remakes of so many movies out there, Netflix, YouTube, Spotify...all this shit happening, while neglecting the importance of old school human interaction! The epidemic of self-absorbed, narcissistic, unreliable, brainwashed, naive, greedy, "in the moment nothing beyond" society continues to cultivate year by year. Fucking lovely.

I hesitated to add this detail into the Spin Cycle *but truth be told this country has gone so off the deep end with our erratic, self-righteous, ridiculous tendencies we might as well re-construct the American flag and include a big pile of bullshit on it. (Positioned faintly behind the 50 stars.) Because let's face it, we've "earned it".*

And this is when you always hear that infamous, ignorant comeback phrase from the naive traditionalists of this country: IF YOU DON'T LIKE IT, THEN LEAVE!

Well FUCK YOU, YOU LEAVE! And leave us sane, wholesome, morally efficient folks alone. We complainers who are actually awake and care will stay, re-group, and mend America back into what it once was for decades; Great. (Prior to the 21st Century Shit Show it's become.) Dumbasses.

Uncomfortable. If I had to describe my life in one word as it stands today, it's uncomfortable. Life doesn't suck, it's not complete "torture" or as bad as some of my ranting might come across as it has throughout the *Spin Cycle*, but overall it's very uncomfortable to live like this. All I want for the remaining years of my life is success in the realms of my interests and talents of course, as well as more comfort. I want to be able to enjoy most situations I'm part of without having continuous thoughts of my painful reality lingering in the back of my mind. I want to quit staying up until the early morning hours each night out of fear of facing the next day, knowing it will most likely be stressful, or uneventful, and I'll be stuck in a lonely, horrific, trance-like state once again.

It all boils down to the truthful realism that only a very small percentage of people born into this world possess a very unusual brain chemistry that brings about special capabilities beyond the "norm". Mostly these abilities are never recognized or commended due to an endless array of factors and circumstances in one's life. The way the world is set up does not cater to the "specialists", and there's been too many people throughout history that "cry wolf" and ruin it for the small percentage of us that really aren't full of shit, delusional, or exaggerating when we speak of our big dreams and special abilities, or anything that's original and awesome. (Which much of the world would most certainly be glad to see in existence!)

The excruciating irony is the more creatively unique and "genius" you are the more fucked up your head is, and likely odds are you will end up living a life of frustrating mediocrity; stuck in a lifestyle well below your capabilities, while sinking into depression, become suicidal, thrown in a mental institution, or maybe luck out and be rescued from this dark reality. You might find inner peace, true love, or become successful and inspirational to the world with what you're naturally good at in the first place. (But who knows.)

This insanity that most of the world never has to factor into their reality or deal with at all, is what reality is for me and a select number of others on the planet who have to deal with this pandemonium for a lifetime. (I had to use the word *pandemonium* at least once before the conclusion of this book. Or did I?)

AGAIN, no one is more special or superior than another. Once that particular sperm hits that egg, it's done. We're conceived and born into the world as who we are and end up a product of our biological genes, upbringing, the times, trends, and so many elements that surround us. The only not-so-special thing about being born a bit more unique than most is the world is set up for the majority who *aren't* very unique and settle into the systems that be and adapt to whatever is happening within the times.

AND AGAIN, more irony with all this is the conformist, happy-go-lucky humans, who don't want to hear us artistic outcasts protest about how much harder we have it than them, *they* are part of the immoral majority that over-praise and over-worship people of fame who happen to get a "lucky break" into stardom. These ignorant, guilty culprits are who created all this "Hollywood dreamer lifestyle" hype into an industry of "Godliness", instead of what it really is; an industry of "uniqueness", and nothing more.

I'm sure many of you by now are thinking **NOT AGAIN**. *Ha sorry. But* A****...)

Like Robin Williams, Sid Barrett, and select others in history, I'm one of these small percentage of special freaks with brilliant ideas meets dysfunctional tendencies, except the major difference is they got to play in the Superbowl while me and so many others with similar mindsets and capabilities stand on the sidelines. Some, like Robin and Sid, honed their brilliance and craft into success, during times in entertainment when it was much more valiant and easier to be discovered and obtain fame from doing what you were born to do. Nowadays, with so much more population inhabiting the planet, so many more artists and entertainers competing for the spotlight, and factoring in the expanding internet and all the clutter it floods onto our dorky digital devices. It's *way* harder nowadays for the next Robins or Sids to be discovered. (Let alone chumps like me who aren't quite as "gifted" but still have something semi-brilliantly unique and cool to offer.)

I live in a day by day nightmare for the most part; knowing what all my capabilities are and where they could take me, yet I'm just dysfunctional enough where I can't maintain basic stability, jobs, focus, or consistent moods each day to move ahead in life at a reasonable fashion. I have *too many* interests and talents and *can't* just choose one to put all efforts into. They all tie in together within the same ballfield of play anyway, so I understand the concept of picking one thing to simplify, and once that thing takes off the flood gates can open for more to stand out and finally receive praise. But picking one artistic skill to roll with is *still* a gamble in the world of arts where *nothing* is guaranteed for a successful outcome, no matter what strategic tactics are involved.

Why do you think DJs and cover/tribute bands are overshadowing most all the great original music out there. Because it's much easier for the average bitch human to go with what's already known and not take time-consuming risks themselves for hopes of discovering something fresh and new that's prevalent in the scene, but unfortunately mixed into the over-saturated, rapid cycling mayhem out there.

Hence why corporate radio lasted as long as it did, (and is somehow *still* going; as strong as that last trickle of urine that runs down your leg after a rushed piss), but it's finally beginning to fade out. We *still* hear the same god damned motherfucking songs from all the same god damned motherfucking bands after DECADES of rotating that stupid dial on our car stereos! So yes, corporate radio should have died years ago.

Now we have other technological means to be become our own DJs, so we can overplay all our personal musical selections for years to come. Thankfully it's not so much revolving around what corporate radio overcooked to hell since the mid-20th Century.

Instead it's now mostly over-produced shittier music that is being heard from Bluetooth devices, personal headphones, earbuds, butt-plugs…all used in order to avoid the redundant, predictable basics the airwave have been torturing us with for decades. To instead become more narcissistic, self-absorbed humans within a zoned-out world of our own selective listening pleasure. (But at least it's FINALLY new, and unique ish.)

These times are tainted cheese, and there's a lot more obstacles to overcome than ever before. I must work that much harder because of it all, yet by lucky chance some get their special talents validated and make big success in life by utilizing the positive, aspiring portion of their inimitable brain chemistry. Otherwise most of us are forever considered "delusional dreamers" to the world. We struggle to prove our worthiness or ever get a chance to showcase our special abilities in this cluster-fuckhole of a reality, so we might very well spend a lifetime exhausting our energy trying to conform and survive within predominately left-brained, societal standards of vanilla coated nonsense. Swell.

Take note, I still exhibit the most empathy and sympathy to those plagued with the worst of the worst in this one precious life we get; PTSD, mental or physical ailments, cancer, and all this awfulness that plagues too many millions of people in this world out of ever living a normally functioning, stable, happy life.

Good upbringing does not make a person whole. It does not make for a perfect being. The most significant times for me have derived from my youthful zest, big heart, open mind, and fun, easy going personality, and numerous experiences I had and adventures I indulged in over the years. I have discovered that my survival mechanisms are mostly inadequate for the world that be, yet keep pushing on within a reality I created. (Huh?)

And so this book must conclude; representing the first half of my wild, adventurous, crazy, fortunate-torturous years on Earth. I have absorbed so much love and friendship, lived through times of excitement and despair, and had a blast documenting and recollecting all these times of my life thus far. Most people look into the past and cherish the good moments while letting go of the bad and don't dwell so much on regrets.

Unfortunately, as you've read and hopefully comprehended, I've had too many regrets and letdowns that impacted the outcome of my life in very powerful and detrimental ways. I would *definitely* change a lot of things from my past no question, but also appreciate so much I've experienced as well. I wouldn't change the great times I've had for anything. (Can't have your cake and eat it. Why the fuck not? Oh yeah, this book beyond summed up the reasoning for being unable to eat any cake presented to me.) Fuck cake, bring me cookies!

Too bad my mental issues, some key missed opportunities over the years, and being a starving artist within these unforgiving times has plagued me more than anyone will understand or ever care to endure. All my photos represent the fun and magnificent times I've experienced throughout my life, whereas many of my journal entries and thoughts concealed within my mind signify the unfathomable.

What an exciting, prolonged, grueling task it's been writing, editing, and publishing this one god damned book. Nineteen (19) years of intermittent writing efforts to complete the entire process concerning this *one* agenda, and finally arrive at the publishing phase. A goal, or mission, I set out to conquer nearly two decades ago is finally a reality?

Life is full of too much game changing surprises, hardships, and struggles for many of us. When certain people, situations, circumstances, and other crap disrupt the natural flow of hard work and years of perseverance trying to establish a worthy life doing what you were literally born to do, it can be an agonizing battle to endure. It becomes hard to forgive, let go, move on, or even want to continue living in some instances.

I'll just continue to drift along in life; gazing at the clouds with my protuberant, persisting thoughts and ideologies, as others prefer the more practical, satiating path in life. (And their tablets over gazing at the sky; Mother Nature's tablet.)

With my creative intuition, natural talents, and innovative capabilities, (that remember, also includes around 50 product invention ideas I've thought of), it's tragic infamy how I haven't been able to reach my true potentials in life and reap the benefits of what all my aptitudes could bring me. Even in the worst of odds there's no question at least a few of my clever invention ideas could bring me fame and fortune. Then I'd be floating *above* the clouds the rest of my life. (And constantly scouting out many people and places below that need to be shit on.)

If you made it through the *Spin Cycle* and were truly captivated by much of what I shared, (the fun creative side of me, and not the incessant griping portions of this book), get in touch, let's team up! Anyone who truly "gets it" and wants to hang out, collaborate, or knows of a valuable source out there I may need to seek out, I'm game! I'm fucking done with this lifestyle I've been stuck in far too long. Fuck this spin cycle!

Even if I ever do "make it", or at least obtain more efficient stability in life, or maybe find true happiness or love during my remaining years alive, I will *still* be disconcerted and angered until the day I die; knowing how unfair and unjust too many things are in this world.

In the days before Kurt Cobain killed himself, he was quoted as saying, "I just don't understand how this world doesn't have more empathy."

True dat, and unfortunately too much of the world is incapable of empathy, or god forbid sympathy. Too many of this world's 7 billion inhabitants don't possess enough heart or intuitive common sense. Humans seem incapable of ever living together in basic harmony, completely deprived of morally efficient means to do so.

The RESET *button for Earth needs to be pushed!*

Kurt, Robin, Hunter, George, and others who have passed on, let me just say you're not missing out on much since you've left us. The world is still beautiful, there's amazing things happening, and it's fantastic to be alive, but it's NOTHING compared to what it was during the times you all were still alive and really "living" the American Dream.

So let us assume there will be many more celebrated times and stories of joy to be shared during the rest of my life, and much less perturbing bullshit to experience and reminisce about. (And hopefully no rhyme or reason for a *Life in the Spin Cycle 2.*)

EPILOGUE

I would like to bring to light that there are prominent figures I didn't talk about much, or at all, throughout the *Spin Cycle* that probably deserved to be mentioned and honored in this book. For this I apologize, but there's only so much I can reminisce about within one book, especially considering how dense with activity my life has been.

It was enough of a time-consuming pain in my rump having to reach out to those I needed to include within the *Spin Cycle,* in order for some of these stories to be fulfilled. I needed to be sensitive to each person's identity and use false names in some cases; as to not burn a bridge or be sued after including anything in my book that wasn't mutually agreed upon from the get-go. (Love that word!)

I'm sure a handful of peeps will feel left out, maybe even angered, after not being included in the *Spin Cycle.* (Especially you Carukus, original #1) Again, I'M SORRY! This was a fucking process and I spewed out as much as I possibly could in order to cover the momentous essentials of my life throughout all these pages of writing. (Hey, I'm sure many are *glad* they weren't included in this mess. Ha-ha, whatever, all good, is what it is...)

I give thanks, praise, hugs, and kisses to my amazing

parents, (mom especially for reading through this book's first rough copy and pointing out I use the words "just" and "that" far too often, so a big thumbs-up thanks to her, just for that), sisters, relatives, friends, and many other interesting persons and animals I've encountered along my life's journey.

And a final high-five to my trusting computers, laptops, Thesaurus, and numerous coffee shops I sat in over the years during much of the time while writing this book. Over- tipping many fine baristas while constantly adding more bits of prose into this boundless memoire.

Overall, I feel privileged to be alive and able to write a book in the first place. Bye now!

Links to my anti-social shit:

www.snowdogsoda.com

www.facebook.com/fizzgig33

www.youtube.com/scarpie33

www.instagram.com/scarpie33

www.facebook.com/groups/dailyshitshow

Made in the USA
San Bernardino, CA
21 March 2020